"Every leader that aspires to greatness and real breakthrough needs to read this book. This book gets to the real guts and gore of leadership."

Carrie Tan, Transformation & Selfwork Coach and politician

"Great leadership is a service. Not a title or position. This book is not interested in confirming the politically correct "facts" of succeeding in the corporate world, but to deep-dive into the "why" behind the success, which is usually unsettling, strange and yet true. Success is the reality bridge to our imagination."

Genevieve Gay, Business & Brand Whisperer, Digital Marketing Maven, Product Marketing Head, Breeze, NCS Pte Ltd

"A refreshing gust of leadership wisdom from Asia; written by an Asian woman to remind us that leadership is not one-size-fits-all. Women have a unique set of leadership skills to bring to the table, and it's deeply personal."

Molly Martel, banking & finance professional, life coach, cancer survivor

"If you're looking to gain clarity in navigating the complexity and organizational dynamics, step up your communication style with stakeholders and sharpen your leadership approach, look no further. Read this book. It's the best thing you can do for yourself and your team."

Monica Tsai, Head of Telco, Auto and Finance, APAC Partnerships Solutions, Google

"Provocative, yet authentic, *Dancing on the Edge of Greatness* reaches inside leaders' heads to reveal what drives them to peak performance. An energizing and motivating read for anyone in search of the thrill of finding their personal edge."

Aman Narain, #BoomerangBanker, ex-Googler, Global Head of Platforms, HSBC

"Like a spa for the mind, each story in *Dancing on the Edge of Greatness* brings you through a journey that untangles the knots that inevitably build up in our day-to-day interruptions, distractions and fire drills, leaving you freshly recharged with renewed clarity, focus and commitment."

Andrew Namboka, Solutions Director, Security, Dimension Data

"*Dancing on the Edge of Greatness* is a refreshing take on leadership and change management. If you are looking for a quick intravenous drip of fist-pumping adrenaline to accelerate your change momentum, read this book."

Carl Hemus, COO, Asia, TMX Global

"Individual success cannot happen in the vacuum of collective failure. This is the leadership survival handbook for ambitious leaders. Sophia's nuanced exploration of being a leader — that it's not a lonely job — is refreshing and a joy to read."

David Simonsen, Director, Amazon Prime Video, Amazon

"This book provides leaders with vital strategies to build great teams and deliver business impact at scale."

Dwayn Lythgo, Operate Leader, Risk Advisory, Deloitte Asia Pacific

"*Dancing on the Edge of Greatness* is a beautifully written and generous meditation; reminding us to act from an entrepreneurship mindset. This book will inspire you to give yourself a shot at doing something BIG or SPECIAL with your life."

Ishan Chatterjee, Managing Director, Product Partnerships, APAC, YouTube

"This is the secret that all successful leaders know: when to stop thinking and start doing. Too many leaders focus too much time thinking about the right strategy, instead of doing and modifying along the way. Change is a constant in this day and age; one needs to be agile. This book shares many examples, and I recommend reading it."

James Koh, talent scout, Founder & CEO, James Kenneth Koh Executive Search

"This book is an invitation to ring in the new era of creativity at work. Making leadership personal is the rocket fuel to bring your creative genius all the way to the boardroom."

João Flores, Regional Executive Creative Director, media.monks

"Insightful, instructive and poetic — Sophia eloquently juxtaposes her own personal journey with a series of mental models tested on the top corporate and tech startup leaders in Asia. An engaging read and a wonderful resource to keep at hand to guide you on your leadership journey."

Karl Noronha, VP, Strategy & Operations, B Capital Group

"If you're passionate about working with people, organizations and the wider community to help them achieve their potential and make a difference, this book is a must-read."

Manoj Menon, Founder & CEO of Twimbit

"This book helps you reconnect with your passion for leadership. "It's a privilege to lead… You have the power to make someone's life better." Sophia Chin covers a range of challenging situations faced by leaders today, highlights potential blind spots and offers practical advice on responding purposefully to these challenges while building a more fulfilling career for yourself."

Thurai Thavasikkannu, Head of Real Estate Funds, Asia, Vistra

"In our busy lives, we can get bound by old ways of thinking. We don't accept and even punish failures. We try to frame the entire organization from performance dashboards to career development, without spending enough time exploring and asking "Why". This is an invitation to kick off your shoes, get grounded and read the book — and feel infinitely alive, finding back that purpose and passion and learn what true ambidextrous leadership is all about."

Walter Kuijpers, Partner, Powered Supply Chain, KPMG

To the gods and goddesses who live, play, love and war

in the modern pantheon of deities.

May you delight the world with your greatness.

DANCING ON THE EDGE OF GREATNESS

Making Leadership Personal

DANCING ON THE EDGE OF GREATNESS

Making Leadership Personal

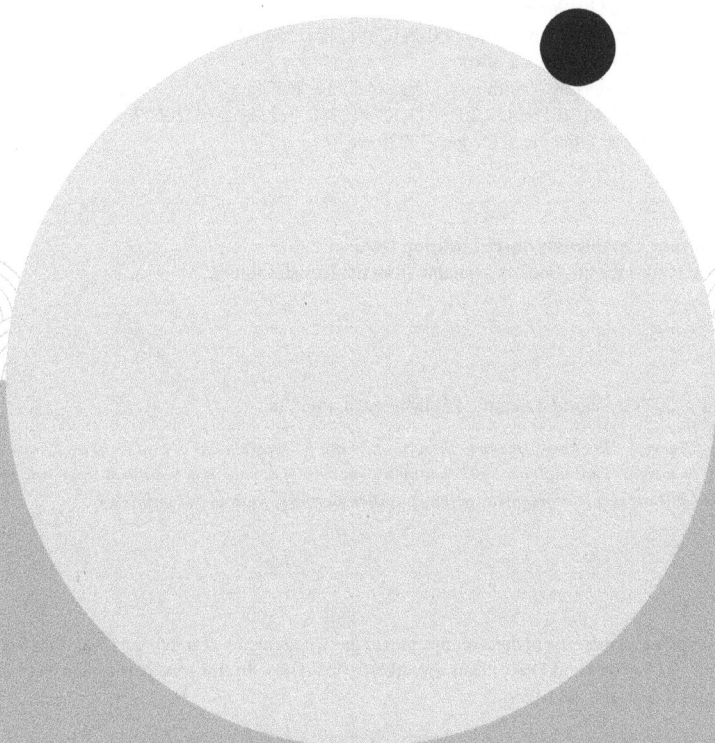

SOPHIA CHIN

PERSONNA, Singapore

World Scientific

NEW JERSEY · LONDON · SINGAPORE · BEIJING · SHANGHAI · HONG KONG · TAIPEI · CHENNAI · TOKYO

Published by

World Scientific Publishing Co. Pte. Ltd.

5 Toh Tuck Link, Singapore 596224

USA office: 27 Warren Street, Suite 401-402, Hackensack, NJ 07601

UK office: 57 Shelton Street, Covent Garden, London WC2H 9HE

Library of Congress Cataloging-in-Publication Data
Names: Chin, Sophia, author.
Title: Dancing on the edge of greatness : making leadership personal /
    Sophia Chin, PERSONNA, Singapore.
Description: Hackensack, NJ : World Scientific, [2023]
Identifiers: LCCN 2022019659 | ISBN 9789811251207 (hardcover) |
    ISBN 9789811251931 (paperback) | ISBN 9789811251214 (ebook) |
    ISBN 9789811251221 (ebook other)
Subjects: LCSH: Leadership. | Authority. | Organizational behavior.
Classification: LCC HM1261 .C457 2023 | DDC 303.3/4--dc23/eng/20220607
LC record available at https://lccn.loc.gov/2022019659

British Library Cataloguing-in-Publication Data
A catalogue record for this book is available from the British Library.

For any available supplementary material, please visit
https://www.worldscientific.com/worldscibooks/10.1142/12693#t=suppl

Desk Editor: Nicole Ong

Typeset by Stallion Press
Email: enquiries@stallionpress.com

Contents

Dear Rockstar, With Love   xv

1. Introduction: Greatness Requires a Personal Commitment   1

Part 1. Born for Greatness   **51**

2. The Sweet Spot for Performance   53
3. Reclaim Your Authority   79
4. Making Leadership Personal   95

Part 2. Personal Leadership   **117**

5. Find Your Calling   119
6. Starting a New Role   131
7. Dealing with a Difficult Boss   139
8. Dealing with Burnout   149
9. Climbing the Corporate Ladder   159
10. Job Hopping   169
11. Being Let Go   177

Part 3. People Leadership   **189**

12. Becoming a New Manager   191
13. Leading People Through Change   199
14. Dealing with a Difficult Employee   209
15. Avoiding NATO Summits and TWOT Meetings   223
16. Letting People Go   231

Part 4. Organization Leadership   **241**

17. Becoming an Entrepreneur   243
18. Becoming an Intrapreneur   251
19. Scaling Your Business   259
20. Restructuring Your Business   269
21. Managing Complexity in Your Organization   277

Part 5. Culture   **287**

22. Why We Hate HR   289
23. Restructuring Without Talent Loss   295
24. Reducing Employee Turnover   305
25. Transforming Your Culture   315
26. Learning at the Speed of Business   323

Part 6. Transformation Tools: What Is Your Leadership Brand?   **331**

27. Leadership Development   333
28. READY: Frame Your Learning Edge   337
29. SET: Define Your Leadership Brand   343
30. GO: Clearly Articulate Your Vision   355

31. GO: Create A 100-Day Impact Plan   361
32. GO: Storytelling   365
33. GO: Listening   373
34. GO: Acknowledgment   379
35. GO: Uncomfortable Conversations   385
36. Culture of Innovation   395
37. Conclusion   403

About the Author   407
Acknowledgments   409
Endnotes   411

Dear Rockstar, with Love

I have a question, and I want an honest answer.

Have you ever harbored a dream of one day seeing your name boldly emblazoned on the cover of *TIME* magazine?

If you have, then great, please read on.

And since we're being honest here... so have I.

I get it. Really. I'm an overzealous devotee of great leadership. I worship at the altar of boldness, charisma and ambition. I've been fascinated with the dynamics of power since I was a kid. Forget the boardroom, that's just a big show of power for everyone else to see. No, the real action happens around the dining table.

I also see myself as a leader. I could say that I love to lead. But to be honest (we're on a streak here!), I like to be followed — a lot. For too long, my fragile ego has depended on the loyalty of others. I've spent my entire adult working life trying to please bosses, colleagues and employees. I've tried in vain to win them over. This has plagued me for years.

And so I'm giving up.

Instead, I'm falling back in love with leading. With the actual craft. And not the disease of fortune and fame. I'm kicking my lust for power. And learning to lead for the right reasons again.

This book is an outstretched hand to others who feel this same tension between people and performance. But a quick word of warning before we continue. In these pages, you will find blood and tears. Be prepared to be called out. And to be titillated. *Dancing on the Edge of Greatness* isn't a leadership book — at least not in the traditional sense. I won't attempt to offer instant noodles solutions that just add hot water and you're ready to lead. Because when it comes to achieving greatness, there are no model answers. Neither will I spew grand leadership altruisms such as "People are our greatest assets," which are true but (mostly) useless in driving meaningful change.

Here's what *Dancing on the Edge of Greatness* is: a leadership book in the non-traditional sense. Satirical non-fiction. It is *Basic Instinct* dressed up as *The 7 Habits*.

The stories in this book are inspired by real leaders who overcame real challenges. There are no famous personalities in this book. That is intentional. Just because these stories are not about some multi-billionaire business magnate does not make them any less iconic. In telling these quotidian but nonetheless dramatic tales of creativity and courage, I hope they trigger some epic moments from your own extraordinary career — when something touched your heart, and you're lifted beyond ordinary experiences. I hope that these stories connect with you in ways that plain facts can never do, and in reading them, they shift the way you look at the world, and you're never the same again. You are changed.

You may be suspicious of the hubris and delusional thinking in this book. But how else do we dance on the edge of greatness? Definitely not by being a bystander to our own lives, a gulf of a misspent life, lived according to other people's rules. Not when you can become the glorious shining star of your very own singularly powerful and beautiful movie.

And like all great superhero movies, your astonishing acts of humanity will inspire those around you to rise up to greatness. Your success brings others up with you.

This book is about making a real change. That means thinking along new lines and doing things differently. The world is magical and full of delightful experiences to be explored. Develop the courage to take that first step into the unknown. To honor the power within. And to lead in the way as only you can.

Let's begin.

Note: The stories in this book are inspired by real people in real situations. Names have been changed so that we can get up close and personal. Some stories have been combined or modified for clarity.

Introduction: Greatness Requires A Personal Commitment

"You must have chaos within you to give birth to a dancing star."

— **Friedrich Nietzsche**

It's 7 p.m. on a Monday. Andrew has just sent off his last email for the day. He shuts his computer and leaves the headquarters office of OCBC Bank (the second-largest banking group in Singapore). But Andrew doesn't head home. Instead, he walks down the block and turns right onto New Bridge Road. Making sure no one is following him, Andrew slips into one of the shophouses. He spends another three hours here creating modifications to the bank's system.

No, this is not a real-life version of *Fight Club*. This is The Open Vault, OCBC Bank's fintech lab. And who's Tyler in this story? Pranav Seth, head of their e-business and business transformation division. He has been tasked with driving corporate innovation for the bank as competition heats up in the industry. Competition is no longer just coming from the other banks. OCBC Bank is going head-to-head against unconventional competitors, from tech giants like Alibaba, Apple and Google to the hordes of nimble fintech start-ups that are looking to disrupt the banking industry and eat the most delectable part of their lunch.

The Open Vault has been quietly taking in incredibly clever maverick bankers like Andrew who slip into the lab after office hours to try out different ways to solve big, deep problems of banking. And it's working. Andrew succeeded in building a pilot blockchain payment transaction between the bank and its subsidiaries.[1] A first for a Southeast Asian bank. The Open Vault also incubated the birth of Emma, a home loans chatbot, that helped close more than S$10 million in home loans before she turned six months old.

1. Safehouse for rebels

With such breakthrough success, why the need for secrecy?

While everyone pontificates about the importance of innovation, in reality, most managers are not in favor of pursuing the ideas, and may even be totally opposed to new innovations. People risk losing out on promotions, even their jobs if they try to do things that displease their bosses. In theory, they may have received their managers' blessings. However, their night-time shenanigans can't affect their day jobs — they still have to hit their KPIs (key performance indicators).

Other managers are not as supportive. They see mavericks like Andrew as troublemakers, rebels, terrorists. That's right — corporate terrorists. And I'm not using that word for dramatic effect. In 2013, a technical glitch brought down the entire online and ATM networks of another bank. There's a lot at stake here. As a leader, how do you encourage disruptive behavior without disrupting the business?

And so The Open Vault is a quietly brilliant idea. It's a simulation center, a digital twin to the banking system, to allow for system enhancements and testing to be done offline without disrupting service. Innovation only happens from engaging with reality. In this case, it's a digital twin. The Open Vault is a safe house in the sense that it provides a secure environment that allows Andrew to tinker safely without the risk of bringing down the banking system. It's also a safe house where Andrew can go to work on his radical ideas without the risk of losing his day job. In essence, Pranav, Andrew and the organization have created a secret garden where wild ideas have a fighting chance.

Let's be honest here. To the rest of the organization that value order and control, transformational leaders like Pranav and Andrew are seen as saboteurs. These rebels create mayhem, rock the boat, and even burn the ship once they reach the other shore. All to support a breakthrough idea. Slaughtering sacred cows — processes and products that made the organization successful but are becoming less relevant today — may be repulsive. It's certainly alienating. But it does not stop transformational leaders from pursuing better innovation. And the results are marvelous. But make no mistake. They move against the institutional grain in a way that makes the rest of the organization twitch with nervous anxiety.

2. At the edge of despair

Every day, we are under immense pressure to perform at the top of our game. But perfection is such a fragile thing. In the chase for greatness, sometimes you can come very, very close but still not get into the perfect rhythm. Instead, you end up overwhelmed and burnt out. Somehow, somewhere, you got derailed.

No matter how hard you try to keep your career, team and organization on the straight and narrow, they just don't seem to cooperate. They constantly misbehave. Like the morning mist, perfection is ephemeral, not something you can grasp or cling to. One minute you are on a rocketship trajectory to rockstar-CEO-dom, and the next you are being told that your job has been made redundant. One minute you are the darling of the venture capital world, the next minute your start-up has run out of cash. Despite your best efforts, you still end up in utter, cataclysmic disaster.

Understandably, we try our best to avoid such crises at work. But no matter how much money and time we throw at them, something will still go wrong. We live with this constant fear that something unpleasant is going to happen. It can feel like the edge of despair. But what if this is also the edge of greatness?

3. Blame the scapegoat

Peter (*not his real name) is the station manager on duty at the Ang Mo Kio train station. It's the evening rush hour and the train has just pulled into the station like clockwork. Peter monitors the closed-circuit camera as people pour out and board the train. Soon the train is ready to move off to the next station. But it doesn't. A fault signal lights up — a train door fault. Peter leaves the station control room and goes to the platform to inspect.

The standard operating procedure would call for him to disembark all the passengers before attempting any intervention. *But this is a simple fix. It's rush hour, and we don't want to cause any trouble.*

Peter goes inside the train to try and fix the door. He makes a mistake, and before he knows it, the train is moving off. With the door still open.

Peter immediately goes into disaster recovery mode. He tells the commuters to stay away from the door. He uses the in-train intercom to inform all the other passengers to keep clear of the door area and hold on to the grip poles.

After traveling around 200 meters, the train stops and returns to Ang Mo Kio station, where all commuters disembark safely. No one was hurt.

Peter acted heroically. His thousands of hours of experience and training to prepare for situations like these kicked in. He should be celebrated as a role model who survived a crisis safely. He didn't freak out, held his composure the entire time and kept everyone safe. In the personal development world where the likes of Tony Robbins are worshipped, they would package Peter up and send him on a roadshow to emphasize the importance of the (dreadfully boring) safety drills and how to stay calm during a crisis. But how did Peter's employer reward him?

He was suspended from his job with immediate effect. He was awarded the Cone of Shame for his bravery. Not only that, the whole country got to know about the shame the next day on the front page of the national newspaper.[2]

When things go wrong, people are quick to blame a scapegoat. According to McKinsey,[3] 70% of transformation programs fail, largely due to employee resistance and lack of management support. As managers, we find it easier to blame our employees for resisting our transformation programs. As employees, we find it easier to blame our managers for not supporting our grand ambitions. You can see how natural it is to blame people when things go wrong. We like to turn it into a people problem. **And that's the first leadership challenge today: what looks like a people problem is often a growth problem.**

4. Cone of shame

Nobody likes uncertainty, and corporations rarely tolerate it at all. The organizational structure, strategic plans, annual budgets, traffic light scorecards and standard operating procedures (SOPs) all serve to add a sheen of certainty to what is, in its glorious truth, an uncertain world.

Intellectually, we know that we can't completely eliminate risk. No matter how well you plan, there will still be a risk that things won't go according to plan. That's reality. Intellectually, we know we should accept some risk, just like we accept the weather. But organizations have a severe intolerance to risk. They talk about managing risk, but that can be a misnomer. Leaders *manage* risk. Pranav manages risk by creating a safehouse where innovators like Andrew can carefully test their daring and radical ideas. Management and corporate bureaucracy seek to avoid risk altogether. In their minds, failure is interpreted as incompetent risk avoidance — Peter failed to prevent the mistake, so he was seen as incompetent.

How will employees behave if they work in an environment that punishes them for failing to prevent a mistake?

For starters, employees will stick to what they already know. *This is how we've always done it.* They'll pursue ideas that serve customers they already know, using infrastructure and skills that they already have. Play it safe. *Just shut up and collect your paycheck.* In other words, be a RHINO: Really Here In Name Only.

A RHINO may not be actively impeding innovation, but they're not helping much, either. Now, the WOLF is a different story. WOLF: Working On Latest Fire. A WOLF will analyze all potential risks, imaginary problems that might occur in the future, and apply avoidance measures. To them, everything — and I mean *everything* — is a potential fire that must be put out before it even starts. They call this "scenario planning." It's not. It's creating pretend solutions to solve imaginary tragedies, dressed up as "scenario planning". They see every little potential fault as a looming crisis and deploy such nitpicking counter-measures, which interrupt people from actually doing their jobs.

The last thing a RHINO or WOLF will do is take a risk to try something different. *What if it bombed?* That will be a deliberate display of incompetence — at avoiding risk.

This environment of avoiding risk is the antithesis of the growth mindset. It's a sort of deception when the Human Resources (HR) department rolls out "growth mindset" workshops across the organization. Only the most ignorant, gullible and clueless will heed the call to prime for growth. But they will learn the lesson fast — when the swarm of corporate sentinels pulverizes any semblance of childlike curiosity and awe left in them. Like a sugar cane press, this is how the juiciest part of disruptive ideas is squeezed out as it goes through the corporate mill. We place boundaries around our thinking before we even begin.

5. The learning edge

I'm not suggesting that organizations throw caution to the wind and break loose. That would be flipping to the other extreme, where anarchy and chaos reign. But there needs to be some courage to do the things that make us feel uncomfortable.

Michael Jordan is touted to be the greatest scorer in the history of the NBA. This achievement didn't come about just because he succeeded more often than other people. Michael missed more than 9,000 shots in his career. He lost almost 300 games. He has failed over and over again. He simply took more shots at the goal and that's why he succeeded.

So, what does this mean for you and your organization? The more shots you take at the goal, the more likely you are to succeed. And this is important to note: you miss ALL the shots you don't make. It's simple mathematics. Being a winner doesn't mean that you never lose. You are simply prepared to shrug off more failures.

Herein lies the real challenge. As over-achievers, our instinct for loss aversion is violently intense. Just thinking of an idea that has the slightest possibility of failure makes us twitch with anxiety. *That won't work! How stupid is that?! You'll embarrass yourself, and all of us!* Anything that threatens to disrupt the warmth and safety of the cocoon will be met with deadly malice. We erect defenses — the Great Wall of innovation — to protect ourselves from the wild ideas that we think will embarrass us in public. We install complicated mechanisms to prevent people from making mistakes, reward people for avoiding mistakes and punish people when they make them. That's how we stop the future from emerging. We don't take the shot. We play it safe. We end up holding on to the past for dear life.

Here's the thing. On the other side of the Great Wall of innovation, there might be all those wild ideas, including some interesting and worthwhile ones. And what if one of the hidden ideas could be THE BIG IDEA that would be really exciting for your organization?

I often hear leaders complain about the lack of innovative ideas in their organizations. The real problem is not the lack of innovative ideas. There is a bottom swell of ideas from innovators like Andrew that can help their organizations tackle real industry problems, but the Great Wall of innovation keeps these wild ideas out... until it can't. And the Great Wall comes crumbling down. Risk-averse leaders get attached to the successes of the past and react negatively to every new initiative. They resist and resent everything and everyone that does not fall into their neat little boxes. But by denying the emerging ideas — trivial ideas that will become so obvious in hindsight — they get left behind in the past. That's how multi-billion-dollar giants fall.

Things change, disruption happens, as they do. With change comes the need for adaptation, for fresh thinking and sometimes a total reboot. What looks like a people problem is usually a wicked growth problem, which will require your best ideas. To get your *best* ideas, you want access to *all* your ideas. It takes a strong dose of courage to lower the Great Wall of innovation. That feeling of fear is intense and real. It can feel like the edge of despair. But this is also the edge of greatness because beyond the Great

Wall is a plethora of wild ideas, promising tantalizing and ingenious possibilities.

The edge of despair is also the edge of greatness if you hold the space to manage the risk instead of avoiding it.

Lowering the Great Wall of innovation is not easy. It can feel scary, but it is not dangerous. It may be the safest thing for your organization to stay relevant. Avoiding risk is the real danger. Pretending the risk is not there does not make it go away. As leaders, we want to celebrate when people manage risk. I find the most inspiring example of this leadership behavior at skateboard parks. When a skateboarder is learning a new trick and he fluffs it, everyone claps! When he fluffs it again, everyone claps again. No one tells him that he's not good enough. No one tells him to give up. Instead, they continue to applaud his attempts. Now, this is a safe place where taking risk is celebrated. And it does not need to be confined to skateboard parks. The Open Vault proves you can bring this into corporations, too. **When you provide a safe environment where people can experiment without the fear of being punished, their innovative ideas then have a fighting chance to create seismic shifts in the industry, without disrupting your business.**

6. The dream factory

Joe (*not his real name) was loading baggage onto the plane at the Cebu airport when his CEO picked him out of the rest. The CEO thought he showed potential and asked him whether he aspired to be a pilot. Seven years later, Joe became a captain of a brand new A320 Airbus.[4] The CEO is Tony Fernandes, and the organization is AirAsia, the largest low-cost airline in Southeast Asia.

AirAsia doesn't see itself as another airline. Instead, they consider themselves a dream factory. Tony's self-proclaimed job is to turn raw diamonds into polished ones. Tony saw a future pilot where others saw a bag carrier. When he said, "Now everyone can fly," he wasn't only talking about the passengers. Tony relies on his instinct for spotting leadership qualities in others. His instinct for talent is so uncanny that he can spot them in the most unusual places.

A dream factory does not happen on its own. It's a deliberate decision to build a company where people can be creative and passionate about what they do. It requires the organization to have a personal commitment to develop and optimize all the talent they have in-house. Every CEO says that people are their greatest assets. So why aren't there more "dream factories"?

7. The corporate machine

Modern corporations are built for scale. It's all about efficiency, cost-cutting, profit maximization and winning at all costs. Processes are compartmentalized and standardized to fit a neat workflow. Managers operate in their own functional silos. They break big problems into smaller chunks and then assign employees to handle each piece. Here's an example. A sales manager carries a sales target of $400,000. The sales manager has four salespeople. So you divide $400,000 among four people. Each salesperson has to deliver $100,000. Better still, make it $110,000 each, in case someone falls short. It's simple maths.

What happens if they don't hit their targets? The sales manager needs to show his boss that he's doing something, so he launches into problem-solving mode. The sales manager sees the delinquent salesperson as the problem. So how do you solve the problem? By removing the problem. *No delinquent salesperson, no problem.* It becomes a witch hunt to prove the person's incompetence, lest the incompetence is pinned on the sales manager himself. Rather inhumane, perhaps? Well, it helps if leaders think of people as objects to achieve their goals, not humans with real feelings.

8. Treating people as objects

People in senior leadership positions are goal-focused. Logical, objective, they do what's necessary to accomplish their goals and achieve results. But maybe in the pursuit of performance, leaders lose sight of something. They stop thinking of people as people, humans with values and emotions. Instead, people are seen as objects or concepts to achieve the organizational goals.

Power blinds us to other people's perspectives.[5] Treating people as people becomes harder the more power we have. Power does very specific things to the brain, and it happens below the conscious level, without you even realizing it. It's not a gender thing; both men and women are afflicted by it. If you have a functioning brain, then you've got the propensity for power blindness.

When things are going well or in nice social settings, leaders smile, they say the right things: *People are our greatest assets.* But when the business is under intense growth pressure, that's when they're more likely to go power blind. The inner tyrant emerges; military orders ensue. They assume people will fall in line. *We just don't have the luxury of time or money to deal with everyone's concerns. Just get on with it.* When the business is in a crisis, leaders fall back to their Excel sheets. At a time when there is a need to upskill people, to empower people to do things differently, leaders do the opposite. The first thing they cut is the "people" budget. This behavior happens like clockwork.

Every CEO says: *People are our greatest assets*. But that can be a misnomer. You invest in assets, and they give you a healthy return over time. The modern organization is designed to extract value — now. Take our performance management system, for example. The dreaded annual performance review is, in essence, an exercise in assessing people's contributions. It's more focused on what the organization extracted from the human "resources", rather than helping them grow.

To understand other people's thinking and feelings, you need to have empathy. Putting yourself in other people's shoes is a very active task. Tony literally puts himself in his employees' shoes. He has worked all the jobs in the airline. Tony has changed aircraft wheels, checked passengers in, carried bags and served food and drinks on flights. He has even flown a plane — albeit in a simulator.[6]

Sometimes it's not safe or practical for CEOs to literally put themselves in their employees' shoes. There are other ways to put yourself in your employees' shoes. Within a few months of taking the helm as the CEO for Singapore train operator SMRT, Neo Kian Hong visited train stations in the day and walked the tunnels in the night. He talked to as many employees on the ground as he could, asking questions about their jobs and suggestions on how SMRT can do better.[7]

This is a very active task. Employees on the ground are not trained in "boardroom speak" or "spinning the truth." A supervisor might try to intervene and answer on behalf of the ground staff. The CEO needs to exercise great diplomacy to gently interrupt the supervisor and revert the attention to the ground staff. This is how you avoid getting second- or third-hand information. "Showing face" is not enough.

This is an exercise of humility in so many ways. Physically, you must strip away your crisp business shirt and don the humble uniform. Verbally, you must drop your impeccable English and sink into colloquial Singlish. Intellectually, you have to believe that the ground staff you are speaking to know how to do their jobs better than you do. This is important. Most CEOs think they know how to do their employees' jobs better than they do. (Likewise, some employees think they know how to do their CEO's job better than they do.) Put simply, you must stop your prodigious and everlasting monologue in order to listen to the other person fully. Emotionally, you have to be vulnerable and deal with unutterably strange and intolerable emotions without judgment.

So this is the second leadership challenge: if you're not actively empowering people, then you're disempowering them unintentionally.

9. The problem with greatness

We say that we want to achieve greatness, but there's this little problem: if you want to achieve greatness, then it must be more than just a job that pays the bills. It must be more than just business. It has to be EXTRA-ordinary. Greatness requires a personal commitment. Put simply, no CEO, athlete or artist has ever reached great heights without putting their hearts into it.

Intellectually, we know this, yet we don't do it. At the moment, our instinct is to protect our hearts. We guard ourselves against feeling any emotions at work. *It's just business. It's not personal.* Our hearts are closed in the guise of being objective. We have not put our hearts into it.

I know I'm treading on thin ice here, but hear me out for a minute. You might be thinking: *Isn't it enough that I'm working 12 hours a day, six days a week? Or that I'm giving it my best? I'm killing myself here trying to do everything and please everyone, doesn't that prove that my heart is in it?*

There can be a sense when we're at work that going through the motions is enough. This is especially true when you're experiencing the challenges of modern corporate life with its impossible targets and ridiculous timelines. You toil to tick all the boxes in your to-do list, which despite your best efforts, never seem to get any shorter. And yet you keep at it. Every day. You do this automatically, without thinking. You don't question it. You're on autopilot, and there's no off switch. Is it any wonder that you feel so overwhelmed, anxious and scared? Things like "leadership development" and "work tech" which are supposed to make your job easier, instead feel like yet another item on your to-do list. Driven by expectations of blatantly commercial promotion, you forge ahead with sheer willpower. *Grit your teeth. Just get on with it. Stop being lazy.* But no matter how hard you work, you still end up back where you started: overwhelmed, anxious and scared.

This kind of behavior doesn't faze us.

10. Breakdown becomes breakthrough

We are strangers to delight. There is a suspicion of joy, as if experiencing pleasure at work is a sin and tantamount to a lack of rigor. We are more familiar with being hard on ourselves. We are highly trained experts at beating ourselves up. We wage a silent war every day, and we can't escape because that tyrannical voice is *inside* us. But ultimately, it's not sustainable. Eventually, we burn out. Willpower is not an inexhaustible resource; it runs out. We end up working very hard, going nowhere.

When we're experiencing the challenges of modern corporate life with its impossible targets and ridiculous timelines, we have every reason to feel overwhelmed, anxious or scared. But we run away from acknowledging these conflicting emotions. We ignore these difficult emotions. We think that being a leader means feeling overwhelmed, anxious and scared, and still meeting the impossible targets within the ridiculous timelines anyway. Just browbeat into submission that gut instinct of yours. Go ahead, tyrannize yourself. Because we think that the alternative — actually listening to our gut instinct — will make us lose our edge. We think we will turn into an emotional puddle; we will look weak. This terrifies us. So we stay detached, logical and unemotional. We glorify the busyness of our lives at work. *It's just business. It's not personal.* Burnout is worn like a badge of honor: *See how tough I am!*

As adults, we have learned to bury our difficult emotions and put up a brave front. A tragic gap starts to form between the brave front we put up externally and how we actually feel internally. We deny our difficult emotions, up to the point where we can't, and the volcano erupts. We say something we can't take back. We do something we'll regret later.

Instead, when you stop running away from the difficult emotions and allow yourself the space to acknowledge them, you spontaneously let go of it, just as feeling the hot handle of a cast-iron skillet makes you let go. You feel a moment of huge relief, like putting down a heavy load.

Aaaaahhhhh...... It's like pressing a reset button. The voluminous and blood-flecked clouds dissipate. Your usual sense of confidence and composure returns. You reconnect to your natural power source. This vitality arises from *acknowledging* the difficult emotion, not *denying* it. It's like magic. The breakdown becomes the breakthrough. Acknowledging your difficult emotions can be the kindest thing you can do for yourself.

Acknowledging our emotions is not easy. Difficult emotions can feel unpleasant. It makes us feel vulnerable like we're on the edge of despair. We forget that emotions are temporary; they don't last. Have you seen how emotionally agile babies are? They can switch from crying to laughing in an instant. When you acknowledge the difficult emotions, you spontaneously let go of them.

The edge of despair is also the edge of greatness if you hold the space to regulate your emotions instead of burying them. The simple act of labeling and validating your emotion changes the brain, and helps you to relax. Paradoxically, the more you deny your difficult emotions, the tighter you hold on to it until you can no longer do it and it erupts — usually at the most inconvenient time.

Managing your emotions is not a descent into an abyss of nothingness. It's the confidence to hold yourself as an intentional calming force in the midst of tumultuous emotions. It's those simple moments when you confidently open yourself to the full range of your cosmic emotions — rather than feel rushed, inconvenienced or anxious — that can make all the difference. You don't freeze your emotions; you dance with them. You live fully in the face of everything you have to deal with. Between pleasure and misery. Between hope and despair. Between greatness and adversity. You're dancing on the edge of greatness.

11. Pure rocket energy

An outdated (yet still popular) view is that emotions make you weak. It gets in the way of making tough decisions. Emotions on their own do not make you weak. Not learning to manage them makes you weak. Staying connected to our emotions unlocks a megatonne of energy. The Latin derivative for the word emotion, "*emotere*," literally means energy in motion. Emotions are automatic responses to dangers and rewards. Emotions prepare us to deal with important events without having to think about them. We don't choose to feel them; they just happen to us automatically.[8] It's PURE ENERGY. The key is to regulate your emotions, instead of being at their mercy. Leading from an open heart makes our mundane day-to-day responsibilities come alive and become a source of joy instead of feeling like an obligation. We have stronger convictions when we encounter unexpected challenges. We are more resilient when we face resistance. We are more forgiving when we experience losses and exhaustion.

Trying to achieve greatness without putting your heart into it is like trying to get to Mars in a horse-drawn carriage when you have a rocket booster in your garage. Without putting your heart into it, you go through the motions using the whip of willpower. *Stop being lazy.* But eventually, the willpower runs out. The corresponding change is superficial. Deep transformation does not occur.

When we don't regulate our emotions, we eat, drink, work, shop or exercise them away. But the change is superficial. Denying our emotions is the real villain — pretending it's not there does not mean it's not there, or that we don't act on it. Instead, take ownership of your emotions, regulate it and unleash your rocket power. Let emotions touch your heart and allow the magic to happen.

12. A company is not an individual

A company is a team of individuals. It's not about propping up the star player at the cost of the team losing the game. The problem occurs when leaders get that confused.

When employees underperform at work, managers think it has little or nothing to do with how they treat their employees — that it's entirely up to the person alone. *The person is incompetent.* But that's simply not true.

Whether a leader blames people for their incompetence or rescues them from it, it threatens and undermines people's mental ability to be at their best. They develop learned helplessness. When people feel like they have no control over what happens, they tend to simply give up and accept their fate. As a leader, you have to understand that you're partly responsible for your employee's mental state and subsequent inability to do better.

There is also a power factor: emotions are most contagious when emanating from the most powerful person in a group. Emotions are as contagious as the Ebola virus. When denial happens as a group at the leadership level, that anger or fear cascades through the organization unconsciously. You're the fountainhead. Toxic water flows downhill.

But so does clean water. As the leader, you have an incredible opportunity to help your employees manage their emotions and feel good about themselves. You can help them get into and stay in an internal state where they can do their best work. Tony saw a future pilot where others saw a bag carrier. When you outwardly state that your employees take pride in their work and come to work daily committed to do their best, you are holding the space for them to show up powerfully at work. And they do. Nobody shows up at work to suck at their jobs; everyone wants to do well.

This might sound fluffy and delusional, but it isn't an excuse to sweep problems under the carpet. People are not perfect. Inter-personal conflicts will still happen. But your typical adverse response to conflicts and difficult people becomes milder and less disruptive. The villain here is denial. The willingness to patiently witness someone's drama queen antics and imperious power trips without resentment, judgment, or fear may be the necessary means to help the person hit their reset button and regain their confidence and composure.

You also hold the space for yourself to rise as a leader. When a power fault disrupted train services in Singapore on 14 October 2020, Transport Minister Ong Ye Kung — Singapore's top transport official — apologized to commuters in a Facebook post.[9] This is an amazing act of grace by a leader. He's sharing the stress, and not stressing others to make himself feel better. It's a very fine line, but it makes all the difference. When things go pear-shaped, will you rely on having the biggest stick or the harshest voice in the room? Or are you going to hone the connection and collaboration skills to operate at the highest level? This requires emotional intelligence. We think that emotional intelligence is a "soft" skill. Try maintaining your composure while facing the full force of ire from 123,000 commuters. There's nothing fluffy or touchy-feely about emotional intelligence. It is absolutely foundational to leadership.

The higher you climb, the more your success depends on making other people successful. It does not mean you have to be a people pleaser. **If you want people to perform at the top of their game, then it must be much more than just business. Engage your emotional side. It's not just business. It's also personal.**

13. CXA story

When running the APAC business for employee health and benefits consulting company Mercer Marsh Benefits, Rosaline would receive complaints from clients about the escalating costs of insuring their employees.[10] Molly, Rosaline's most demanding HR client, pointed out how her insurance premiums were doubling every three years as her middle-aged factory workers had chronic diseases. She lamented how only the healthy attended her wellness activities, whereas the sedentary and obese never showed. And how despite all the money she spent, she couldn't see the link between her wellness efforts and her insurance premiums!

Molly was the first of many HRs to say to Rosaline: "You're my broker — why can't you help me fix this?"

Rosaline came up with a simple and radical idea: rather than wait for employees to get sick and be hospitalized to benefit from insurance, why not shift part of that insurance money into early detection and disease prevention?

Rosaline didn't stop there. She even figured out how to solve this issue using technology. It just needed an investment of US$10 million. Rosaline pitched the idea to her global bosses in New York. They rejected her idea. She didn't give up. She tried again. And again. And again. After trying for five years, in 2013, she finally gave up and left Mercer to build it on her own.

Little did she realize that the US$10 million would come from her own pocket. Rosaline ended up investing her family's entire savings of US$5 million and signed a personal guarantee for another US$5 million loan to build the technology and acquire an SME insurance broker.

CXA began by capturing employees' health data — blood tests, lifestyles, claims and activities. With the data, they created functionalities that benefit everyone. Employees are given a personal recommendation on ways to be healthier and a wallet to choose the health benefits that work best for them. HR receives anonymized data and tools to offer targeted interventions, attacking their highest-cost claims, addressing Molly's diabetic factory workers. The insurance brokers use the data to negotiate reduced premiums from insurers.

Molly, of course, demanded that CXA do this without adding work for her HR team. So CXA consolidated all of Molly's vendors onto one platform, thus capturing data at the source and eliminating the paperwork between her company and employees, insurers and all her providers.

And since Molly's such a tough negotiator, like every other HR person, CXA's flex and wellness platform come for free when CXA is appointed as the broker.

CXA was valued at $107 million after its Series B funding round in 2017. As of 2020, CXA was serving more than 600 enterprises and more than 700,000 users across 20 countries in Asia.

14. Analysis paralysis

Note how Rosaline spent five years navigating the corporate bureaucracy in Mercer but getting nowhere. On her own, Rosaline built CXA into a $100 million company in four years.

This is not surprising. Launching a new product in large corporations is laborious and expensive. Corporations spend years in conceptualization to launch a new product. They invest significant amounts of money, time and brainpower to estimate market size, conduct focus groups, scan the competitive landscape, analyze the capacity to execute, draw up a fancy 35-page business plan and go through multiple budget rounds. *Everything must be perfect. You can only rob the bank once.* Approval is by consensus, so the team has to make sure *everyone* is happy. APAC, EMEA and the Americas have to sign off on it. Everyone — Product, Sales, Marketing, Customer Service, IT, Finance, Legal — has veto power over every little detail. By the time they get to launch, they have invested significant time and money on theoretical models. They've cut their own time windows short and created a much lower margin for error. They almost *have* to succeed right away or leave the market. This approach makes it harder than it needs to be to experiment or pivot.[11]

The 35-page business plan provides a sheen of confidence that people actually know what they're doing — even when they don't. This is the Dunning-Kruger effect:[12] a cognitive bias whereby people who are incompetent at something are unable to recognize their own incompetence. Not only do they fail to recognize their incompetence, but they're also likely to grossly overestimate their abilities. Essentially, be a ZEBRA: Zero

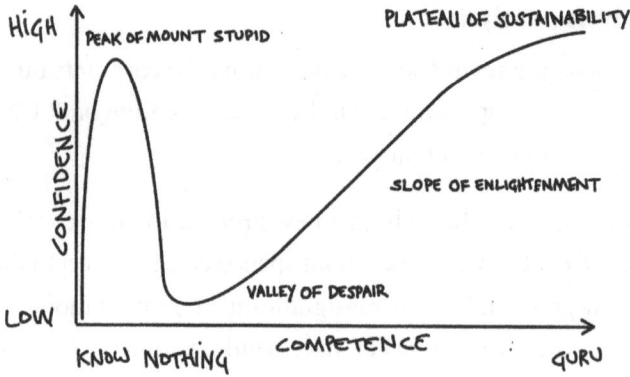

Figure 1.1: Dunning-Kruger Effect

Evidence But Really Arrogant. The Dunning-Kruger effect is typically depicted as the diagram in Figure 1.1.

And here is the third leadership challenge: think big, act big, and you'll grow smaller.

15. Find the bright spots

When developing an idea, transformational leaders like Rosaline move quickly from concept to prototype, which they then test with a *small* group of customers. They get their prototype into customers' hands as quickly as possible, find the bright spots — the first signs that things are working — and then rework the prototype based on that real market experience. They handcraft to find out what works — the bright spots — and then they scale it. **Think big, act small, and you'll grow bigger.**

This might sound ludicrous to you. After all, you are an alpha red leader with global ambitions. Rosaline couldn't possibly have personally invited

700,000 users onto her platform. You might be tempted to think that Rosaline had one brilliant idea, built a fantastic product and customers just poured in, right? Here's the thing. Changing people's attitudes and habits is incredibly complex. It requires trial and error. Not recognizing how difficult it is takes you out of the action, and is *truly* delusional. No theoretical business model survives first contact with reality. Instead of naïve idealism, Rosaline gave her business concept a fighting chance by creating small prototypes and quickly engaging with real situations and real customers. When you engage directly with reality, the solutions that emerge from *within* the complexity are inherently realistic and sustainable.

16. Gravity problems

This might sound contradictory, but in order to scale, you first need to do the things that won't scale at all. When trying to solve big complex problems, it seems logical to seek a solution that befits the scale of the problems. *Big problem, big solution.* But these are gravity problems: problems we can't do anything about because they're just reality, like gravity. Or it's a really, really hard problem that will require significant effort and sacrifice and runs a high risk of failure.

If I analyzed what's causing the escalating costs of insurance premiums, I may deduce that it is a direct result of escalating healthcare costs, of which a contributing factor could be the over-consumption, over-servicing and overcharging of medical services. It may be logical to think: regulate the medical costs, and insurance premiums will drop. But healthcare is one of the most complex industries to manage. This would mean reforming the healthcare system. If addressing escalating insurance premiums required reforming the healthcare system, then it would never happen. Especially not in four years, and with US$10 million. Reforming healthcare is a gravity problem — it is not actionable for Rosaline. Instead, Rosaline accepted the realities of the complex healthcare ecosystem, which freed her to reframe the problem: Rather than wait for people to get sick and be hospitalized, how do you keep them away from the hospital in the first place?

Humans are an odd bunch. We fight reality. We fight it tooth and nail. Accepting reality can feel like the edge of despair for us. We think that accepting reality is synonymous with surrender and giving up. Our insufferable puffed-up ego has to eat humble pie. **But this is also the edge of greatness if you hold the space to accept the reality of the things you can't change instead of fighting it.**

When you're trying to solve a gravity problem, you're stuck permanently, because there's nothing you can do. Solving a gravity problem is not actionable. No matter how much money and time you throw at it, reality will win. Instead, when you accept the reality of the things you can't change, it liberates you to work around the situation and reframe the problem to be actionable. In truth, it's the constraints we face every day that force us to be innovative. If we want to solve big complex problems, we have to accept the gravity problems (the things we can't change), and find the bright spots (the things we can change). Now that's empowering!

17. How David beat Goliath

You may say that thinking big and acting small only works for start-ups with no encumbrances. It doesn't work for monolithic organizations that are ungovernable and unwieldy, where more energy is devoted to navigating the labyrinth than achieving results. It may seem like naïve idealism to think that small solutions can solve large complex organizational problems given their scale, legacy systems and conflicting priorities. We want to believe that there is *one* perfect bureaucratic solution that will fix *everything* that is broken in the organization. The panacea to all corporate ills. Sure, with infinite patience, time and money, we could fix anything. In theory. The reality is... we wouldn't. With all that freedom, we would try to do everything, and end up moving an inch in a million directions. *Think big, act big, and you'll grow smaller.* In actually believing there is one perfect solution to fix all your organization's problems, now who is the naïve one?

The modern organization was built upon a production line approach to achieve economies of scale. This works wonderfully when things don't change. But what happens when a large complex organization has to go through change? A lot of things will go wrong. Their leaders will see problems everywhere. If they asked, "What's broken and how do we fix it?", they'll simply spin their wheels.

Instead, think big, act small. In this respect, we can find a bright spot at the SMRT. From the first day taking the helm as CEO of SMRT, Neo brought things back to basics. He set a clear mandate for everyone in the organization: deliver safe, reliable and comfortable train services. Within months, Neo reorganized the organization to bring the focus back to its primary business, which is to manage and operate train services. "Delivering safe, reliable and comfortable train services" is a tangible and measurable outcome. There's nothing subjective about it. Neo provided crystal-clear direction, showing people where to go, how to act and what goals to pursue. It spelt out in no uncertain terms what is most important to the organization. Let's be crystal clear here. The CEO did not say, "Deliver safe, reliable and comfortable train services, but not at the cost of profit maximization."

This empowers cross-departmental teams to resolve conflicting priorities and overcome stalemates. *Will this make our train services more safe, reliable and comfortable?* If the answer is yes, then they can proceed. If the answer is no, then they know they had better re-evaluate what they're doing.

This also empowers employees to prioritize their work. *Will this make our train services more safe, reliable and comfortable?* Whether they are a janitor, a station manager or a head of the department, they know in no uncertain terms what is most important to the organization. More importantly, it empowers them to say no to requests that will take them away from the primary goal. That's how the entire organization stays focused.

This is a change from the inside out. The changes emerge from *within* the complexity. There is greater accountability. The changes are inherently realistic and sustainable, and thus more likely to stick.

18. Dancing on the edge of greatness

You are an extraordinary force for positive change. You have tremendous potential to make a difference. But this potential does not unleash itself. Greatness requires a personal commitment.

No extraordinary journey is linear. You think a successful strategy starts with the perfect idea, followed by a tonne of hard work and capital flush, and then the straight line slope to enlightenment (Figure 1.1). That's a myth. In reality, the straight line slope of enlightenment is a series of

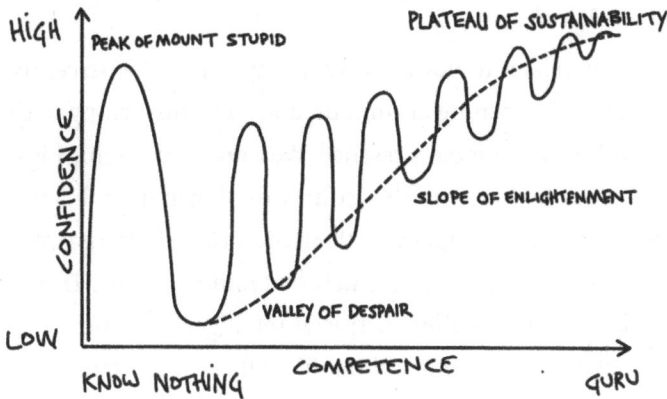

HIGH

PEAK OF MOUNT STUPID

PLATEAU OF SUSTAINABILITY

CONFIDENCE

SLOPE OF ENLIGHTENMENT

VALLEY OF DESPAIR

LOW

KNOW NOTHING   COMPETENCE   GURU

Figure 1.2: The 14 Peaks

bumps. It's a continuous sequence of peaks and valleys, flush with uncertainty and struggle. It's more like climbing the 14 Peaks (See Figure 1.2).

On the jagged slope of enlightenment, every advance reveals a new shortcoming. You meet the hesitation, unwillingness and raw fear that comes when we go beyond the confines of our conditioning. **It can feel like the edge of despair.** Change is not easy. When we try to change things, we're tinkering with behaviors that have become automatic — we do it without much thinking and feeling. Changing ingrained habits makes us feel uncomfortable. But this is exactly where it becomes exciting. This is the gateway to our next level of performance. **This is also the edge of greatness if you hold the space to learn from your experience instead of running away from it.** By your gifts and under the authority of a higher calling, you are compelled to lead. You can't *not* do it.

18.1 *Open Mind*

An open mind relates to our intellectual capacity to be perceptive to the changes that are happening around us, and to be discerning to distill the disruptive ideas to its simplest essence. We think that solving big complex problems requires big complex solutions that befit the scale of the problems. We develop complicated theoretical models. We go into analysis paralysis. We end up creating products that nobody wants. **Think big, act big, and you'll grow smaller.** Artificial intelligence is such a buzzword these days; everyone is talking about big data. I'm not talking about big data, but deep data. Notice how Rosaline did not try to directly mitigate the escalating cost of insurance, which is a gravity problem. Rosaline accepted the realities of the complex healthcare ecosystem, which freed her to reframe the problem and create a solution that is inherently realistic and sustainable. **Think big, act small, and you'll grow bigger.**

Being open-minded requires us to have the humility to face the uncomfortable truths, rather than perpetuate the comfortable lies. We fight reality. We fight it tooth and nail. **It can feel like the edge of despair. But this is also the edge of greatness if you hold the space to accept reality instead of fighting it.**

18.2 *Open Heart*

An open heart relates to our emotional intelligence and how we feel, which allows us to connect with ourselves and others as social beings. Our instinct is to protect our hearts in the guise of being objective. *It's just business. It's not personal.* We treat people as objects. We go through the motions, driven by the whip of sheer willpower, but it's not sustainable. The corresponding change is superficial. Deep transformation does not occur. **If you're not actively empowering people, then you're disempowering them**

unintentionally. If you want people to perform at the top of their game, then it must be much more than just business. Tony didn't see Joe as just a bag carrier. He could also see the future pilot within him. It's those simple moments when you confidently open yourself to emotions that can make all the difference. *It's not just business. It's also personal.* **Engage your emotional side. Make leadership personal.**

Being open-hearted requires us to drop our corporate bulletproof vest and be emotionally sensitive. This makes us feel vulnerable. **It can feel like the edge of despair. But this is also the edge of greatness if you hold the space to regulate your emotions instead of burying them.** Emotions are PURE ROCKET ENERGY. Not learning to manage them makes you weak.

18.3 *Open Will*

An open will relates to our capacity to make decisions and choose how we respond to a situation. When transformation fails, management blames it on employee resistance. Employees blame it on lack of management support. We play the blame game. **What looks like a people problem is often a wicked growth problem.** But we don't take the shot. We play it safe. We build the Great Wall of innovation. Avoiding risk is not the same as managing risk. Pranav manages risk by creating a safehouse where innovators like Andrew can carefully test their daring and radical ideas. **Provide a safe environment where people can test their ideas without the fear of being punished.** This gives you a fighting chance to create seismic shifts in the industry, without disrupting your business.

Being open-willed requires us to have the courage to confront our fear of the unknown. **It can feel like the edge of despair. But this is also the**

edge of greatness if you hold the space to manage the risk instead of avoiding it.

19. Biggest leadership mistake

Achieving greatness is not easy. It requires a personal commitment. But in today's modern corporate world, it feels unsafe to be personal. *It's just business. It's not personal.* We go through the motions. We don't rock the boat. We turn a blind eye. We're very busy working really hard, but not getting the results that we want. And yet we persevere. We don't allow anything to touch our hearts. We're on autopilot, with no off-switch. In the truly fascinating but nonetheless endless pursuit of profit maximization and winning at all costs, we may lose touch with what it means to be human. We become more machine-like. *Being machine-like is safe.*

Let me make this vivid for you. The three biggest leadership mistakes we're making today:

1. We are not clearly articulating our vision.
2. We are not listening.
3. We are avoiding the uncomfortable conversations.

And the single biggest mistake we're making as leaders today? Well, we're only throwing away something that means so much to us — our *humanness* — just because being overwhelmed and burnt out *feels* safe.

Here's my challenge for you. When working harder is not getting you the performance you desire, STOP. Don't work harder; work smarter. This will require a leap of faith. But do it anyway. Bring your full self to work: open your mind, open your heart, open your will. Engage fully with the world and drink up its life-giving juiciness. Make leadership personal. The result is magic.

20. What this book is about

The theme of change will pervade this entire book, but this is not a change management book. This is a leadership book, albeit in the non-traditional sense. It's a piece of satirical non-fiction. It's *Basic Instinct* dressed up as *The 7 Habits*.

In its essence, this book is about *you*. Its sole purpose, its whole reason for being, is to unlock the best way for *you* to lead. While there are plenty of captivating books on how to lead, this book focuses on the best way for *you* to lead. To step towards *your* learning edge and lead in the way only *you* can, given your experience. To be the first leader like *you*.

Of course, this seems rather preposterous. I don't know you. I've never even met you. So how can I even begin to write a book about you? One way would be for me to stop right here, give you sheets of blank pages, and ask you to start writing.

In my own experience, staring at a blank piece of paper trying to figure out who I am and what I'm here to do is one of the most daunting things I've ever had to confront. Most people run away from it; they don't think they have the answers. But I believe we already have the answers. No, you won't find it on the internet. It lies within. Our heart already knows what it wants. But it's something else altogether to articulate it. Think about all the things we can do without really being able to explain them. We rely on our non-conscious brain for all our habitual behaviors, from walking to doing our jobs. Ask someone to describe how they walk (or work), and they will struggle to describe the actual process to you. But they can do it without even thinking.[13] That's why our wisdom does not communicate in words. Instead, it communicates through our emotions and the intestines (those good old gut feelings). It's literally back to basic instincts.

When it comes to making our big career or work decisions, we think that feelings are a nuisance; a distraction that gets in the way of logical thinking. In fact, having an emotional reaction *during* the decision-making process is indispensable. That's the way your wisdom communicates with you: *Hey, this is important to us*. Without emotion, we'd be left floundering; we can't tell the forest from the trees.

And for this reason, I wrote this book for you. I offer up real-life stories with the hope that something will resonate with you and trigger those butterfly-fluttering gut feelings. You may read something that makes you go, "Oh my gosh, that's me!" Tune into your gut; your wisdom center is trying to communicate with you. *Hey, this is important to us*. Hold the space, don't rush, be curious, and you may get an aha moment, a sudden realization, one that you didn't see coming, that you know viscerally to be true. You will have tripped over the truth. Or not. Doing it this way takes some of the seriousness out of it. The heavy lifting has been done for you. You just need to sit back, relax and tune in to your gut. This makes the experience a whole lot more light-hearted and fun.

21. Leadership is deeply personal

The *Harvard Business Review Must Read Series* will have us believe that there is a standard formula for becoming a successful CEO. A model answer for CEO excellence. They make effective leadership look almost effortless. Just add water, and instantly ready to lead.

They are all lies.

Sure, we've come across great leaders who make effective leadership look natural and effortless, like Pranav, Andrew, Rosaline, and Tony. They have that... *je ne sais quoi*. An X-factor. That winning leadership persona. They look so effortlessly confident. Working with them feels easy. They bring out the best in everyone, helping teams and organizations prosper. They're the dream bosses. They achieve extraordinary success, and they make it all look easy. And we want to be like them. But I've learned, from personal experience, that simply copying their behaviors *does not work.*

Here's the thing. What you see — their winning leadership persona and extraordinary success — is just the tip of the iceberg (See Figure 1.3).[14]

We are often inspired by what we see, which are their winning behaviors and results. That lies above the surface of the ocean. But what we see is

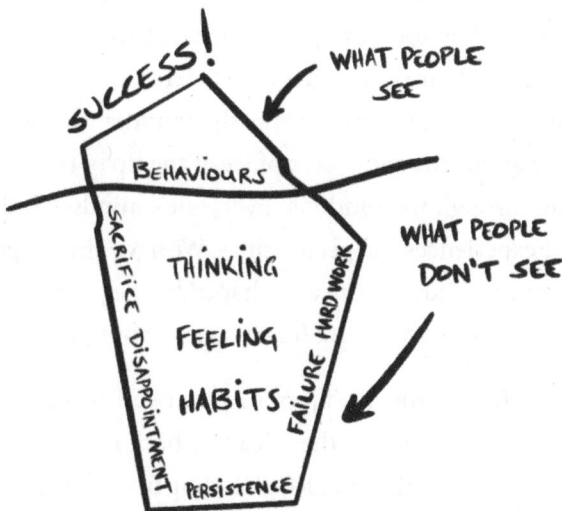

Figure 1.3: The leadership iceberg.

shaped by their mindsets — how they think, feel and make decisions — which lie below the surface of the ocean. We also do not see the sacrifices they made, the disappointments and failures they endured, which brought them to where they are today. It's invisible to us. Making leadership *look* easy is the result of a lot of hard work and careful cultivation of good mindsets over a long period. These leaders have been through the school of hard knocks, and that makes them very wise. They have built a stable, unshakeable inner wisdom through their own direct and personal experience. Wow, wisdom... that elusive genre of knowledge, unlike academic knowledge, which is necessarily acquired through blunders and mistakes, where the most enlightening lessons are recalled with deep mortification and a tinge of regret.

Like it or not, you already have a leadership persona. You have an original and ripe reputation based on how you get things done and interact with others. If you want to have that *je ne sais quoi* like these leaders, simply copying the way they look or speak won't cut the mustard. Wearing monogrammed cuff links or carrying a Chanel handbag does not automatically turn us into an effortlessly confident leader. That's like chipping away at the bits and pieces of ice at the tip of the iceberg. You'll only be going through the motions. Everyone's mindset is different. It's shaped by our experiences and peculiarities. We have distinct personalities, motivations and aptitudes. We're also shaped by the people we work with and the environment we work in. It's not one-size-fits-all.

For deep transformation to happen, you need to shift the lens of discernment from focusing on these leaders back to you. That *je ne sais quoi* comes from within. The practice of leading from the inside out means that, in every uncertain moment, you turn inward and *feel* for what is true. That's why leadership is deeply personal.

This book is about making that deep transformation journey. And our modern corporate world provides us with many opportunities to do so. We are constantly in conflict with the difficulties we face at work. Our greatest mistake is not recognizing these difficult situations as the opportunity for learning and growth. This IS the learning edge.

This book covers the most common edgy situations that leaders face. The ones that people complain about and lose sleep over. The things that people whisper about in the corridors, but never see the light of day in the boardroom. The stuff that people talk about behind your back, but never directly in your face. It's those parts of ourselves or our organizations that we sweep under the carpet and keep in the shadows because bringing it into the light causes anxiety. This is the 14 Peaks; the series of bumps. The practice of leading from the inside out means that we stop sweeping these difficult situations under the carpet and confront the elephant in the room. **It can feel like the edge of despair. But this is also the edge of greatness if you hold the space to reflect and learn from the experience instead of running away from it.** When you can see the elephant in the room, you can pull the rug out from under its feet. You understand things for yourself, beyond anything anyone can explain to you, and your behavior changes naturally. Deep transformation occurs. You solve your problems *permanently*. You stop chipping away at the tip of the iceberg.

Each chapter will guide you through a deep transformation journey of going over the edge and coming back, completely transformed. I hope that some of these stories will come too close for comfort for you. I want you to *feel* that frisson of excitement. It's by design. So a quick word of warning before we continue. In this journey, you may come face to face with inner demons and dysfunctional mindsets that have kept you disconnected and playing small. You can see now where the satirical non-fiction flavor comes from. I don't do this to be sarcastic or critical, or to mock anyone's weaknesses. Especially when there is none. The villain here is denial. When you stop turning a blind eye, the truth emerges. Then the solution becomes obvious. That's wisdom. You will have tripped over the truth. It's a defining moment that changes the way you see the world in an instant. It's like magic.

Of course, this is up to you. But whether you like it or not, those underlying habitual thought patterns are at work. You can pay attention to it and transform it into your superpower. Or you can deny it and have it become your kryptonite.

22. What this book is NOT about

Many leadership development programs today provide model answers based on one-size-fits-all leadership models. Having intellectual knowledge is important, but on its own, it's not enough to move us into action. That's like learning how to ride a bike by reading a book. Knowledge by itself does not change behaviors. You end up going through the motions. Deep transformation doesn't happen.

This book is about bridging the gap between knowing and doing. For deep transformation to happen, you have to make it personal. So you won't find cliched model answers, rules to be obeyed, authoritative claims guaranteeing results, nor over-simplified five-step formulas guaranteeing success. I personally know how mentally frustrating and worrying it can be not to have a "model answer," and I apologize in advance for not giving you one. We've become so reliant on an external authority to provide us with a model answer. Somehow, somewhere, we lost that connection to our primal need to lead. Instead, we turn outwards and go shopping for model answers, judging and comparing to see which is best. The model answer of model answers. That's how we confuse ourselves.

When it comes to greatness, there are no model answers. It's deeply personal. What this book offers are lots of transformational stories, lots of ideas, within a simple framework. This is the starting point. I hope that this sets you off on your reflection process so powerfully that you can finish it on your own. Your leadership journey then becomes this wonderful deepening of your wisdom based on your experience; the authority comes from within. You're no longer adding more fuel to the fire of self-judgment — *I'm not good enough* — based on some model answer created by some outer authority.

You might ask about the model answers we learn at business school. Case studies, best practices and management models are developed based on reflecting on past experiences and studying the successes of previous leaders and organizations. This is good, we learn how not to repeat the same mistakes. We don't reinvent the wheel. However, there are times when we face challenges that cannot be addressed solely by reflecting on past experiences. Sometimes the experience of the past is not relevant. It becomes the very obstacle that stops us from coming up with a new way to respond to an emerging future. We become A ZEBRA. We work very hard to dig in our crampons on the peak of Mount Stupid (Figure 1.1), unable to recognize our own incompetence and grossly overestimate our abilities. We end up taking a giant leap… into the past.

I am not disregarding the model answers we learned at business school. You need to know how to read P&L statements accurately to run your business successfully. The mechanics of business management are technical and strategic; they are not personal. It's the same with leadership theories. Theories are systematic and based on general principles; they are not personal. When you experience the most powerful revelations, whether through reading a book or attending business school, that is actually *you* connecting with *your* wisdom. A new piece of information touches your mind, and suddenly, your heart is transformed. It's like magic. In an instant, the way you see the world changes. Your behavior changes naturally as a result. But let's be clear here. The magic actually comes from you. The leadership theory is simply a tool to unlock the magic that is already within you. When you integrate aspects of different leadership theories from a deep place of wisdom and experience, then the theories can support each other dynamically and be incredibly powerful.

So, be prepared to be called out. And to be titillated. That's why this book is *Basic Instinct* dressed up as *The 7 Habits*. This book has been designed to bring your magic alive. But it requires your full existential participation, basic instincts and all. The magic *only* comes from you. Without it, this book becomes just another boring book. Which is my worst nightmare as its author.

23. Structure of the book

Part 1: Born for Greatness

Part 1 covers the theory and science of performance. You may be suspicious of the hubris and delusional thinking in the book, so I've added this section to allay your concerns upfront. The research findings are unanimous. Making leadership personal is not just the right thing to do — it's ESSENTIAL to unlocking growth and performance in a high-pressure, highly disruptive work environment.

Part 2: Personal Leadership

When you hold a personal commitment to scale your impact in the world, you activate the best in yourself to perform at your peak. As a personal leader, you grow by holding the space to learn from your experience. Each chapter in this section covers a learning edge to stop playing the victim who feels powerless without direct authority. Instead, they become a creative who is committed to scale their impact in the world by partnering with others. Leaders do not need the biggest teams or fanciest tech to deliver results. They know, without question, that the greatest adversary and ally is themselves.

Part 3: People Leadership

When you hold a personal commitment to empower others to scale their impact in the world, you activate the best in yourself to activate the best in them. As a people leader, you grow by holding the space for people to make their own decisions and learn from their experiences. The higher up you climb on the corporate ladder, the more your success depends on the success of others. Each chapter in this section covers a learning edge to stop playing the hero who rescues others and provides temporary relief without dealing with the core issue. Instead, they become a coach who is committed to empower others to scale their impact in the world. Leaders do not become a hero to everyone. They make everyone a hero. Everyone wants to be the hero of their own story.

Part 4: Organization Leadership

When you hold a personal commitment to your vision, you activate the best in your organization to make that vision a reality, at scale. You articulate this vision to everyone in such a vivid and inspiring way that performance follows naturally. There's nothing more exciting than being part of a team rowing in the same direction to win the bigger game. As an organization leader, you grow by holding the space for the organization to start, grow and sustain in the market. Each chapter in this section covers a learning edge to stop playing the villain who blames others for not being smart enough or fast enough to keep up with them. Instead, they become a challenger who feels personally responsible for making the world a better place, and staying committed for an insanely long time. This is a sad fact of innovation: nobody will ever be as excited about your great idea as you are — until you get them hooked, that is.

Part 5: Culture

Whilst organization leadership is about vision, culture balances that orientation with a focus on people. You believe that your people are your organization's greatest asset; people are your secret sauce. As an organization leader, you work with your HR department to build a culture of innovation and continuous improvement within your organization. You create the right environment for people to do their best work, where people come to work every day to make a difference. You role model the desired behaviors you want to see in the organization. With a culture of innovation and continuous improvement, people can take an idea — *any* idea — and make it great. This is an agile organization that can spin on a dime. Each chapter in this section covers a learning edge to stop treating people like resources to be extracted for profits. Instead, they become a more human organization where people become better off by working with them — happier, healthier, smarter, and naturally, more productive.

Leadership development is a life-long journey of self-discovery, and you transcend through the different stages. In other words, even when you are the CEO, you don't stop trying to be a better personal leader. In fact, being a better personal leader becomes even more important as you transcend. The lower levels are foundational. You're never done with the foundational stages. The higher you climb, the harder the job becomes; not easier. For example, suppose you are joining a new organization as the CEO. You will face a learning edge on all four levels. For example, as a personal leader, you'll be onboarding to a new role (Chapter 6). As a people leader, you'll be reboarding the team to your new leadership (Chapter 12). As an organization leader, you may be scaling the organization (Chapter 19) and trying to reduce employee turnover (Chapter 24) at the same time.

Part 6: Transformation Tools: What Is Your Leadership Brand?

This section offers simple and practical tools that you can use immediately to transform everyday challenges into an unbelievably golden opportunity for learning and growth. These tools were designed and tested to be effective with real leaders in the real world, in their stressful everyday lives. I understand that asking busy people to do more work does not work.

What's much needed but woefully lacking in professional leadership development today is a broad spectrum of social and behavioral skills, which are more complex, emotional and experiential than business management skills. I explain these complex social and behavioral skills in such a simple way that *anyone* will dare to give it a try. The tools are designed to help you get started so powerfully that you can easily continue on your own. In essence, they are an easy way for you to do hard things. They look deceptively simple, but punches above its weight in terms of impact. Most of these tools are strategically designed to be completed in 15 minutes, the time it takes you to transition between meetings. If time is money, then these tools give you the biggest bang for your buck.

24. Frame the learning edge

In Parts 2 to 5, each chapter covers a specific difficult situation and brings you through a deep transformation journey. Each chapter follows a U-structure to frame the learning edge. See Figure 1.4.

Situation: The difficult situation the leader is facing.

Old Mindset: The dysfunctional behavior pattern that has become automatic but is no longer relevant and keeps the leader disconnected.

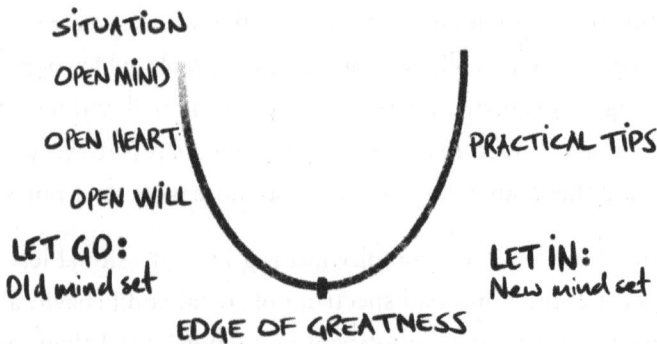

Figure 1.4: Frame the learning edge.

Open Mind: The leader stops denying the the inconvenient truths that prevent the future from emerging and engages with reality to uncover bright spots that emerge from *within* the complexity.

Open Heart: The leader stops running away from difficult emotions and unlocks the source of joy, love and wonder.

Open Will: The leader stops avoiding making the hard decisions, thus managing the risk of failure instead of completely avoiding it.

New Mindset: The new positive behavior pattern that helps the leader stay connected and make a meaningful impact.

Practical Tips: Practical suggestions on how to apply the new mindset to the situation and do things differently.

Each chapter starts with the external perspective of the situation. This is the tip of the iceberg. We then turn the lens inwards and dive below the surface of the ocean, making the invisible visible. This is where the mindset shift and real learning happen. *Open mind. Open heart. Open will.* We then resurface on the other side, transformed, and end with practical tips on how you can address the situation with the new mindset. Each chapter, therefore, has both breadth and depth. You don't need a big solution to solve a big problem. Using this method, you can identify the micro-changes within your control that you can make *now*, which are too small to fail, but when done consistently, lead to something bigger. Now that's practical AND powerful.

The change frame as shown in Figure 1.4 provides guardrails to guide you through a deep transformation journey. These stories are NOT model answers. They merely serve as a reference to get you started reflecting on *your* experiences. I hope that these stories trigger some epic moments from your extraordinary life at work. You start off so powerfully that you can complete it on your own.

So sit back, relax and tune into your body. Don't just read from your head. That's like trying to run a 100-meter race with one leg. The story may *look* different on the surface, but the underlying patterns resonate at a deeper level. Remember that our wisdom is made available to us emotionally and intestinally. That magical butterfly-fluttering feeling — that's all from you. That's you unlocking your wisdom. These insights are precious. Write down whatever memory bubbles — thoughts, emotions, situations, people — that arise as you read each chapter.

Another quick word of warning here. It's only natural that you will resist carrying out this instruction. After reading the chapter, you might say:

I agree.
I disagree.
I am confused.
I have nothing else to say.
There's nothing to say.
This is ridiculous.
I don't have a pen.
Let me read another chapter first.

The list goes on, but you get the point.

Hold the space. Be curious. Don't run away from it. Do not censor it. Write it down. Whether it's positive or negative, ridiculous or reasonable, funny or serious, write it down. Because everything you experience — your thoughts, your feelings — is data. If nothing comes up for you, write it down, too. *Everything* is data. Your task is to defer judgment and simply observe the data.

Here are some prompts to get your creative insights going if you get stuck:

What struck me?
What annoyed me?
What's different here?
How does this make me feel?
How does this validate what I already know?

Remember, when it comes to greatness, there is no model answer. There are no absolute "right" or "wrong" answers. Our wisdom is brilliantly intelligent. It is exquisitely contextual, time-sensitive and personal. And it has its own priorities. It's not interested in being right or wrong according to some model answer from outside. It's only interested in what *feels* true and powerful inside. Hold the space to have that strategic conversation with yourself. Crystallize the intuitive ideas that come up for you and take your best step forward into the future with intention and purpose.

25. How to engage with this book

My wish is for this book to be practical. Read through it once, then keep it handy as a go-to survival guide. The best way to engage with this book is to go directly to the most relevant chapter when you encounter a similar situation — in the moment of need. For example, if you're about to have a difficult conversation with your employee, take 15 minutes to read Chapter 14: Dealing with a Difficult Employee. Then take another 15 minutes to frame the Uncomfortable Conversation (Chapter 35).

Past: As a leader who went through a similar situation in the past, you can use this book to reflect on that experience. Maybe it was a stressful experience at that point in time, but now you have regained equilibrium and it's safe to understand what actually happened. You may gain a newfound perspective about yourself. It helps to know that the experience made you stronger; you're clearer about your values. You may realize that you've forgotten what it's like to do something extraordinary. Maybe you've been playing safe for too long, and your wisdom wants you to reconnect with your authentic power.

Present: As a leader going through a similar situation right now, you can use this book to see things from a different perspective. Stop being a bystander to your life; a gulf of misspent life, lived according to someone else's rules. Not when you are a glorious shining star. Stop going through the motions. Get unstuck and lean into the adversity with calmness and resilience. Center yourself and show up powerfully. It helps to know that you are not alone. You've got this!

Future: As an ambitious up-and-coming leader who has not encountered these situations, it helps to know that this is the royal road to performance. It is not something to avoid. Uncomfortable and distressing as it may be, it is a golden opportunity for growth and self-development. There is a real leadership gap. It does not look like it to you, with so many "senior" leaders ahead of you, but looks are deceiving. Ramp up your leadership skills. Seek out those uncomfortable challenges that most "senior" leaders shy away from and leapfrog in your career.

You can also use this book to empathize with someone who is going through a similar situation.

Employee: As an employee dealing with a difficult boss, this book can help you understand where the boss is coming from. The same applies to a boss dealing with a difficult employee. Remember, you're on the same team. If you support your bosses, they will pull you up. If you support your employees, they will push you up. Everyone wins.

Friend: As a concerned friend, partner or family member, you may notice someone close to you going through a similar situation, but they may not be able to articulate it. This book can help you understand what they may be experiencing, so that you know how best to support them. Being overbearingly positive without understanding the difficulty is not helpful.

26. Everyone can lead

You may not feel ready to lead the change. You think there is a better person out there who should take the lead. Someone more knowledgeable and qualified. Someone who actually has all the answers.

But how true is that? Why not you?

What if you're brilliant, talented and powerful? What if you have a hidden superpower and you're meant to bring something extraordinary into this world?

At your best, you're a powerful force for positive change: driven, conscientious and highly motivated to make the world a better place. You don't accept the status quo, not when the future can be so much better. You're ambitious, but your ambition is not self-serving. Rather, you feel personally responsible for making the world a better place. This drive gives you tremendous potential to make a difference.

There's an element of greatness in everyone. We all have the potential for greatness within us. We are all meant to shine. It's not only in some of us; it's in every one of us.

27. You have to choose (to engage with the book)

Whether you realize it or not, you are standing at the edge of greatness on all levels of scale: as an individual, as a team, and as an organization. But this potential for greatness does not unleash itself. You have to choose to unleash it. That's the problem with greatness: it requires a personal commitment. In the vile and terminally exciting modern corporate world, it can be a fight to switch off the autopilot mode. It requires you to turn the lens inwards and dive into the unknown depths of your mind. You'll meet the hesitation, unwillingness and raw fear that you encounter when you go beyond the confines of your conditioning. The fight is within. No one else can do it for you. Some will even try to stop you. Change is not easy, but easy is not the goal. Greatness is.

And ultimately that's what this book is about. To help you recognize that you already have greatness within. You simply have to reconnect with it. My wish is that you enjoy the life-changing stories, gain an epiphany or two, and fundamentally change the trajectory of your professional career and your organization.

As you dance on the edge of greatness, people will be inspired by your example, and they will want to do the same. You empower others to reconnect with their power. Like how a rising tide raises all ships, your success brings others up with you. It begins with you.

So take that leap of faith. Don't shy away from ambitious goals. Once you understand what's important to you, you'll be relentless in turning your dreams into reality. The result is magic.

Part 1

Born for Greatness

2

The Sweet Spot
for Performance

*"Beyond the very extremity of fatigue distress,
amounts of ease and power that we never
dreamed ourselves to own, sources of strength
habitually not taxed at all, because habitually we
never push through the obstruction."*

— William James

It was 11 a.m. on 4 January 2010, the first working day of 2010. Also, the first day for me as a first-time entrepreneur. After working two years for recruitment agency Aquent, and receiving a rather unpleasant letter from the boss two months earlier, I decided to strike out on my own. Together with another colleague, we started our own headhunting business. We were in our new "office," Starbucks at Plaza Singapura.

The first order of the day: pick a company name.

Check.

The second order of the day: figure out how to survive.

This one's going to take a while.

Headhunting can be a very lucrative business. Companies that are extremely choosy about who they hire are willing to pay top dollar to find the best talent to fill their most important positions. Those big deals can make it worth your while. But there's a catch.

With contingency recruitment, companies pay a fee *only* for a job well done. Whether you get paid is contingent upon a successful placement. You have to find the right person, see them through the interviews and salary negotiations, and make sure they transition into the organization properly, before getting paid. If it falls apart at any point, you get nothing. Zero. Not a cent. You invest your time and effort upfront, with no guarantee of a return. It becomes a gut-wrenching investment gone bad when either party gets cold feet. It's a high-stakes game. When you win, you roll in the big dollars. When you lose, you lose *everything*. It's all or nothing. Black or white. Nothing in between.

I already had some experience placing sales and marketing roles in the consumer tech industry. *That's where I shall start.* I reached out to all the consumer tech companies that I could think of. I waited with bated breath, and… nothing happened.

I wanted to give up. But I couldn't give up. *Find the breakthrough.* I continued reaching out. One day, I received a reply: "We're interested to hear more. Let's chat."

I was excited. It's a cool, sexy, up-and-coming tech company called Apple. *This can be fun.*

I met up with their internal recruiter. After a little chitchat, she shared that Apple was expanding their e-commerce team in Singapore, and she asked me whether I would be interested in working on a merchandising role.

Hell, yeah!

Back at my office in Starbucks, I started my five-step headhunting protocol:
1. Source
2. Screen
3. Engage
4. Track
5. Case closed. Roll in the big dollars.

With the merchandising role, I didn't even get past step 1. After sourcing for a few hours, my initial enthusiasm shriveled up as I came to a realization: *the talent pool is very, very small.* More like non-existent. This was 2010. Just to give you some perspective. Lazada, the leader of e-commerce in Southeast Asia today, dubbed the "Amazon of Southeast Asia," was not founded until two years later.

The standard five-step rules of headhunting won't work here. I had nothing to show for my work. I shared that with the internal recruiter. "We're open to considering out-of-the-box candidates," she said.

Find the breakthrough. Unleash that freewheeling imagination...

I started sourcing and screening different groups of professionals and sent them to interview with the internal recruiter. How about merchandising candidates from brick-and-mortar stores? They were rejected.

Unleash that freewheeling imagination...

How about product marketing candidates from consumer tech companies? They were rejected.

Unleash that freewheeling imagination…

How about digital marketing candidates? They were rejected. I was waiting for the axe to fall where the internal recruiter tells me that I have failed, I am wasting her time, and she no longer wants to work with me.

Instead, one day, she calls me up and asks, "Do you have the bandwidth to work on another role?"

Err… hell, yeah.

And that's how one role became two… three… roles, and so on. Before I knew it, I had a six-figure revenue pipeline. Not all the roles were like that merchandising role. When I was briefed on a sales role, I couldn't believe my luck. *I can do this!*

My enthusiasm was, again, short-lived. One after another, the candidates were rejected. Some of them were rejected in the first round. Others made it to the ninth round, only to be rejected in the tenth round. Rejected in the *tenth* round! Going through ten rounds of interviews is unfathomable, but rejected at the *tenth* round? It never happens! It shouldn't happen. This is an anomaly. *The standard five-step rules of headhunting really won't work here.*

He's perfect! It was so close! Why did he get rejected?

"It's not something glaringly wrong. He's a really great candidate. That's why he got so far. But it's a red flag. And we're just not sure whether we should proceed," shared the internal recruiter.

Other times, the response would be as follows:

He's not a good fit with the culture.
He's not a good fit with the team.
He's not a good fit for the role.

But what's the right fit?!! Can someone tell me what "it" is? What's the secret sauce?

Apple sort of became my lab. Every day I was meeting amazing people with super-impressive academic and professional qualifications. I mean, they are the gods and titans of the industry. *But it wasn't enough.* Every time I met someone who works in Apple, I would ask them what "it" is. If I asked ten people, I would get ten different answers. I took each response seriously. I would test each of the responses to see whether it rings true. I was like a mad scientist experimenting with specimens in the basement lab, defying every known principle of talent sourcing, screening and engagement. Some days, it felt more like gambling than expert precision: Just *tikam-tikam, lah!* (Malay for "choose randomly," commonly used by impatient people queueing to buy 4D lottery tickets).

I paid close attention when candidates went through interviews. I took down copious amounts of notes.

She has T-shaped skills: deep expertise in one area and empathy for the other related disciplines.

He is really senior, and yet he is willing, no, not just willing, he is actually gleeful about getting his hands dirty.

She is an amazing storyteller! I can sit here all day and listen to her.

What a thrill seeker! He runs towards challenges. He is not afraid to stir up trouble!

I made many observations. But what really caught me off guard were the smiles on their faces. They would burst out laughing when they talked about their biggest failures. It was so infectious I couldn't help but laugh, too.

I would be ecstatic: *That's it! I found it!*

Except I was not sure exactly what "it" is. It was right in front of my eyes, but I couldn't quite grasp or explain it. I need to figure this out. And I need to figure it out FAST.

Earlier on, as part of my research on Apple, I came across a little speech made by their CEO, Steve Jobs:

"Your work is going to fill a large part of your life, and the only way to be truly satisfied is to do what you believe is great work. And the only way to do great work is to love what you do. If you haven't found it yet, keep looking. Don't settle. As with all matters of the heart, you'll know when you find it."

"Do what you believe is great work." I get it. Totally. No pain, no gain.

But "love"? "Matters of the heart"? Really?

Steve is not some spiritual guru or *rah-rah* motivational speaker. He is the CEO of a global multinational *tech* company. A successful one at that. Which CEO talks like that? "Love"... *really*? He makes it sound so... *personal*.

So, here's what I was trying to figure out: *was he just saying it?* I mean, it sounded cool, radical and all, like he's some maverick CEO out to provoke a reaction from the audience. *Or does he really mean it?* And if he really meant it, would that make "love" a must-have for anyone who joins the company? Was his speech hiding the secret code for me to unlock my headhunting wizardry? I couldn't quite put my finger on it, but my own instinct kept telling me that there was some fuzzy connection between "love" and "great work." Both require sacrifice, putting up with short-term pain for long-term gain. Both require patience, taking time and effort to cultivate.

Let's say Steve Jobs really meant what he said. But how would you go about screening for something as intangible as "love"? It's not something you can keyword-search through a resume, is it?

And so here I was, thinking… What if Steve Jobs wasn't trying to be provocative in his speech? What if he was being obsessively and compulsively precise: *"You'll know when you find it."*

Yes! That's it! I found it! In that moment, the sky split open and the sun shone through. I felt a burst of immortality.

I thought back to all the candidates who succeeded in getting a job offer from Apple. When they recounted their experience during interviews, they radiated with positive vibes. They laughed about their failures. They are humbled by their own achievements: *I was lucky.* They waxed lyrical about their teams. Here is the thing: it wasn't *what* they did or said, it was *how* they said it. It was how it made me *feel*. I felt uplifted and inspired. It made me think: *Wow… they seem like really happy people.*

As with all matters of the heart, you'll know when you find it. The penny dropped. Everything made sense now. All those feedback from the internal recruiter that seemed so random: "He sucked all the energy out of the room." "He lectured *at* me." When viewed from the perspective of "love," these were not red flags, more like red cards!

I stumbled across something big. I realized I had been fixated on the obvious: the achievements, the titles, the salaries, the educational qualifications, the size of their teams, the P&L they carried. Don't get me wrong. All those things are important, but they only get you to the starting line. That is just the tip of the iceberg; it isn't enough to win the race. To win the race, it's about how they *feel* about their work. It was literally right in front of me the whole time!

This leader shared:

There's nothing more thrilling than having a very fast-moving team where everyone is rowing in the same direction. That feeling of power. That feeling of excitement. It's addictive. You feel like you can do anything. And you do! And you want to do it again.

1. Sweet spot for performance

Think of the last time you felt completely absorbed in your work. Your attention is entirely focused on the tasks at hand. You are living in the moment, so utterly immersed in the work that time flies by without you even noticing. You're in the zone. Performance flows quickly and naturally. You're tired, but you barely notice. And when you emerge from the zone, you realize it's already 2 a.m.; you've reached new levels of performance and made a great deal of progress.

Researchers have known for a long time that there is a "sweet spot" for peak performance. Our brain gets a delicious cocktail with just the right balance of two specific neurotransmitters: dopamine, the chemical of interest, and adrenaline, the chemical of alertness.[1] Dopamine and adrenaline: I call it DOPE. You feel greater enjoyment, energy and connection. This is the leader's high.

In this elevated state, we're more open to learning and change. We stretch to reach new levels of performance. Our brain is delighted because it loves making new connections. This ability is called neuroplasticity.[2] Our thinking is sharper. We are totally engaged in our work with deep, unremitting focus, even when we're under pressure. It feels like the most natural thing. In this state, even things that can kill us look thrilling and exciting (skydiving, anyone?).

2. Hitting the sweet spot for performance

So far, we've heard the good news — the sweet spot for performance actually exists. We hit the leader's high, we do our best work. But this might sound delusional and totally alien to what you experience at work. Every day, you are under immense pressure to meet unreasonable expectations and impossible timelines. In the diabolical chase for perfection, sometimes you come very close, but more often than not, you end up burning out. So how exactly do you hit the sweet spot for performance without burning out?

Here's the catch. The magic only happens when there's just the right level of stretch. When there's little stretch — there's no immediate deadlines to meet, for example — our performance is not that great. But when we

Performance

Sweet Spot For Performance

Bored

Overwhelmed

Stretch

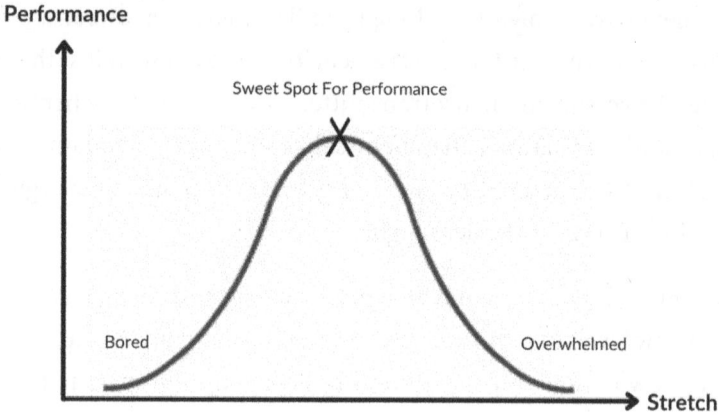

Figure 2.1: On the edge: Sweet spot for performance.

stretch ourselves — we are fixated on our target, for example — we rise to the challenge. We experience the DOPE effect, which is a powerful motivator that challenges us to overcome obstacles, push harder and strive for excellence. At this point, it's really: No pain, no gain. This is a powerful engine for performance that drives and focuses us all the way to the very top of the chart, the sweet spot for performance. See Figure 2.1.

We want to stay here for forever. But we're only human. Staying at this optimum amount of stretch over a long enough time automatically pushes us over the edge and into the long downward slope into the overwhelmed zone.

Too much stretch and you would be overwhelmed. Too little stretch and you would be bored. The sweet spot for performance happens within a Goldilocks zone: *not too hot, not too cold, but just right.* Individuals vary in terms of the stretch they need to feel engaged and alert — or tip them over the edge. It's personal. You are literally dancing on the edge of greatness. One wrong move and you go over the edge. So, what does it look like when you go over the edge?

3. The overwhelmed zone

We see ourselves as high achievers. We believe anything is possible with a clear vision and sheer hard work. We are virtuosos at the art of multi-tasking. We pride ourselves at managing many things at one time.

You're like a juggler balancing many balls in the air. Initially, you feel good because you're on top of it. You're in the zone, all jazz hands and spirit fingers. Your boss throws you a new ball — a problem that needs to be fixed. *No problem, I've got this.* And then your boss throws you another ball. *No problem, I've got this.*

At a certain point, it gets edgy because you're reaching the limit of what you think you can handle. It feels like you're about to lose your edge — you're going to drop some balls. And then your boss tosses you one ball too far.

Internally, there's just too many balls in the air for your brain to handle, and it puts up a wall. *No! I don't accept!* Your brain rejects the new ball from your boss.

But this is your boss, so of course you say yes. This creates a disconnection. Internally, you've put up a wall: *No! I don't accept!* But externally, you go: "Yes, boss!" You don't want your boss to think that you're incompetent or being difficult. So you browbeat your feeling into submission. You push yourself to work harder through sheer willpower. *Stop being lazy. Just get it over and done with.* You try to deny this disconnection, which only makes it worse. The stress keeps ratcheting up. It feels like you're banging your head against the wall. You can't run away because the stress is *inside*

Performance

Sweet Spot For Performance

X

Overwhelmed

Stretch

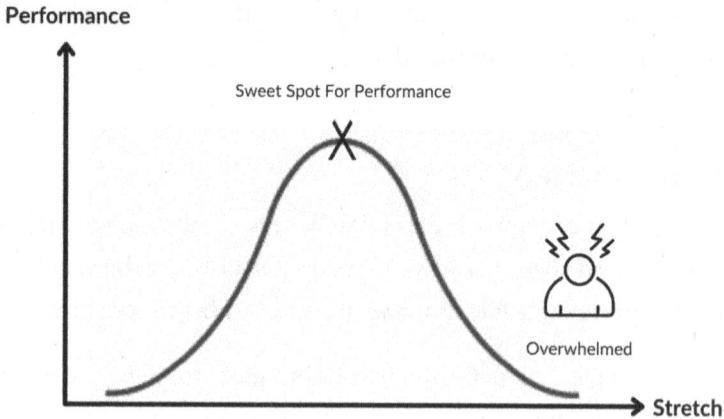

Figure 2.2: Over the edge: Overwhelmed.

you. Congratulations, you have disappeared over the edge into the overwhelmed zone (see Figure 2.2).

Being in the overwhelmed zone is like driving with your handbrakes on. Your foot is slammed down on the gas pedal, but you're hardly moving. You see smoke coming out of the engine. You hear this awful screeching sound. You're stressing the engine: stress in your mind, stress in your body, stress in your relationships. Your creativity runs dry. Chats start to have negative vibes. You think that everyone wants a piece of you: employees, leadership team, board members, even the press. You check yourself not to amplify the bad juju, but your knack for energizing people with fairy dust becomes like a dead cat bounce. Never in your life have you been so surrounded by people yet felt so isolated. *No one understands me. No one appreciates how hard the job is.*

And of course, you're dropping balls. You make foolish, dreadful mistakes, which then gets blown into a melodramatic calamity. Every day it's like a bomb has gone off somewhere in the business. *We're f*cked! It's over!* This is the classic WFIO (pronounced whiff-eee-o) moment — a term borrowed from Silicon Valley to describe that horrible moment when an entrepreneur is certain their start-up is dead. A typical entrepreneur experiences three of these per week.[3] Your head spins. Your heart pounds in your chest. You gasp for air. You break out in cold sweat. *Am I having a heart attack?*

When we are overwhelmed, we are hit by an overdose of cortisol, the chemical of stress. *We're in danger!* Our fight-or-flight response kicks in. The more automatic, primitive brain systems take over. We go into high-alert mode, automatically scanning the environment for danger, real or perceived — *five times* per second![4] We get "tunnel vision"; focusing on problems and details, and then exaggerating and blowing them out of proportion. Every minor inconvenience becomes a life-and-death situation. Our attention gets hijacked by the loudest voice — which is not necessarily the most important. In this overwhelmed state, we struggle to maintain control of our emotions and we frequently lose our temper. *Hulk stay. Banner go.* Or we go into freeze mode: we can't concentrate, we become paralyzed and we senselessly follow the five-step protocol again and again. We've got our noses so stuck in the details and drama that we're *not even aware* when we've completely lost it.

4. Stress is bad for you

Companies are facing an employee burnout crisis. 76% of employees experience burnout at work.[5] And the cost is enormous. We're not just talking about absenteeism, dissatisfaction and job-hopping. Job burnout also carries major health risks like diabetes, heart attacks and even death.

But this is hardly surprising to you. We are a stressed-out generation. Psychologists, doctors and scientists have been warning us against the harmful effects of stress. *Stress is bad for you. Stress makes you sick.* Like chickenpox, it's a dangerous epidemic that must be stopped.

This is the thing… we ignore the stress. This is the Achilles heel of dominant Type-A personality types, the overachieving workaholics: when we are stuck, we just keep going. *Overwhelmed? Nah… there's just a lot happening right now. No big deal.*

Intellectually, we may know that working harder is not the best solution, but we push through anyway. At the end of the day, we try to relax by distracting ourselves from the stress. We binge-scroll through Facebook, binge-watch on Netflix, binge-eat chocolates and binge-drink alcohol.

When we can no longer ignore or distract ourselves from the stress, we try to get rid of it. You've probably heard stress-reduction advice a thousand times: relax, practice deep breathing, exercise regularly, get more sleep and manage your time. When done correctly, these techniques are effective. But we take a radical approach to reduce our stress. Relax…. RELAX!!!!!

5. The bored zone

What does it look like when we flip to the other extreme end and we're under-stretched? This is where boredom lurks.

When we think of boredom, we typically think of someone lazy like a couch potato. We think of stress in engineering terms. Too much pressure and the bridge collapses. Remove the stress and things start to float, light as a feather. Human stress defies engineering norms. That person watching TV, stuffing his face with potato chips and doing no exercise? That's not boredom; that's relaxation. It's not the same. Boredom is "the uncomfortable feeling of wanting, but being unable to, engage in satisfying activity."[5] When you're bored, you yearn for connection with the environment, to engage your heart and mind, but somehow the environment prevents you from doing so. Put simply, bored is what the unengaged mind feels like when there's too little going on.

If this is the case, then most leaders may be bored. 89% of leaders feel they would be happier in their careers if they were allowed to act more purposefully.[7] It's not that they are unhappy. Most of them regularly feel a sense of purpose at work. But there is a sense that they can do more and be happier for it. Internally, they are saying: *Yes, I want to act more purposefully*. But externally, they are blocked. There is a wall, and they can't see a way forward.

This creates a disconnection within the mind. Internally they are saying yes, but externally they are blocked.

We ignore this disconnection. *Just shut up and collect your paycheck.* Over time, we drift into this grey twilight zone, lurking around the office without much care and intent. We go through the motions and watch the clock in the office. We dread waking up for work and are just counting down till retirement. Work becomes a necessary evil, and you are paying penance. In other words, you're comfortably miserable at work.[8] There is a paralyzing need to maintain the status quo but you dread every minute of it.

Congratulations, you have disappeared over the edge into the bored zone. (see Figure 2.3)

You can be very busy and still be bored. Boredom lurks where people avoid taking risks. Like when they follow the five-step protocol again and again like a broken machine. Or when they are constantly fighting the same fires,

Performance

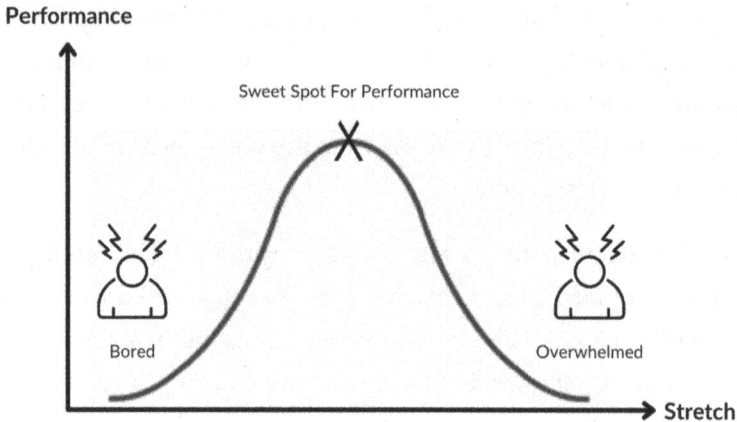

Figure 2.3: Below the edge: Bored.

but on different days. *Same, same, but different.* Or when they say polite words that people want to hear, but not what they really think. Or when they stay in the same job for a long time because of the overwhelming fear of the unknown and the belief they won't find a better job.

The new research is showing that boredom produces self-destructive feelings — try waiting two hours at the doctor's office without your mobile phone. You just want to poke your eyes out or chew your arm off. Boredom is "aggressively dissatisfying." It causes a lot of tension in the mind. Boredom has been associated with increased levels of cortisol. In other words, boredom can be stressful, too! Boredom can cause headaches, stomach aches and backaches. We try to relieve our boredom by calling in sick, taking long breaks, doomscrolling Facebook and gossiping with colleagues.

So, while being overstretched can be stressful, it looks like being under-stretched can be equally stressful.

6. Stress can be good for you

Health psychologist Kelly McGonigal[9] is having an existential crisis. For 10 years, she has been telling people that stress makes you sick. But she came across a shocking scientific finding that made her rethink stress. The researchers concluded that it wasn't stress alone that was killing people. It was the combination of stress and the *belief* that stress is bad for you that makes it bad for you. And here she was, spending all her time and energy trying to convince people that stress is a villain and needs to be eliminated. She thought she was helping them. But what if she was doing more harm than good?

This is what the new science of stress reveals: How you think about stress matters. When you change your mind about stress, you literally change your body's response to stress. While stress is definitely unpleasant to experience, it is a natural and biological response that has evolved over millions of years to keep us safe and warn us of danger. Not inflict it. The feeling of stress by itself is not the most challenging for us. It's the critical, judgmental way we treat the feeling of stress that is unhealthy. Put simply, stressing about stress makes us sick.

When we change how we think about stress — viewing the stress response as an ally to help us overcome challenges — we are less stressed out, less anxious and more confident.[10] Your heart is pounding? That's your body pumping more blood to give you more energy. How about the butterflies in your stomach? That's your wisdom telling you that this task really matters to you (remember that our wisdom does not communicate in words, but through our emotions and gut feelings). Our stress response automatically prepares us to deal with events that are important to us — without having to think about them. How amazing is that?!

7. Rethink stress

So, how you think about stress matters. What I'm about to tell you next is mind-blowing. The term "hitting the sweet spot for performance" can be a misnomer. It implies that you must apply force and "hit" something. Hitting the sweet spot for performance is not *another* thing you have to do. It's not *another* task to add to your checklist. It's not *another* goal you have to attain. Here's the thing… you already have it. **Hitting the sweet spot for performance is our natural state of** ***being***.

Stress by itself is not the villain here. Stress can be positive, *eustress*, triggering growth and new levels of performance, or it can be negative, *distress*, causing damage and harm. Here's the thing. The effects of stress depend almost entirely on the dose — how much, how long — and how you perceive it.[11]

You learned earlier that the sweet spot for performance only happens when there's just the right level of stretch. *Not too hot, not too cold, but just right.* There is stress that comes along with the stretch, but it's a healthy stress — eustress — like when we're exercising. (See Figure 2.4).

Here's the caveat: there's a limit beyond which the stretch becomes unproductive, even destructive, like over-exercising or over-training.

When too much is going on, we become overwhelmed. We are hit by an overdose of stress — distress. We have gone over the edge. It's not that you're lazy or unmotivated. You're exhausted.

When too little is going on, we become bored. We are hit by an overdose of stress — distress. We have also gone over the edge. It's not that you're unhappy. You regularly experience fulfillment at work. But you can be happier if you are allowed to act more purposefully.

In the distressed state, our more automatic, primitive brain systems take over. We keep having the same negative thoughts. *The standard five-step rules of headhunting won't work here.* Yet we lean harder into the same habitual mistakes. We become trapped in a negative cycle. Our stress response system, constantly on guard, becomes overworked and fatigued. We end up creating even more unnecessary stress. **We can stay in this distorted stressed state for a long time.**

Holding ourselves in this distorted stress over a prolonged period is not cool. It suppresses neuroplasticity. It becomes harder for the newer, evolved frontal regions of our brain to operate.[12] The energy that would normally go into proactively managing risks gets diverted to avoiding risks. We're exhausting precisely the same mental energy needed to think creatively, exercise self-control, stay focused, make tough decisions and persist in the face of frustration or failure. In other words, we're working very hard to stop ourselves from getting out of the funk! When we're in this distorted stressed state, it's like petrol gushing out of the petrol pump, free-flowing onto the ground. This is NOT our natural state of being. This is a ridiculous, nonsensical, cyclical aberration.

That's how we lose our edge. Now, how do we get it back?

8. Stress + Rest = Growth

In the 1990s, psychologist Mihaly Csikszentmihalyi wanted to study creativity, so he interviewed hundreds of groundbreaking inventors, innovative artists, Nobel Prize-winning scientists and Pulitzer Prize-winning writers to explore commonalities among them.[13] He learned that the brightest minds spend their time either pursuing an activity with ferocious intensity or engaging in complete restoration and recovery where they are not thinking about work at all. This approach, Mihaly discovered, not only prevents creative burnout and cognitive fatigue, but it also fosters breakthrough ideas and discoveries.

It's a no-brainer: when you're tired, take a break. But here's the thing… we disregard the need for a break. We think that taking a break is only for wimps. We are much more familiar with the "ferocious intensity" part, to the point of overwork and deterioration.

Ambitious leaders don't have a problem throwing themselves into the work, intensely pursuing a goal or challenge. The idea of stress as a problem doesn't really resonate with them. They see stress as a powerful motivator. It has gotten them pretty far. But this powerful engine for performance has a limit. Eustress turns into distress. The automatic, primitive part of the brain takes over. They make the same habitual mistakes. No matter how hard they work, they remain resolutely stuck.

At this point, though it seems counterintuitive, the best thing they can do is stop trying.

Often, when we step away from the stress and rest, the missing piece we have been looking for mysteriously emerges out of nowhere. It's an "aha" moment. You have a sudden realization, a shift in your thinking, and you see the world in a whole new light. *This is not the end; this is where it all begins.*

9. The "aha" breakthrough moment

That moment for me when the sky opened, and the sun shone through? That was a breakthrough moment. *Yes! I found it!* The feeling is unmistakable — it's the greatest feeling. Such aha moments or insights are defined as "powerful experiences that expand our understanding of the world and ourselves. They can confer both enlightenment and practical advantage."[14] *Wow... enlightenment.* In that breakthrough moment, our brain makes new wide-scale connections. We literally see things in a whole new light — a paradigm shift. It's a game-changer. As a result, our behavior changes, and it leads to important discoveries and innovations.

Here's the thrilling part... when you're hit by that proverbial aha moment, you are shot up with another DOPE hit. That sense of euphoria? *Eureka!* That's the DOPE effect. You feel motivated and committed all over again. This becomes a virtuous cycle of healthy stress and rest, operating in the "sweet spot" to achieve your desired outcome.

So, the next time you're stuck, no matter how hard you try, *stop trying.* This often surprises people, especially the dominant type-A personalities; giving up is the last thing on our minds. Maybe this piece of information will convince you otherwise. Neuroscience research has shown that breakthrough insights are often inhibited because people are focused on the wrong answers; these have become the dominant thought.[15] When you keep trying to solve the problem, you are only zooming in on the wrong answers, and get more tangled in a Gordian knot. By holding on so tight, you are actually working very hard to *prevent* the breakthrough insights from emerging.

Be kind to yourself. The next time you feel stuck, take a rest. Do something else. You have to LET GO of the wrong answers ... so that the right ones can emerge. STOP grasping at the standard five-step rules ... so that your freewheeling imagination can run wild. *Unleash that freewheeling imagination...* This explains why we often gain breakthrough insights while doing other things, like walking, showering or driving. We're "mind wandering," which allows the co-mingling of ideas in the subconscious where unusual connections can be made.

10. Nervous breakdown

Some of us are such hardened corporate warriors that we have to experience a nervous breakdown in order for us to let go. We throw up our hands in despair: *I give up!* It packs an emotional wallop. But somewhere around the time when our arms fall back down to our sides, we spontaneously let go of this excessive unhealthy stress. *Aaaahhhhh.....* It's like pressing a pressure relief button. We spring back like a rubber band. We pop out of the deadlock and eject into a space of possibilities.

The experience can be quite dramatic and exhilarating. But you don't have to wait until you are in the back of an ambulance with the sirens blaring, experiencing chest pains, to pop out of the deadlock. Surprise, surprise, the dominant type-A personalities don't have a problem turning it ON; they have trouble turning it OFF. Instead, pursue rest and recovery with the same intensity you dedicate to your work. Rest IS Work. Strategically plan cycles of stress and rest in your most important pursuits. Commit to off-days, long weekends and vacations following periods of heavy stress. Insert short breaks throughout your day.

Ruthlessly guard your 8-hour window of opportunity for sleep. As sleep researcher Matthew Walker aptly puts it in his book *Why We Sleep*: "The best bridge between despair and hope is a good night's sleep."[16] Sleep deprivation degrades the complex functions of the brain, including learning, memory, emotional stability and complex reasoning. Those 24-

hour no-sleep hackathons — fueled by caffeine fumes — compromise precisely the mental muscles you need to be an *effective* dominant Type-A personality!

11. Surrender to your sweet spot for performance

So, the term "hitting" the sweet spot for performance can be a misnomer. It's more accurate to say "surrender" to the sweet spot for performance. *Let go. Stop trying.* It's not about doing more. It's about doing less to achieve more. You do this by balancing laser-focused work with complete rest and recovery. Not only will you prevent burnout, you will also be priming yourself to generate breakthrough ideas and discoveries. And it feels so good... it's the DOPE effect. You will also be making a profound statement. You're acknowledging the presence of a greater power within which holds the holy grail and it longs to get you back to feeling joyful, loving and powerful — your natural state of being. You simply have to trust this greater power within, unclench your fist and just let go.

This is a story from the late Herb Kelleher, CEO and co-founder of Southwest Airlines. Southwest Airlines was conducting stress management classes many years ago. The instructor invited Herb to speak. The instructor told the class: "Herb undergoes a lot of stress all the time. Herb, tell the class how you handle it." And Herb said to the class: "I don't handle it. I like it." That was the last time Herb was asked back to the class. Herb worked 100 hours a week. People would ask him why he doesn't get burned out. His response: "Well, it's easy. When you have a passionate joy in what you're doing, you don't burn out."

"Passionate joy." It's that "love" word again. It throbs within you, and it wants to be unleashed. Let it laze around, and it'll blow up in your face. Instead, balance between laser-focused work and complete restoration and recovery. Find your sweet spot and activate the powerful eruption of "love," which will propel you forward naturally.

12. Dancing on the edge of greatness

We're wading at the deep end of the pool here. Hitting our sweet spot for performance means that we must *feel* our irrational emotions. It's uncomfortable for us; we're more used to wielding blunt tools. Dancing on the edge of greatness means reaching for those big, hairy, audacious goals, without compromising yourself. You're in control, but you're so close to losing it. It can feel like the edge of despair, but that's exactly where you *feel* it. It helps you connect to your soul. That's exactly where we feel most alive.

You felt it before. When you were a kid, and you had to be yelled at to slow down. Every game you played, you played at top speed, sprinting like crazy, daring your little pumping heart to its limits. And the sense of awe and wonder, the endless why's. When you dreamed of being an astronaut and being the first to go to Mars.

That's the beauty of stretching yourself and mastering your craft well enough to give you that feeling. You have forgotten what it is like. But it is all still there. We all have this internal switch that changes us back into the natural-born leaders we once were. You just have to reconnect with it.

But a word of warning. The combination is potent and wild. It can *easily* overpower you. We have become strangers to this crazy little thing called "love." We've been conditioned to stay detached, serious and unemotional. We tend to associate greatness with some kind of stoic self-sacrificing journey, one of hard work, obligation and responsibility. As if having pleasure at work is a sin. We glorify the busyness of our lives at work. We close our hearts in the guise of being objective. *It's just business. It's not personal.* But we're only going through the motions. Eventually, the willpower runs out. That's how we stop ourselves from playing big. It's like trying to get to Mars in a horse-drawn carriage — when you have a rocket booster in your garage the whole time.

We're running away from our greatness. "Love" is that rocket booster. Hitting the sweet spot for performance is a dynamic balance of high-intensity work and calm divine rest. It's like a ballerina dancing her heart out, every move is conscious and deliberate, alternating between high-intensity movements and complete recovery, to create a devastatingly beautiful effect.

The self-sacrificing martyrs out there might be thinking: *yeah, yeah, easier said than done. Sounds wishy-washy.* Well, I did warn you about the delusional thinking. What I'm really saying here is that you have a *choice.* What would you rather be? Exhausted? Depressed? Maybe a little bitter? All the sacrifices you made for the company, for the team, gone unappreciated. This is the modern corporate world; it is reasonable to feel this way. You are not alone in feeling this way. But that doesn't take away the pain. The suffering is a huge price to pay, and no amount of money will ever adequately compensate for the pain you endured.

Making leadership personal is an alternative way. Observe how staying numb to the excessive stress is what keeps you stuck and playing small.

Stewing in that combustible combination of grievance and ambition is just a hotbed for petulant tyranny. See how a gentle brisk walk or a good night's rest liberates you from all that unnecessary tightness and neurotic thinking, and brings you back to "love" and playing big. Experience the mind-altering magic that is intrinsic to who we are. This is the easier way — a kinder and more compassionate way. You dance, not for great performance, nor bonuses and fancy titles, nor for fortune and fame. Instead, you dance on the edge of greatness out of pure self-interest because you want out of the stress, pain and suffering. Being constantly overstressed is NOT our natural state of being. It's an aberration and totally unnecessary.

When you dance with wanton abandon, like no one's watching, people will be touched by your leadership. They will recognize it. They will respect it. Bonus and fancy titles will follow. Fortune and fame will follow. Someday.

Until then, you and I are not excused from leading.

3

Reclaim Your Authority

"Use things. Love people. Worship the divine."
— Arthur C. Brooks

I grew up with a stoic, no-frills lifestyle. Ballet was out of the question: "It makes you vain." Barbie dolls were frowned upon. Instead, I played with Lego. And took part in a lot of sports. Not quite made of sugar and spice, and everything nice. Well, if I can't be nice, then at least I shall be smart and successful. *Study hard. Get a good job. Work your way to the top.*

At 15, I arrived in Singapore on an ASEAN scholarship. At 20, I won the JTC Corporation scholarship. At 23, I joined them as an accountant and rose through the ranks on the "scholar track." I met a boy, got married and bought my first property. I was 25. *I am set for life.* On the surface, my life looked like a fairytale ending. This is where the story ends: and they lived happily ever after. *But why didn't it feel like happily ever after?*

I grew up standing on the shoulders of giants. My whole life was geared towards working hard, winning medals and accolades, climbing the academic and corporate ladder, achieving status and wealth, and feeling powerful in the world. Anything less than doing "important work in the world" had no intrinsic value. Under the guidance of my mentors, I donned my bulletproof vest and headed into many battles. I made huge progress very fast. I claimed the spoils of war: the degree, corporate title, money and property.

And it was never enough. As soon as I achieved my target, I would look for the next hurdle, the next promotion, and fill every spare moment with getting things done. I didn't know how to stop. I didn't know how to say no, achieving had become an addiction. But somewhere in the back recesses of my mind, there was a niggling feeling: *what is all this for? I've achieved everything I've set out to achieve. But why doesn't it feel like a win?*

1. Power corrupts

In the world today, the word "power" has a subversive, almost dangerous, connotation. We read about the successes and shenanigans of the infamous uber-rich like Donald Trump and Jho Low, and we say they are "power-hungry." We say that power corrupts, and absolute power corrupts absolutely. We believe the world is separated into two groups of people: you're either at the table or on the menu. Eat, or be eaten. The winner takes all: the top job, the offshore bank accounts, the $40 million penthouse, the partying with celebrities. The power, sex and money are there for your taking, but only if you're the predator.

That's a narrow and highly fictionalized definition of power modeled on ruthless and vindictive megalomaniacs like multi-billionaire hedge-fund king Bobby Axelrod in the TV series *Billions*.

In simple terms, power is the capacity to do something and make things happen. Power gives you a sense of control; you're not a powerless victim at the mercy of what's happening around you. Having power means that you have choices; you have freedom to choose how you want to show up in the world. It's amusing when I hear senior leaders say they are not interested in power. Without power, they can't carry out their responsibilities. They can't influence the behavior of others or the course of events. Without power, they may be forced to make tough decisions that they would rather not make. How much can you achieve if you have no power?

The idea of having absolute power does stir a little penthouse-office lust for me. Deep down, I know I want it. I just don't know how to get it. I see two types of power: extrinsic power which comes from an outer authority, and intrinsic power which comes from our inner authority.

2. Extrinsic power

With extrinsic power, the source of power is external to you. Extrinsic power is given to you by others, and you can give it to others. Money is a form of extrinsic power. If you have a lot of money, more things are accessible to you. You have more choices about how you want to spend your time. You can choose to get a suntan on the beach, gin & tonic in hand, while monitoring your smartphone as your money spontaneously multiplies in front of your eyes.

Formal titles and positions are another form of extrinsic power. Companies have CEOs. Governments have Prime Ministers. We create organization structures and institutions — power structures — and entrust power into the hands of a few people. This gives them the authority to make decisions, and everyone else is expected to comply. This is a good thing, especially if it's a large complex organization which needs to be efficient. Without power structures, the place will be chaotic, people won't know what they're supposed to do, and things won't get done.

With extrinsic power, the more tangible you can make the show of outer authority, the better. That's why universities issue degree certificates, police wear uniforms and companies have fancy executive floors. And why is the Birkin such a covetable item? Well, it's an understated piece of arm accessory that screams, "Don't mess with me," which by the way, also holds your belongings. It imputes power for everyone to see and behave accordingly.

The show of outer authority can be intangible, too. There is the "blue-eyed boy" of the CEO. You treat this otherwise rather ordinary person differently. This person has the ears of the CEO. And never, ever make the mistake of under-estimating executive assistants. They are powerful gatekeepers. They have the power to promote or kill your projects. Ignore at your own peril.

Extrinsic power is transferable. It can be acquired or lost, just like our jobs. CEOs come and go. Today, you're in favor; next day, you're out. Extrinsic power fluctuates, going up and down like the stock market. Extrinsic power can be bought or stolen, making it highly susceptible to abuse.

Extrinsic power is a zero-sum game; one person's gain is another person's loss. After all, there can only be one CEO. Only one person singled out and promoted over the rest. There are clear winners and losers. The world is split between those who have power and those who don't. There is a clear hierarchy: top to bottom. Those at the top have the most power and therefore are the most valuable and least vulnerable. The manager is more valuable than the employee. The doctor is more valuable than the nurse. The degree is more valuable than the diploma.

3. Intrinsic power

With intrinsic power, the source of power comes from within. It's intrinsic to who you are. When someone is moved to act by an inner authority — love, for example — the work itself brings a lot of joy. They care deeply about the work. They strive to do their best work, even when no one is watching.

An inner authority grants them the courage to confront their fears and risk failure. By their gifts and under the authority of a higher calling, they are compelled to move. Not because someone told them to, but because they believe it's the right thing to do. They can't *not* do it. This inner authority drives them to reveal themselves in an authentic way — without caring how depraved they look to others. It has its own authority that's not dependent on the approval of others. That's how they can act with unusual intensity and clarity without regard to how everyone thinks of them. They are ruthless, but not necessarily evil. By their absolute self-confidence, they can spark confidence within others.

Think about the last time you were struck by inspiration and felt compelled to get off your comfortable armchair and do something with a messianic zeal. Everyone has experienced this intrinsic power at some point in their lives. You feel joyful, loving and powerful, for no apparent reason. The mundane day-to-day tasks transform into something magical. When things get tough, you're inspired to survive, even thrive. At your most inspired, you perceive a crisis not as an unfortunate event, but a divine sign from heaven to pounce. The experience is unmistakable — the greatest feeling in the world. It feels like the most natural thing. You're not pushing or struggling. Instead, it's like you relinquished control, stepped aside and let this higher force take over.

When you wake up and your usual knack for bouncing out of bed is more like a dead cat bounce, a little voice in your head says, "Your work here is not done." That's the inner authority speaking from beyond.

This is the stuff of dreams. The Jedi call it the Force. It's hard to describe, largely because it is so limitless. The actual experience of touching our intrinsic power defies description, but it has not stopped people from trying: love, passionate joy, unshakeable confidence, almost hare-brained courage.

Intrinsic power cannot be bought, transferred or hoarded. It comes from the deepest core of our being. Intrinsic power is intangible. It can't be seen, it's hard to describe, and doesn't fit conveniently within a nice, tidy concept. So how will you know if you have it? As Steve Jobs puts it, "As with all matters of the heart, you'll know when you find it." That's how you know — the feeling is magic.

Unlike extrinsic power, intrinsic power is limitless. One person having intrinsic power does not make another less powerful. In fact, one person expressing their inner authority encourages another to do the same. Like how a rising tide brings up all ships, they bring others up with them. It's addictive. Everyone can be powerful at the same time.

Here's the thing. You can give away your inner authority by choosing to play the victim. But no one can take your inner authority away from you. It is intrinsic to who you are.

4. Extrinsic versus intrinsic power

So, which is more powerful: extrinsic or intrinsic power?

We are more familiar with extrinsic power. We are constantly striving for more fame, fortune and powerful friends. We have this intense need to dominate over others — we think we can only gain at someone else's loss. We control and manipulate people and situations to achieve visible, measurable results for ourselves. We place a premium on winning medals and accolades, climbing the academic and corporate ladder, and achieving status and wealth.

As children, our parents were terribly concerned for us to transition as quickly as possible into the adult working world. They taught us from a tender age to be responsible citizens who set and achieve ambitious goals. They encouraged us to forge an identity based on our accomplishments — how many A's we score and trophies we win. *But don't get too full of yourself,* they warn us. Any wonder why our ambition is so passive-aggressive?

As adults, we strive to become somebody important in the world. We believe that we only become *somebody* when we are famous. Otherwise, you are a nobody. We demand a slightly grandiose title and a merely legitimate salary because people defer to the highest-paid person in the room, thus the acronym HiPPO: highest-paid person's opinion. We don't think we can do the job until we've been given the Vice President title.

It may seem like extrinsic power like fame, fortune and status make us more powerful, that's why we crave it so much. But it hides one tiny flaw. When we rely on an outer authority to make us feel powerful, we give them power over us. Since young, we have been told what's good or bad for us. We learned to rely on others' wisdom and knowledge to navigate the world. We have been educated on how we should think, how we should feel and what we can and cannot do. We have been provided with oversimplified model answers on how we should lead our lives. *Study hard. Get a good job. Work your way to the top.*

And we comply. When I was young, I dreamt of earning $10,000 a month. When I got there, I realised to my dismay: *$10,000 can't be the magic number, I'm still not happy.* I then dream about making $20,000. *Only then it'll be enough. Only then I'll be happy.*

That's how the source of authority over our lives comes to reside outside of ourselves. When faced with uncertainty, we look to outer authority for model answers. When we feel insecure about ourselves, we look to outer authority for approval and validation. We look outside ourselves for some evidence of our worth. On Facebook, people cast their thumbs up or down in what seems like a final judgment on our worth. In this way, our fundamental existence is questioned every day. That's how we become powerless.

For too long, I've been worshipping at the altars of wealth, celebrity and power. This is the hard truth: no amount of fame, fortune and status can make us feel fulfilled. It's like trying to fill a black hole. *It is never enough.*

5. Disconnection (aka The Black Hole)

We have grown so accustomed to living in a culture that privileges and emphasizes external power like fame, fortune and fancy job titles, that we don't even realize what we're missing until it's right in front of our faces. Somehow, somewhere, we lost connection to our primal need to lead.

Instead, like Pavlov's dogs, we've been conditioned to salivate at the ring of the cash register.

Leaders understand that true power comes from within. It does not come standard issue with the position you hold in the organization. I've set foot inside the corridors of power. I've sat in hallowed boardrooms, the pantheon of the most powerful individuals in the organization. They are like the gods who rule from their celestial thrones on Mount Olympus, gliding sleek in their power. You'd think that they will be generous, wise and magnanimous. Some are. But here, you will also find the finest folie de grandeur.

Commanding power is not the same as demanding it. Demanding power is akin to a little tyrant throwing a tantrum. For the most hardcore, there is really only one way to wield authority, and that's with a stick. Fear is wielded as a weapon to get others to submit to their authority. Empathy is seen as a sign of weakness. When they don't get what they want, they become angry. They raise their voices and blame others.

Arguing the point doesn't command authority. It breeds fear and resentment that eventually weakens it. Demanding power comes from a place of fear that power will be withheld from them. And that fear is justified for their sense of self-worth is dependent on external validation, which can be taken away from them at any time.

When we're disconnected from our inner authority, holding on to extrinsic power is not sustainable. Jho Low has been charged with multiple counts in connection with a money-laundering scheme that raised billions of dollars from banks and wealthy investors. Jho Low's modus operandi was based on cultivating an image as a billionaire, giving the impression that he is super-rich and can make *you* super-rich. On the surface, everything was shiny and dazzling. And it worked. It made him a billionaire. But it did not last long. Like a house of cards, his "fraud of unprecedented gall and magnitude"[1] crumbled and fell. Look here, I'm no ascetic monk. The idea of ultimate control and total domination does arouse the dormant Olympian ambitions in me. But ultimately, extrinsic power on its own is unsatisfying because it doesn't last. All the partying with celebrities and supermodels, luxury apartments, Van Gogh and Monet paintings, and $200 million superyachts were not enough to fill the black hole.

6. Connection

At the moment, we feel powerless because we're so disconnected from our inner authority. We think that power lives outside of us. We think we can only lead if we're granted a position of power. *I can't do the job unless you promote me.* The job title confers importance on us. Like we need permission from some outer authority to influence others.

We are familiar with this aggressive feeling of powerlessness. We become power-hungry and plot exploitative Machiavellian schemes. This feeling of powerlessness leaves us achingly vulnerable to temptation. When we fail to acquire the power we desire, we comfort ourselves with deep-fried chicken, bubbly champagne and sparkly diamonds. We continue to indulge in these rampant but insatiable cravings to distract ourselves even when we already know it won't fulfill us ultimately. The black hole can never be filled.

Commanding power comes from the steady and stable connection to your inner authority. Being powerful is our natural state of being. No one can take it away from you, but you can give it away. There's a way to be a powerful leader without resorting to fear. You express your daring ideas freely and adopt whatever manner the situation calls for without regard for what people will think of you. Instead of wielding the stick, you seduce the world into giving you what you want. People in your presence feel like a million bucks. You make them feel special; all becomes accentuated beyond the ordinary when you pay them special attention. You are ambitious, but your ambition is not self-serving. Rather, you feel personally responsible for making the world a better place.

Our inner authority arises from dominion over our mind, and not over others. You have absolute power over your mind. When you change your mind, the way you experience the world also changes. You rely on your inner resourcefulness to organize external resources to derive the best benefits for as many people as possible, including yourself. As it turns out, extrinsic power follows intrinsic power. It doesn't work the other way round. Money is a bad master, but it makes a great servant.

7. Redefine success — on your own terms

So, back to my quarter-life crisis. Externally, my life looked like a fairy-tale ending. I was on the rocket ship trajectory to *happily ever after*. But internally, I was struggling. I felt like I was not achieving my potential. I didn't feel like I was ahead. Instead, it felt like I was falling behind. I can't seem to cultivate a desire for my boss's job. Or my boss's boss's job. I had no idea what I wanted to be, but I knew this perfect life that I had worked so hard for — to "set me up for life" — was plainly not it. The potential losses were clear, but the future was not.

It was unlike any struggle I have had before. I did not want to play by someone else's rules anymore. I did not want another perfect execution of another model answer based on someone else's authority. *Throw the model answer out the window.* I wanted the freedom of believing in myself, and not let myself be led by someone else. I want to be the master of my own destiny. I had to come face to face with my inner authority. *I want to know for myself.* This is uncharted territory. It's exciting — and terrifying.

I chose to bite the bullet. I broke up my marriage, becoming the first divorcee in my family's entire history. I refused to play the yes-man to the CFO, unlike everyone else, and stuck out like a bad smell. I left the scholar track.

I dived into the wild unknown. I changed careers four times. I did the entrepreneurship thing. I fell and hurt myself many times, but I learned to get back up and become better.

Today, I'm an entrepreneur, leadership expert and writer. I live in a testosterone-driven home with the love of my life and our three young gentlemen-to-be, co-creating our dream beach villa at the Tip of Borneo with the local Rungus community. Being in business for myself feels like the most natural thing. Growing up, I never saw myself as an entrepreneur, but I've always been attracted to big dreams. I'm happiest when I'm seeking inspiration and expressing my creativity. It's not likely that I would be fulfilled with a safe, well-trodden career path.

When I was young, I had wonderful mentors, people I admired and looked up to. Work was part of their identity. They loved their jobs. They looked happy, and I wanted to emulate them, be like them. With their guidance, I rose through the ranks very fast. But it was a dismembered way of living. My mind was always somewhere in the future. Someone else's future.

At some point in life, you have to bring yourself back to the present and find your own personal path. It turns out, the last thing our titan-like mentors want is a replica — not when they can help shape original masterpieces. While you may ask others for their opinions, ultimately, you make your own decisions. When you stop trying to become somebody important in the world, you start being… *you*. You stand for something. People who stand for the same values will gravitate towards you. In their eyes, you snap out of the blurriness into sharp relief. Like when your camera comes into focus. *Snap!* When you rise, you bring people up with you. You're like a mirror reflecting their inner authority back to them, which makes them feel truly alive.

How do you know when you've found "it"? You'll know — it's powerful stuff. Heaven opens, and the light shines through. And you're humbled because you've been called to a purpose greater than your spectacularly overdeveloped ego: *Oh, that's why I'm put on Earth.* That's how you know — the feeling is magic.

8. Reclaim your authority

Maintaining our own sense of authority does not happen overnight. At the moment, we are disconnected from our inner authority because we're so singularly focused on external things. We must have the fancy job title, the big team, the big budget. Otherwise, we can't do our job.

The fast, modern world is full of pleasurable distractions. At every corner, there is a new restaurant to try, a new "It" bag to possess. The craving for delicious food and beautiful objects is hard to kick. When you've tasted its seductive powers, it's very hard to give up. But no matter how much we indulge, it can never fill the black hole. There's nothing immoral about partying with celebrities and supermodels, luxury apartments, Van Gogh and Monet paintings, and a $200 million superyacht. Status and money, on their own, do not corrupt. But aren't you getting tired trying to fill that black hole? Instead, reconnect to your inner authority. Extrinsic power follows intrinsic power, not the other way round. When you're fully in touch with your natural state of being, even the most mundane thing can transport you to a whole new level of consciousness. Everything else is a bonus. Revel in your luxury apartments, fast cars and sparkling diamonds, but they don't define you. The Ferrari does not drive you; you drive the Ferrari. The Chanel suit does not wear you; you wear the Chanel suit.

The world wants you to show up in your glorious uniqueness. There is a more seductive power within. Call upon it. Give yourself the space to reconnect with it. There is so much noise around you, people telling you how to do your job, glitzy ads telling you who you should be. Instead, turn the lens inwards and find that sweet spot for peak performance. This is your true calling; it comes from an inner authority. It throbs within you and wants to be unleashed. Reconnect with your inner authority often. When you connect regularly with the hidden force, you have the immense satisfaction of mastering yourself in a deep way. You start to believe in your self-worth. You will feel more in control. This is real power, not the carrot-and-stick illusion of control.

Unlike outer authority, everyone has inner authority. As a leader, you sense this human potential for greatness. We are all meant to shine. It's not just in some of us. It's in every one of us. But this power does not unleash on its own. It's a fight to unleash it. The wisest leaders call upon this power, taking the time to learn how to wield it well. They encourage others to discover their own inner authority, and they do this every day.

If there is one thing I learned observing these transformational leaders: when it comes to greatness, there are no model answers. I learned that CEOs (and everyone else, actually) don't like being pigeon-holed into who they *should* be based on someone else's expectations. Instead, follow your heart and forge your own path. Have the courage to hold the tension of not knowing the model answers and the willingness to listen to your inner wisdom. This is the work of a lifetime, and it starts in small, everyday ways. It's the little things we do every single day that create the biggest impact. Be a lifelong student of leadership. Fall back in love with leading.

4

Making Leadership Personal

"The workings of the human heart are the
profoundest mystery of the universe."

— Charles Chesnutt

I see myself as a leader. I could say that I like to lead. But it is more accurate to say that I like to be followed — a lot.

For too long, my fragile ego has depended on the loyalty of others. I have tried in vain to please bosses, shareholders, employees, clients and business partners, and win them over. I worked hard to meet their incredibly high standards and exceed their expectations. This has plagued me for years. And made my life rather unpleasant. It's exhausting trying to make everyone happy.

So I'm giving up.

Instead, I'm falling back in love with leading. With the actual craft. And not the disease of fortune and fame. I'm kicking my lust for power. There, I said it. I've got an addiction — I'm powerless against power. But not anymore. I'm changing, turning over a new leaf, and learning to lead for the right reasons again.

1. The drama triangle

The drama triangle was created by psychologist Stephen B. Karpman to describe dysfunctional situations at work (Figure 4.1). It illustrates the power game that most leaders in most organizations spend most of their time playing. Like all good dramas, the drama triangle has three roles: a villain, a hero and a victim. Each role represents a common and ineffective response to conflict.

Let's use a simple example to drop into the drama triangle. Imagine a seven-year-old boy named John. It's in the morning, dad is rushing to send John to school, and John is fluffing with his shoelaces. Dad blames John, "You're seven, and you still can't tie your own shoelaces!" John freezes in fear and thinks: *I can't tie my own shoelaces.* Mum, noticing the conflict

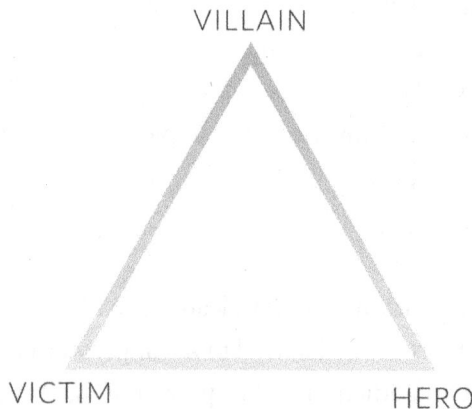

VILLAIN

VICTIM   HERO

Figure 4.1: The drama triangle.

situation, swoops to the rescue, "Don't worry, John, I'll tie your shoelaces for you."

The villain: Someone who is critical, controlling and manipulative, who blames others or themselves for their problems. Dad is playing the role of the villain: "You can't tie your own shoelaces."

The victim: Someone who feels powerless about their situation and complains about it, but does nothing. John is playing the role of the victim: "I can't tie my own shoelaces."

The hero: Someone who does not want people to feel bad, so they say or do things to make the immediate pain go away without addressing the core issue. Mum is playing the role of the hero: "I'll tie your shoelaces for you."

Imagine it's the next day. Dad is rushing to send John to school. John fluffs with his shoelaces. Dad blames John. John freezes. Mum goes to the rescue… again. The drama triangle is the perfect machine. It never breaks down. The same situation happens again and again. It keeps everyone locked in the drama triangle playing the small game, re-enacting the same scene every day. We can play this small game for a very long time.

2. The bane of every leader's existence

Now imagine this typical scenario. Jacqueline receives a call from her client. The client has a beef to pick with Jacqueline's project team. Missing deadlines. Shoddy work. The only thing that's consistent about Jacqueline's project team is delivering too little, too late. After reassuring the client, Jacqueline hangs up and calls her project manager, "Move aside. I'll fix this. I can deliver the work twice as good as you, in half the time."

In this context, the client is the villain, the project manager is the victim who can't seem to do his job, and Jacqueline is the hero who swoops in and saves the day.

Jacqueline can be tying more than one person's shoelaces. Another employee approaches her: "I don't know if I'm ready to present at that client meeting today." And Jacqueline says, "Move aside. I'll fix this. I can present the work twice as good as you, in half the time."

Jacqueline's employees become dependent on her to tie their shoelaces. They are afraid to act on their own. They come to believe that they can't control or change the situation, so they don't even try — even when opportunities for change become available. Organizational psychologists call this learned helplessness.

That's how Jacqueline ends up spending the whole day tying other people's shoelaces. Jacqueline carries around a backpack full of other people's problems. She bears the burden, up to the day it becomes too much. This is where she tells the project manager that he's not driving the project like he needs to. He must shape up, otherwise, it leaves her no choice but to ask him to leave. Now, the role has shifted. Jacqueline has just slipped into the role of the villain. Subsequently, the project manager may approach the client to ask for help to get him out of trouble with Jacqueline. The client wants to help because it makes him feel like a hero.

The roles shift so dynamically — sometimes within the same breath — that you don't even notice it. You can start anywhere in the drama triangle, it doesn't matter, and everyone goes around in circles. It's a game of musical chairs. The drama triangle is a big race to the bottom to prove who's the biggest victim. Everyone's burnt out. No one wins.

Why do we play such childish games? We cannot help ourselves. The response is automatic. We do it without conscious thinking. This is how we learned to do relationships. We are pulled into the drama triangle like moths to a flame because we know these scripted roles too well. You never question why the villain harms or the hero rescues. That's just what heroes and villains do. That's how the story goes. You don't need any more information; you know the script and intuitively act out the role. That's why we find *Game of Thrones* so fascinating; it's the drama of our lives! We do so love our Netflix melodramas. Like drugs, playing in the drama triangle can feel like heaven — you feel like James Bond. But it's a fake heaven. It temporarily takes away the stress and pain, without solving the core issue.

3. Trapped in the drama triangle

Now let's make this more interesting. Let's say things don't improve and it leaves Jacqueline with "no choice" but to replace the project manager. She approaches the HR manager to fix the problem.

Notice here that Jacqueline has just framed herself as the victim. She complains to the HR manager (the hero) about the project manager (the villain), and asks the HR manager to fix the problem.

See what happens next. The HR manager puts the project manager on the "pip" — Performance Improvement Plan. The HR manager is now the villain blaming the project manager. The project manager may then plead

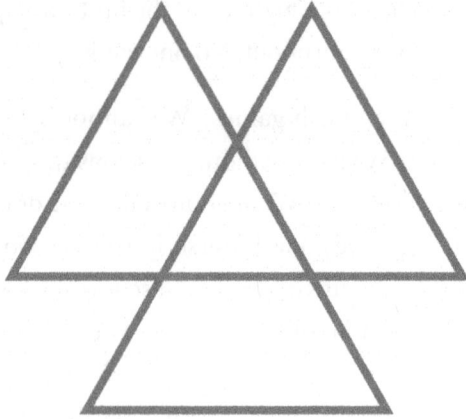

Figure 4.2: Complex web of drama triangles.

with Jacqueline to help him get out of trouble with HR, making Jacqueline the hero again.

Like *Game of Thrones*, new characters are constantly added to the grim and tumultuous saga. In a meeting, everyone brings their own drama triangle. We end up in a complex web of drama triangles where people are frustrated and venting, no one grows, some regress, and we're all overwhelmed (Figure 4.2).

I have always imagined myself to be the poster child of enlightened leadership, promoting the virtues of delegation and empowerment. I will be the paragon of virtue, exercising godly patience and divine wisdom. But too many times, I have fallen into the Bermuda drama triangle. It feels schizophrenic. One minute, I'm the hero who saves the day. It feels so good to be the hero — until it becomes too much. Dr. Evil emerges, and marching orders ensue. One minute, I'm on the charm offensive: *cajole them,*

Figure 4.3: The inner tyrant.

encourage them, do whatever it takes to win them over. The next minute, I fly into a great rage, puffed up with a sense of indignation and entitlement.

At the end of the day, I'm tired, prickly, over-sensitive and prone to violent outbursts of anger. My closest pals say I'm "intense." They are being nice. What they're really saying: "psycho." Erratic and volatile. Mercurial. Short-tempered. Sophia? More like So-Fierce. Generally, not a nice person to hang out with.

There's just no disguising the lack of leadership gravitas. I'm more like a petulant child throwing tantrums when I can't get what I want (Figure 4.3). It's unbecoming, and I've got to brush it out. Detox it out. I simply can't have it.

4. Why we lead

This book is an outstretched hand to other leaders who feel this same tension between people and performance. Between doing what is right and what is popular. Leaders who feel the burden of trying to be all things to all people. This is a clarion call for all of us to start leading for the right reasons.

This is the first and only lesson every leader must learn: real leaders don't lead for fame, fortune and powerful friends. They do it because they cannot *not* lead.

When you ask them, "Why do you want to lead?" At first, the answer will be rational: to solve a world problem, to close the gender gap, or simply, to get a return on investment on my MBA. But those are not the real reasons.

The truth is: they simply can't *not* do it. They can't imagine doing anything else. There are a thousand good reasons not to do it, but yet they do. It's hard to explain this without sounding impulsive or whimsical. It's not rational.

But by their gifts and under the authority of a higher calling, they are compelled to lead. They are taken over by a force greater than themselves against their rational judgment.

To see a world of possibilities.
To connect deeply with people.
To take courageous action.

But most importantly, to empower people to reach new levels of performance. They sense the potential in others and want to do what they can to unleash it and help them achieve their dreams. They stay out of the drama triangle, not by denying it, but by accepting that no one is immune to the seductive call of the Sirens. Even the best of us are instinctively drawn into the watery depths of the Bermuda drama triangle.

Instead, be like Odysseus. Chain yourself to the mast, revel in the Sirens' songs and pass unscathed. Leaders are bold. They are ambitious, but they are not hoodwinked by it. Their ambitions are not self-serving. Rather, they feel personally responsible for making the world a better place. They have the imagination to conjure up a vision of a better future, and they are relentless in turning it into reality. Leaders wake up every morning feeling: "There's something bigger I'm meant to do."

Even if they can't yet articulate it.

Under immense pressure from all sides, when it is so tempting to call it quits, they discipline themselves to persevere. Questions of how long or how much is irrelevant. What is imperative, what cannot be emphasized enough or belabored upon, is that they show up — one day at a time.

As leaders, they are called to work each day to chart the right course, rally the team up the craggy slope of enlightenment, and make corrections when they inevitably fall into the valleys of despair (Figure 1.2). The little voice in their head says: *you must not be afraid of it. You must accept it, just as you accept the weather.*

5. Brush out that peccadillo and come clean with the ego

The desire to be admired is natural, of course, as it is to want to be acknowledged as a force that changes the world. We worship at the altars of wealth, celebrity and power. But ultimately, it corrupts the art — the pure craft of leading. Achievement becomes an addiction; we become power-hungry. We develop a rather nasty narcissistic streak. We feel terribly superior to others and come across as egotistically ambitious, viciously competitive and overbearingly positive.

From my own experience, this comes from a place of deep insecurity. Maybe it's because, as a child, I never had enough attention from my hardworking Chinese parents. They were distracted by other things, like their work. I couldn't disagree more. *What can be more important than me?*

Suffering is a way of life. Stoicism is a given, to be worn proudly. We're made from hardcore, gritty Chinese immigrant stock. It's in our blood. Dad was constantly testing our limits. *Just ran five kilometers? Do one more.* Whatever I did, it was never good enough. There was no acknowledgment, no pat on the back. *It's not good enough.* He always expected more. Mum's a super-achiever, too: Managing Director of a pharmaceutical company, first in the family to get a university degree, beating the boys to it. "Be independent," Mum drilled into me since I was young. *Do it yourself, because you can't depend on others. They will let you down.*

I grew up with a no-frills lifestyle. Ballet was out of the question: "It makes you vain." Barbie dolls were frowned upon. I went to a private school, and I still blush, thinking about my old-fashioned geeky jeans next to my well-heeled friends. As a girl, life was not quite made of sugar and spice, and everything nice. Well, if I can't be nice, then at least I shall be smart and successful: *Study hard. Get a good job. Work your way to the top.*

As a kid, I learned how to present a more confident and happy face to the world than how I actually felt. It neatly covered up the gawky awkwardness and low self-esteem. I became a master at attracting more than my fair share of attention and hogging the limelight. I studied hard and achieved straight-A's. I went into competitive swimming and won medals and trophies. Externally, I looked like the model student, but underneath the surface, I was becoming dangerously addicted to the hits of attention I received from these badges of honor. It feels so good.... I'm whole and worthy. It's like I'm shouting out to the world: *I'm the best.* (And you're not.)

Unlike teen acne, I didn't grow out of this narcissistic streak. Instead, it grew stronger. And more dangerously sophisticated. As an adult, I am always rushing into difficult situations to save the day. My inner hero wants to relieve other people's suffering and restore happiness. But if I look deeper, it boils down to control. *Do it yourself, because you can't depend on others. They will let you down.* I'm compelled not by the need to connect with people but to control and manipulate. That's the inner villain in charge. It's fake empathy, finely-honed over decades.

But despite the trophies and accolades, the lovely family and the beautiful home, I still feel a sense of lack. The inner victim rules the day. It brings out the imposter syndrome:[1] feelings of inadequacy that persist despite evident success. It's *never* good enough. The black hole can never be filled.

I've been playing in the drama triangle for a long time. It's never going to be enough. So, I'm turning over a new leaf. I must stop terrorizing people with my insecurities before karma returns and bites me for my childishness and selfishness. Put these ideas of fame and fortune to death. They have no place in the act of leadership. I've got to stop my insecure diva's manipulative meanderings and pay deeper attention to people. Reverse the hero's normal impulse to pontificate and give its opinion on everything. Erase those egotistical shortcomings. Brush out that peccadillo and come clean with the ego.

6. Sparkle like you mean it

Leaders do not need the biggest teams or the fanciest tech to deliver performance. They know, without question, that their greatest adversary and ally is themselves. And that they are not alone. Leaders recognize the inner authority acting upon them, guiding and leading them.

And everyone has this inner authority. As a leader, you sense this human potential for greatness. We are all meant to shine. It's not just in some of us. It's in every one of us. But this inner potential does not unleash on its own. The wisest leaders call upon this inner authority, taking the time to learn how to wield it well. They encourage others to discover their own inner authority, and they do this every day.

You may not feel ready to lead.

But this is not an excuse to wait. It is a call to begin. To honor your gift. To show up for yourself, as your best and elevated self, and for others around you. Even without invitation. Show up in an extraordinary way. In the way, only you can.

To truly be a leader, you need to believe that you are destined for greatness, even if it requires a crazy leap of faith. You must believe that your life has a more destined quality than you, perhaps, realize. You need to make this decision over your own most strenuous and reasoned objections. The evidence is slim, you say? The jury's still out? Well, you're missing the point. You have to be your first and biggest cheerleader; your greatest ally is within. And as you must know by now, your greatest adversary is also within. The insecure inner victim taunts: *who are you to be brilliant and fabulous?*

Well, who are you not to be? Don't look externally for the evidence of your leadership appeal — how many likes and tweets you have. Create it with your towering self-regard. Even if you must fake it. Treat it like a performance. You have never been a conformist. You are a tremendous force for positive change, cutting through the ignorant and preconceived ideas of the masses. You have incredible power to influence and seduce people into new ideas and inspiration. You ignore criticism, ridicule and vilification, while simultaneously using your influence for the greater good. Step up and play the leading role in your blockbuster movie. Dress the part. You are meant to illuminate. You are meant to be seen. You are the pathfinder, shining the way forward for others. This is the performance of your life, so sparkle like you mean it!

Wait a minute, you're telling me to fake it. That doesn't sound very authentic. You're skeptical. It's just another form of manipulation.

We are seeing the movement of authenticity and vulnerability in leadership literature. We overshare about ourselves, professional and personal, exposing more than we should.[2] We practice "radical candor", with a penchant for wry self-deprecation... at the expense of others. We dish out "incisive" criticism, because we believe it improves performance and productivity (admittedly, it's also fun to write and entertaining to read). All this is evidence that we humans are evolving, becoming more honest and truthful. I think differently. If I dug deeper into the motivations behind my own behavior, I became more forthright not out of some deep moral calling, but out of increasing self-absorption combined with overall scepticism and cynicism.

This creates a false sense of vulnerability. *Is this person genuine or doing it to go viral?* There is no vulnerability in posting emotional stories to get more likes. And here's the thing... there's no shame either in being personal. Share your glorious achievements, but also give a hint about the mortifying but oh-too-common mistakes you made to get there. That's something worth sharing. You're sharing your wisdom, not gloating. Let it come from your heart and soul, without all that serious moralizing judgment. Learn the talk, from colloquialisms to oratorical flourishes. Treat it like a performance — make an impression. Get off your high horse and sparkle like you mean it.

Sparkle like you mean it? It's so whimsical and wishy-washy. That's so beneath me. This is "leadership" we're talking about. It goes against our training. We have been taught from a very young age that life is serious business; everything must have an ROI; anything less than doing important work in the world has no intrinsic value. We're taught that we must accomplish so many things and excel at everything because the winner takes all. We develop such high standards for ourselves and others: we must be perfect, otherwise, we are worms. We develop unreasonable expectations of our work, our house, our partners, keeping up with the Lees. Such a competitive, goal-oriented mindset sucks the juiciness out of life as we rush through each day, each moment, chasing a never-ending dream. We become so tight physically, mentally, and emotionally, we become stiff-necked. Literally and figuratively.

Drop the loaded backpack, people. Keep it light. Reconnect with your inner authority. Spring back to your natural state of being. When you allow yourself a touch of levity, something quite wonderful happens. That solidity and seriousness start to melt. You experience the youthful fluidity and spontaneity again. You remember the natural-born leader you once were when you were a kid, and you had to be yelled at to slow down. You have forgotten what it is like. But it is all still there. You just have to reconnect with it. You begin to dance with your experience. Dance with abandon. Don't care what the snarky diva thinks. Allow yourself to be brilliant. Allow that inner light to shine through. Be the life of the party. Take your shot. Laugh at your own mistakes. Shake it off. Treat it like a performance.

But I don't want to play this game. it's so beneath me.
You have no patience for theatrics.

Well, I don't need to play this game.
You've played the charm game long enough to get to where you are today.

Why do I have to charm others when it should be the other way around?
You are the CEO, after all.

If you want to keep playing in the drama triangle, then hang on tight to that heavy seriousness. But if you no longer want to play the small game, then you need to give yourself some levity. Find the space and unlock the drama triangle (Figure 4.4).

Figure 4.4: Unlock the drama triangle.

You may refuse to play this game, but in the end, you are the one who is marginalized. CEOs are rendered ineffective, not through overt acts of defiance from their employees, but through very low-grade negligence. Your employees may comply with your wishes, but secretly hope it fails. At best, they willingly comply. But no one sticks their neck out. People don't take the necessary risks that will help the organization to stay relevant.

There is also a very practical reason why we treat it like a performance. We need it for survival. Our success depends on it. In challenging situations, real leaders understand what can make the difference between success and failure: people's attitudes. It is better to engage them, understand their inner motivations, charm them (or isolate them), without them realizing what you are up to. If you behave in public exactly how you behave in private, and you say out loud whatever occurs in your despotic power-hungry mind, you will offend almost everyone and reveal qualities that are best concealed. *Keep it light. Dance with the experience.*

But all this is rhetoric. We play scripted roles in society. We're expected to maintain professional decorum and respect. We all have on our bulletproof vests. So, if we're putting on masks anyway, why not derive some pleasure out of it? It's exhausting trying to keep up appearances out of fear of being found out. Why not be more strategic about it and shape it for maximum effect? Own the stage and see yourself transform into the brilliant superstar on the stage of life. Enjoy your moment in the limelight. *Keep it light. Dance with the experience.*

7. Crazy leap of faith

Taking the leap of faith does not mean dismissing core issues and telling people that everything is hunky-dory. In a time that is grim, leaders think they need to be positive and roll out the five-point-emergency-response strategy. "Within a couple of days, infections are going to be down to close to zero," the President says. "One day, it's like a miracle. It will disappear." *We have everything under control.*

That's not faith. That's just denial. Not recognizing how difficult the situation is takes you out of the action. It's irrelevant idealism.

If you're trying to get a grip on the new reality, know that you're not alone.

If you're hunkered down, trust that you've got what it takes to get through this.

If you've had to make some tough decisions, take solace that you chose to act. Because the right decision is usually the hardest. And that requires a leap of faith.

Faith is not a substitute for facts. When you deny reality, a horror vacui emerges in a dense cloud of water-cooler gossip and Chinese whispers — bad juju. Nature abhors an empty space. Rumors fill it up marvelously.

Faith is the belief that things will get better. Faith is the trust that you can handle whatever arises. You don't ignore or run away from difficulties. You acknowledge the difficulties, no matter how grim the situation is. You give yourself permission to feel those difficult emotions without thinking that something is fundamentally wrong with you: *it's okay to not be okay.*

We think faith is wishful thinking: fluffy and wishy-washy. From my own experience, taking a leap of faith is a very active and conscious choice. Those who actually take a leap of faith are often the most moved to take bold and conscientious actions, despite the strife and difficulties. You'll find that the hairiest obstacles that keep us stuck are imagined. Instead, you'll find that the obstacles melt away the instant you accept the reality and reframe the problem to be actionable.

8. Ejecting into greatness

Again, the whole point of this is simply … leaders don't lead to be loved. They lead for the pure joy of leading. Because if they were not leading, they wouldn't know what else to do. Of course, there is a great irony to all of this. As you wean yourself off this constant need for validation, you discover something: that this fasting from popularity liberates you to create remarkable works of greatness.

You no longer tie yourself up into a Gordian knot, worrying what other people think of you. You can stop taking their insinuating comments, shows of coldness, or overzealous interventions personally. You realize that people are generally dealing with their own self-absorbed neuroses. You crossed their path at an inopportune time and became the convenient target of their anger or frustration. In most cases, they are not relating to you as an individual. You have just been cast as an unsuspecting victim in their drama triangle.

When you're liberated from your self-obsessed neuroses, you can see the drama triangle game that you spend most of your time playing. You come to a place of self-acceptance: hero, villain, victim and all. *Want to be perfect? No thanks, that's too boring.* It is the most liberating experience to be drawn out of our narrow, overly critical, moralizing, self-obsessed world. Freed from your self-imposed neuroses, you can more easily direct your attention outward.

First, your mind opens. This frees you to see the inconvenient truths without all that insecure moralizing judgment. You direct your focus out into the world with wonder and childlike fascination. You see things in a whole new light. **You are no longer the villain stuck in the drama triangle blaming others for not being smart enough or fast enough to keep up with you. You are liberated to be a challenger who feels personally responsible for making the world a better place.** Instead of saying "You can't tie your own shoelaces," you say "Tying your own shoelaces is not easy, but easy is not the goal, greatness is." That is the essence of boldness and being a visionary, which lies at the heart of being an organization leader.

Second, your heart opens. This frees you to be genuinely interested in whatever people have to say without being distracted. When people vent their frustrations, rather than jumping in with the solution or fixing the problem for them, you ask questions like, "What would you like to happen?", and listen patiently. You sift for the gold in what they just said, polish it, and offer it back to them. This has a tremendous seductive effect. **You are no longer trying to be a hero to everybody, offering temporary relief without addressing the core issue. You are liberated to be a coach who makes everyone a hero.** Instead of saying "I'll tie your shoelaces for you," you say "You are more than capable of tying your own shoelaces. Will it help if I show you once, then you try it?" That is the essence of leading others, which lies at the heart of being a people leader.

Third, your willpower opens. This frees you to make the tough decisions, to let go of the past and let the future emerge. You stop feeling powerless about what is happening — or not happening — to you. You take ownership of that natural born leader within you and unleash your self-expression.

You are no longer a victim stuck in the drama triangle complaining about not having direct authority. You are liberated to be a creative who engages fully at work by partnering others. You make your own decisions. You learn by making mistakes — and that makes you very wise. Instead of saying "I can't tie my own shoelaces," you say "I can tie my own shoelaces. I am powerful beyond measure. This is my natural state of being." You will experience the immense satisfaction of mastering yourself in a profound way. That is the essence of empowerment, which lies at the heart of being a personal leader.

The empowerment triangle has three roles: coach, challenger and creative. All three roles are motivated by a bigger purpose, which is depicted by the X in Figure 4.5. This is the bigger game. There's nothing more exciting

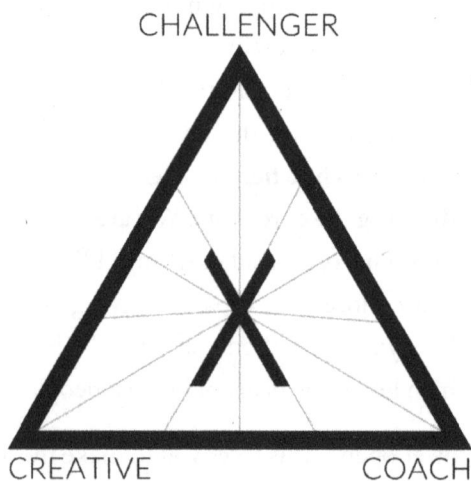

Figure 4.5: The empowerment triangle.

than being part of a fast-moving team rowing in the same direction. The feeling is magic!

9. The Empowerment Triangle

To get into the empowerment triangle, you must *first* pop out of the drama triangle. Just being aware of the emotional drama can snap you out of the drama triangle. It's a moment of enlightenment, and it's available to you in an instant, like waking up from a nightmare.

Of course this is easier said than done. When you awake from the drama triangle nightmare, you'll see things in a whole new light. You will see emotional drama everywhere. You will see it more clearly in others than in yourself. DO NOT go around the office labeling people as villains, victims and heroes. That automatically drops you into the drama triangle. Instead, teach people how to use the drama triangle and let them trip over their own truth. Now, that's empowering!

Keep in mind that the drama triangle is a self-awareness tool to see your own role in creating dysfunctional situations at work. In other words, it helps *you* trip over *your* own truth. It can taste a bit salty to admit that you play in the drama triangle. It packs an emotional wallop. It can feel like the edge of despair. Leadership can bring up old childish patterns — demanding attention like a little tyrant. But this is also the edge of greatness because you can't solve a problem that you're not willing to have. Sometimes you must do the uncomfortable things that don't look pretty. Face up to the challenge and enter boldly through the main door. Leadership presents a golden opportunity for us to outgrow our narcissistic streak and become a more conscious adult. We begin this process by fully accepting ourselves — diva tantrums and all. The villain here is denial.

But that's not all. At a deeper level, this work is about transforming generations of bad behaviors that we have inherited from previous leaders. We see oversized ego at work all the time. When we deny it, unintentionally, we are giving permission to successive leaders to behave the same way. *The drama triangle needs to go.* In its place, you have the empowerment triangle: challenger, coach and creative. Leadership means, ideally, that you will empower people, the future leaders of your organization, and they, in turn, will do the same for their people. Over time, this becomes a "thing" in your organization. People will come to say that you have an amazing culture, and it is your best competitive advantage.

10. Related chapter

Chapter 35   Uncomfortable Conversations

Part 2
Personal Leadership

5

Find Your Calling

*"Here comes 40. I'm feeling my age and I've
ordered the Ferrari. I'm going to get the whole
mid-life crisis package."*

— Keanu Reeves

Richard is a senior and respected business executive in one of the largest technology companies globally. Over the last 20 years, he has taken on various regional and global roles across the world from Asia to Europe. Today, he manages a team of 110 people. Richard earns a generous salary, bringing home in a month what some make in a year.

Richard enjoys the lifestyle of a high-flying business executive. He has the landed property, European car, trophy wife and doting kids. He eats at the hottest tables in town. He owns the latest electronic gadgets — boys toys. Superficially, Richard's life looks fantastic. Yet he's not happy. There is a niggling feeling at the back of his mind. It feels like a big gaping void. *This is not "it." There's something else I am meant to do.*

Richard has always been tapped on the shoulder for greater opportunities. He doesn't even have a CV. He never needed to apply for a job. He was always invited. His career skyrocketed on the boosters of the fast-growing tech industry. But now he's questioning whether this is something he wants to do for the rest of his life. Sure, he's living the high life, yet he feels trapped by his circumstances as if he's not in full control of his life — like a bird in a gilded cage.

And then Richard catches himself, ashamed for even thinking like that. His hardworking blue-collar father's voice booms loudly in his head. *Your life is great. You have everything. What right do you have to complain? You should be grateful.*

So Richard keeps that disturbing thought to himself. *Bury those pesky thoughts. Continue your semi-charmed life.* Richard invests all his energy into climbing the corporate ladder, pretending to be happier, more successful and more in control than how he actually feels.

But that feeling doesn't go away.

Richard always feels tired. He's on back-to-back calls from morning to night. By the time he's finished with work, he's completely exhausted. His young children are growing up too quickly, and he's becoming a stranger in his own home. Quality time with his family only happens in the weekends, Richard collapsed on the floor, while the kids hop on pop.

Richard always feels hungry. He craves for a sugary snack at 1 p.m. every day. His business shirts are getting tighter around the middle section. He dreads the day his Hugo Boss pants tear at their seams when he sits.

At bedtime, Richard tosses and turns in his bed. He can't go to sleep, no matter how tired he feels. Most nights, he spends alone in front of his laptop, a bottle of wine in hand, trading online. He has been watching those Internet video ads. *From passion to profit: How to make money doing what you love. The 4-hour workweek. Imagine working 4 hours a week, anywhere in the world, for the rest of your life.* Richard dreams of the day when he can lie by the pool sipping cocktails, the hot spouse lying next to him, angelic kids splashing in the pool, while his online business makes money for him.

That dream feels like a million light years away from the glorious busy-ness of Richard's life right now. Richard is gritting his teeth, working hard to maintain the status quo, but dreading every minute of it. Comfortably miserable. A bunch of boring Thursdays stitched together heading towards a cliff. There's a niggling feeling that he's avoiding the inevitable, and he's running out of time. *I gotta get out of this.* Richard can still ignore that niggling feeling for now, but he knows he's only chipping away at his sanity, and one day he'll wake up and realize that he's been disrupted to the core, simply because he was not prepared to confront the elephant in the room.

1. Old Mindset: Chipping away at the tip of the iceberg

Are you grown-up but unsure what you want to be "when you grow up"? Don't worry, you're not alone. I once interviewed the Managing Partner of a big-four consulting company managing a $10 million practice across Asia. He said, "I don't know what I want to be when I grow up."

Some call Richard's dilemma a midlife crisis. It occurs in middle-aged individuals, typically 45–55 years old, who feel trapped by the lives they have built for themselves. In their bid for freedom, they quit the job, relationships and responsibilities that keep them trapped — cue in the mistresses, toyboys and sports cars. Such life changes are usually not welcomed by the people around them. They get dirty looks from people. They are called nasty names. Some are so ostracized by their own kin that they have to move to a different country!

This is not surprising. Society is not supportive of change. It's not in the interest of society to encourage life changes. It's inefficient. It disrupts people and resources from flowing smoothly. So society resists such changes: by encouraging people to conform to the norms of society, and alienating people who disrupt it. *Be grateful for what you have!* As if it's a sin to expect more from life.

Even if people resist the temptation, the thought itself upsets them, and they blame themselves for even thinking that they want more. They take it as a sign of personal failure: *There must be something despicable with me.* They withdraw from interactions with other people. They pull away inwardly to try to figure out what is wrong with them. This often creates a time of confusion. *Am I a selfish narcissist?!* People can stay in this state of confusion for many years.

Maybe Richard does not know what he wants to be when he grows up. He's not alone. More than half of us don't really know, too.[1] Most people's careers have been dictated by opportunity more than what they really want. Richard thinks that he should be somebody who is ridiculously successful and happy by now, and he's falling short. It's not that Richard is unhappy. It's still a gilded cage after all. But there is a niggling feeling that he's barely scratching the surface of his potential, and he's running out of time.

2. Open Mind: What uncomfortable truth are you denying?

This is the moment of truth for Richard. How much longer more does he want to play the imposter game? The tank is empty. He's running on fumes.

Richard spent 20 years building up his semi-charmed life and giving it meaning. His possessions and achievements, the blue-chip company he works for, the powerful people he hangs out with — they were once all Richard cared about. What he lived for and was willing to sacrifice for. But for some inexplicable reason, the pleasures that he used to derive from these things have become rather unsatisfying and unreliable. These "things" that he absolutely needed to feel powerful in the world are now not so important anymore. This gives way to an eruption of a deep sense of meaninglessness. A big gaping void.

I don't understand this feeling. I've done everything right. It feels like he's missing something he'd always imagined he would have by now. Richard feels the fatigue of old age coupled with a restless unfulfilled spirit. It feels like death, like he has reached the end of the road.

Of course, death is painful. But what is really dying here for Richard is the whole conceptual framework of how his life *should* be. All his life, he has been told to be a good person. A good son. A good husband. A good father. A good boss. He has been told how to behave and what's expected of him. It got him to where he is today. But somewhere along the way, he stopped trusting himself.

It's exactly this conceptual framework of how his life *should* be that is breaking down. Nothing real is actually dying. It's just the flabby learned conditioning melting away — the weight that he used to need to throw around to show others how successful he is.

Crisis is about a breaking point. "Breaking" connotes damage and something tragic. That's what society wants us to think. *Change is inefficient.* I prefer to see crisis as a process of transformation. Transformation causes damage, but it's not tragic. It can be exhilaratingly liberating. Transformation is about letting go of the past that we've become very attached to but is no longer useful. This creates space for the future to emerge. Before, Richard relied on handsome gratuitous ads to tell him what makes him happy; but more shiny new toys no longer hold Richard's attention. The mundane no longer interests him. Richard's mind is unengaged. In fact, he's bored. His potential is under-utilized. That's Richard's brain sending him all sort of ache bombs to seek out mental engagement, re-evaluate his personal goals and change his overall course. Richard is waking up to the truth that the most profound authority on what brings him happiness and fulfillment lies within and not in the glorious extraneous distractions of the outside world.

3. Open Heart: What difficult emotions are you ignoring?

When our external conditioning goes into meltdown — when what we held to be true for so long no longer rings true — it's like our foundation is being rocked. The ground underneath your feet moves. It can be a destabilizing experience.

Richard denied that deep sense of mundaneness and meaninglessness. He ignored it. He avoided it. He tried to run away from it. He thought that if he confronted it, he will *lose* his ultra-high-definition macho edge — he will turn into an emotional puddle; he will look ungrateful, weak and vulnerable. This terrifies Richard.

But denying it just makes it worse. It undercuts his energy. He feels depressed because he is resisting activities his heart truly wants to start. It makes him irritable, lashing out in anger at the things that are holding him back in life and weighing him down. Secretly, he feels oppressed by the role society expects him to play — always having to be responsible, in control and rational.

When Richard stops running away from his emotions and confidently acknowledges them, he pulls the power from them. This is the moment of truth for Richard. He finally calls foul on himself. *How do I get back to doing work that energizes me? How do I change?*

The villain here is denial. Denying those feelings of boredom and mundaneness keeps Richard repeating the same mistakes, working hard going nowhere. It makes him achingly vulnerable to cheap temptation. We can stay stuck here for a long time. But this is not our natural state. Our brain throws all sorts of ache bombs to let us know when we've gone over the edge. There's a natural power within which longs to fully engage with the world. It wants you to stop playing small, and unleash that freewheeling imagination.

4. Open Will: What hard decision are you avoiding?

"What do I want to be when I grow up?"

The innocence of the question. It triggers the imagination. A sense of hope, anything is possible. It conjures up all sorts of images of exciting adventures and tantalizing delights.

Richard used to complain: *I should be somebody by now; I'm falling short.*

Richard's not falling short. Behind what? Behind whom? Maybe Richard feels he is falling short of some expectation set by a glitzy ad that tells him he needs that latest red sports car in order to feel powerful in the world. Maybe Richard feels he is falling short of some expectation he set for himself: bigger title, bigger team, bigger salary — the bigger, the better — and reality got in the middle of that plan and it didn't work that way. But I'll bet Richard spent time doing something that was incredibly valuable, so he's not falling short. He's not behind his timetable; he's not behind anyone else. Richard is right here, right now, and this is the perfect place that he can move from.

When Richard accepts that this is the place he can move from, it opens his mind to the possibilities from here going forward. It dawns on Richard. *This is not the end. I'm only just beginning.*

It's a time for playful learning, to try different things with childlike curiosity. Richard has always harbored dreams of becoming an entrepreneur. He never entertained that idea, pushing it to the dark recesses of his mind. *It's too risky.* He decides to take on a risky role within the organization to build a new business from scratch. From managing 110 people, he becomes an independent contributor, managing a team of one: himself. It may look like Richard is regressing, the opposite of progressing. But sometimes, you need to step back to move forward. This is the very essence of transformation: *metamorphosis.* Adopt the view of an innocent — an open approach to exploring life. When you look upon the world without all that harsh moralizing judgments and expectations, you'll find innovative answers to your most pressing and intimate problems. Within six months,

Richard will be putting up plans to hire 60 people for this new fast-growing business.

5. New Mindset: Diving to the bottom of the iceberg

What looks like a mid-life crisis is more like a mid-life transition. Our brains change as we approach middle age.[2] With fluid intelligence, you're a cowboy. You're a ninja. You're the best at what you do. You can solve problems faster than others. Unfortunately, fluid intelligence peaks in your late 30's to early 40's, and then it goes into decline.

Crystallized intelligence doesn't rely on those skills. It's your ability to teach others, synthesize ideas and recognize patterns. In other words, crystallized intelligence is wisdom. And if you can jump to a new career or a way of doing your current job that favors crystallized intelligence, you'll get better and better through your 50's, 60's and even 70's. And the big bonus is that you'll be doing something that serves others more. Now, that's cracking the code.

Richard's heart already knew what it wants. It no longer wants Richard to stay a passive passenger in the ride of his life. It wanted Richard to flex his entrepreneurial muscles. Richard couldn't quit his job and do his own thing. He had an expensive lifestyle to maintain, and he has mouths to feed. But with a shift in perspective, Richard got the entrepreneurial experience that he wanted, albeit with the might of a multinational organization behind him.

This crisis of identity isn't limited to middle-aged people. Similar to the midlife crisis, the quarter-life crisis is a period of uncertainty and questioning that typically occurs when people feel trapped, uninspired and disillusioned during their mid-20s to early 30s. We're seeing the Great Resignation, where people are quitting traditional 9-to-5 jobs to start their own businesses, side hustles or part-time gigs. Some are quitting to take a break or care for family.

Growing up is a lifelong process of discovering your truth and becoming more conscious about what really matters to you. This is one benefit of aging: you realize that very few things matter. You learn to trust your intuition more. You follow the intuitive breadcrumb — one intuitive clue leads you to the next thing, and the next. And before you know it, you're all shiny and glorious again, but completely different.

You just know it is time — time to start something new and trust the magic of beginnings. There is alchemy within the transformation. So when that deep sense of mundaneness and meaninglessness visits you, adopt the view of *The Very Hungry Caterpillar*. Be curious. Follow the trail of intuitive breadcrumbs. You'll reach a place where you know what's important to you and what makes you happy. The truth will set you free — but first it will pack a punch. This becomes your core — your home that you can always return to. You deserve to be happy. You are meant to shine. The best is yet to come. And you are only just beginning.

6. Practical tips

Do nothing. Don't quit your job. Don't sell your house just yet. Take a simple retreat. Do nothing. It's the most difficult thing to do — and the most intellectual. Hold the space for the mind to wander. Sometimes to pause is the change people need!

Do less. You may be trying to do everything in order to please everyone, and becoming overwhelmed. Narrow your responsibility to where you can make the most impact. Do less and accomplish more.

Do more. Apply yourself to projects that align with your values. Take on opportunities that allow you to use your talent for innovation. This may sound perversely counter-intuitive as you're already overwhelmed. But working on something you love actually energizes you. It gives back energy, not drain it from you.

Quit. You have reached the glass ceiling in your organization. You have learned everything you need to learn. You have made significant contributions to the organization over the years. Applying your domain expertise and leadership in a new arena may be the learning & growth you need.

Entrepreneurship. Before you decide to go at it on your own, define your bare minimum standard of living. Calculate the baseline cost to maintain a level of experience that will keep you just comfortable enough.

Support. Choose your allies wisely. Unfortunately, society is not supportive of true change, including some who are closest to you. Surround yourself with people who understand what you're going through and support you in the change you want to make.

Learn. Read voraciously. Pick up new skills. Seek new answers to old questions. Discover new truths and perspectives from surprising places. Remain resolutely open to the void of the future.

Don't rush it. Deep transformation is not a quick event of a few months. This is not a fling. It may take two to three years, sometimes even longer, to master a new skill or attain a larger goal.

6

Starting a New Role

"Goodness, like evil, often begins in small steps.
Heroes evolve; they aren't born."

— Ervin Staub

Sean is grinning like a Cheshire cat. He has just landed the job of his dreams: Business Director for a technology services company. He has to pinch himself. Even as he was going through the advanced stages of interviews, he didn't think he would get the job. He went along with the fantasy. *Why the heck not? For the fun of it. See how far it goes. What can go wrong?*

Sean tickled the elephant, and by gosh, the elephant has turned and now looks him straight in the eye. Deep inside, Sean is in perfect ear-to-ear panic. The mandate is to grow the business five times to $100 million in three years. This is a highly lucrative and fast-growing business. Gaining early market leadership is vital. Sean is transitioning from an individual contributor role to managing the P&L and a large team. He was planning to be conservatively bullish: *let's focus on doubling the business for the first year.* His future boss tells him, "Think longer-term and think bigger." Sean was planning to take incremental steps: *let's start with a small team*. His future boss tells him, "You are inheriting a large team."

This is a moonshot for Sean, and he needs to push himself out of his comfort zone to be successful. *I have a feeling we are not in Kansas anymore.* He knows that what got him here is not going to get him there. Sean is playing in a different league now. It feels like mission impossible, and yet failure is simply not an option.

Sean's unreasoning, heart-pounding panic monster is having a field day. Then he hears what to his strained senses sounds like Michael Jordan: *You're tougher than you think you are. And you can do more than you think you can. Pack your bags for the next level. There's a bigger game to be won here.*

Now, whether it was Michael Jordan, his aunt May or the spirit of the universe, Sean has just been called to something bigger.

1. Old Mindset: This is how we've always done it

Sean is not starting this business from scratch. The technology services company has been trying to get this new business up and running for two years, with very little progress. And as Sean starts his first day at work, he's about to learn why.

The first thing that hits Sean is the joyless slog of corporate bureaucracy. The organization says they want to get the business to $100 million in three years, but then they have a hundred rules to stop people from getting there. They have highly complex work processes whose sole function is to create "busy work" for everyone.

The next thing that hits Sean are the fiefdoms across the organization, run by little bureaucrats with their checkboxes. This new business is a rising star, but for now, it is so small that it does not even ping on their radar. The bureaucrats think it warrants neither their attention nor their budget. Sean does not have *carte blanche* to push decisions through. He's the new kid on the block. He has zero political standing and no strings to pull. He needs to lobby the other departments to his cause, pushing paper up the hierarchy layer upon layer.

Finally, there is the cliquish high school behavior happening along the hallways and in every meeting room. Any suggestion to improve things is met with the same response. "This is how we've always done it." "Don't rock the boat." "If it ain't broken, don't fix it."

Transitioning into this new role is already a steep curve for Sean. But, on top of that, he has to grapple with the "infrastructure" that seems to be geared toward holding the organization to the past than propelling forward into the future.

2. Open Mind: What uncomfortable truth are you denying?

Onboarding is challenging. Even if Sean was doing precisely the same job as before, he'll still have to learn the new organization's processes, culture, people, all of which may feel very strange compared to where he was from. Sean is quick to point out to his new colleagues: *This is not how we do things in my previous organization.* This type of thinking does not go down well with Sean's new colleagues. They remind Sean that he's no longer in his previous organization: *This is how we do things around here.*

If Sean is reactive and waits to be told what to do, he will be overwhelmed by the highly complex work processes. There will be a lot of busy work, but little progress. Sean needs to be proactive and strategic. It can't be business as usual. However, removing the corporate bureaucracy is not an option — it's a gravity problem. If growing this business to $100 million required reforming the organization's processes, culture and people, then it would never happen. Especially not in three years. It's not actionable for Sean. This frustrates him, but his inner Michael Jordan reminds him: *You can't hate the Beast and expect to beat it. The only way to truly conquer something is to love it.*

Sean accepts the realities of the "infrastructure". This frees him to reframe the problem: *how do I create a bright spot?* Instead of trying to sell to everybody, Sean starts by narrowing the target niche for the new business, going for the highest value and fastest-growing client segments. He projects the market demand and figures out how they will take a significant chunk of the pie of that market. He takes in the complexity of the organization and isolates the goals that will make the most impactful gains within the first 100 days. Sean knows that he needs to get his most important ducks in a row within the first 100 days to hit the 12-month gate.

Instead of trying to work with everyone in the organization, Sean maps out the key sponsors he needs and launches an all-out charm offensive to lobby for their support. He evaluates carefully what value each stakeholder brings to the table, what excites them, and what triggers them. Sean chooses to work with stakeholders whose vision aligns with his and who are not resistant to change.

3. Open Heart: What difficult emotions are you ignoring?

What Sean is doing is compressively stressful. He's hit regularly by panic attacks and sweaty armpits. He has his three WFIO moments per week. His inner Michael Jordan says: *You got this.* Against his rational objections, Sean finds himself replying: *Yes, of course, count me in.* He takes a deep breath. He stops trying to run away from his panic monster and faces it with kindness. The moment Sean acknowledges his panic monster, the tidal wave subsides. Sean's trademark Cheshire cat smile starts to break. His game face comes back on, emanating perfect calm and wisdom.

Sean shares the championship-winning vision with his team and stakeholders. He provides clarity and shines the light forward. Sean's authenticity establishes instant rapport and credibility with his customers, employees, peers, and bosses. It resonates deeply with them. It's like Sean can read their minds and articulate what they already know deep down inside, even if they don't have the words for it. Sean can describe their desired future even better than they can do it themselves.

Fundamentally, no one wakes up every morning thinking "I want to suck at my job." Deep inside, everyone wants to be part of something epic in their life. Otherwise, life becomes a bunch of boring Thursdays heading toward a cliff.

4. Open Will: What hard decision are you avoiding?

If Sean conforms to the highly complex work processes and tries to do everything, he will be overwhelmed. He will be torn by the conflicting priorities. He will get stuck by the corporate bureaucracy. That's the spray-and-pray method: *Just observe what everyone else is doing, grab a bunch of ideas, throw it on the wall, and see what sticks.* It's very ordinary behavior. But Sean will end up moving an inch in a million directions.

Instead, he creates space for himself to approach the situation strategically. Every Saturday morning, he sits down to reflect on what happened during the week and review his progress. This pulls him out of the minutiae of his day-to-day work and gain a broader perspective. He looks for bright spots where things are working. He figures out how to scale these bright spots and do more of it. He looks at what didn't go well and decides what course-corrections he needs to make.

He respects the sabbath on Sunday. He takes a complete rest. He does not check emails. On Monday morning, he hits the office with a messianic sense of mission and absolute clarity on what needs to be accomplished that week. He does this every week for three months.

In the beginning, Sean is barely crawling. But he stands up and starts walking. One step at a time. The next thing you know, Sean is running. As a high-performance athlete, Sean goes in for the kill; every move is conscious and deliberate. He produces significant gains in the business in a very short time.

5. New Mindset: Pack your bags. There's a bigger game to play here.

To others, Sean looks like a swan gracefully moving across the lake, a picture of elegance in motion. He makes the hard work look ridiculously easy. Sean can turn the most demanding tasks into something sublime, giving the impression that it is effortless. People don't see the intense paddling beneath the water's surface propelling the graceful motion that everyone sees and admires.

Sean wasn't always this smooth. In his youth, he tickled a fair few elephants, requiring constant reinvention. The atom bomb of transformations, puberty... ugh... acne... first teeth bang kiss. Sean learned how to meet these challenges with the grace of a swan. Through his experiences, he built an unshakable faith that he has all the tools he needs to handle what comes at him. He learned how to overcome that panicky run-until-you-drop struggle mindset and meet these challenges with a deadly calm. He knows instinctively that if you want to play bigger, fighting the "infrastructure" won't work. It's not sustainable. Instead, you accept it, which frees you to look for breakthroughs. One breakthrough opens up to another, like following a trail of breadcrumbs. You learn your way to the top.

All great leaders are constantly reinventing themselves. They don't stay the same; they are constantly learning; they evolve. And it's personal. It's not the same for everyone. Leadership is a lifelong practice of powerful transformations, of boiling down the essence of your leadership.

6. Practical tips

Day zero. People think onboarding starts on the first day. But really, from the first interview, the onboarding has started. You'll even start your new job while serving your gardening leave. When you're inspired, you can't help yourself. There's obviously a conflict of interest, so you'll do it secretly.

Learn, unlearn, relearn. In a rapidly changing world, the ability to unlearn and relearn matters more than ever. This is difficult to do. We need to *actively* stop thinking one way — the dominant thought — before another train of thought can arrive. It's not about adding to your suitcase of skills and knowledge; it's about letting go.

Be humble. A lot of things will be new for you. You'll fall from the peak of Mount Stupid into the Valley of Despair. There will be some degree of awkwardness, fear, and uncertainty. But this is exactly where it gets exciting.

This is the royal slope to enlightenment. The villain here is denial. Instead, recognize this as a learning journey. You're dancing on the edge of greatness. Be kind and patient with yourself and others.

Allies. Choose your allies wisely. You were hired to build a business; not to win an election. It's not a popularity contest.

Stakeholder interviews. Engage your stakeholders in a creative conversation. Step into the shoes of your stakeholders and see your role through the eyes of these stakeholders. *How can I seduce my stakeholders so that they will give me what I want? What do my stakeholders want? What do they need me for? How best can we work together?*

Goodbyes. In the excitement of the new role, we can forget about the old one. Goodbyes are always difficult. Seize the opportunity to immortalize the achievements and good times you had with the team. You may be blamed for betrayal. Speak your truth quietly and clearly. Listen to their harangues — even if it's slanderous and dull — they too have their story.

7. Related chapters

Chapter 12   Becoming a New Manager

Chapter 26   Learning at the Speed of Business

Chapter 31   Create Your 100-Day Impact Plan

7

Dealing with a Difficult Boss

"He who blames others has a long way to go on his journey. He who blames himself is halfway there. He who blames no one has arrived."

— **Chinese proverb**

Joanne is the head of IT service delivery for a tech company. Her boss has just closed the largest sale in the history of the organization. And while he is still basking in the glory, he asks Joanne to manage the account. Joanne is all fired up and ready for the challenge. She leads the tedious onboarding process to set up the new service and get into operational mode. But within two months, she realizes that her boss failed to bid for the project properly, and she is now personally accountable for a project that will be lucky to break even. This is a complex project requiring special expertise, but Joanne can't afford to hire the external resources she needs to deliver the services properly. Mistakes happen regularly. It's like a bomb goes off somewhere in the project every other day. The implementation drags on and the project becomes drastically behind schedule.

And clearly, the client is not happy. Every day, seagulls arrive with a fresh load of problems to add to the existing list of 50 improvement items. Flame emails ricochet across the organization, copying everyone. Joanne's boss is not shy in telling her where she's going wrong: "The platform is unstable." "You are drastically behind schedule." "The work is shoddy." Instead of taking the time to get the facts straight and work with Joanne to find solutions, he swoops in squawking, dumps orders riddled with formulaic advice, and tells her to "get on with it!" Before Joanne can set the facts right with her boss, he abruptly takes off, leaving her behind to clean up the mess. It's so intense to the point that any WhatsApp message or email from Joanne's boss will trigger profuse sweating under her arms.

1. Old Mindset: Command and control

"I'm going to take away all the excuses until there is only one left: you."

"If you don't think you're cut out for the job, then do me a favor, and leave."

"Someone is going home today and not coming back."

These comments are NOT uncommon. It feels isolating and demotivating. And seems rather unfair. In Joanne's case, it's like she was set up to fail. Huge unreasonable expectations have been placed on her shoulders, coupled with a lack of resources. When milestones are not met, Joanne's boss blames her, "Why are we missing the milestones? Are you doing the right thing? Are you working hard enough?" He's oblivious to the constraints placed on Joanne.

Joanne is exhausted and overwhelmed. She can't turn to her boss for an energy fix; she'll get her head bitten off. The whole situation makes Joanne feel incompetent: *Maybe I'm not cut out for this job.* She doesn't like feeling this way. Joanne has always been a top performer. She's intelligent, ambitious and hardworking. She receives flashes of quitting. *Yes, but no, I actually like my job.*

The truth is Joanne's deeply, deeply tired. She's tired of confrontational conversations with people who are not on the bus and still don't get it. The business was like a Disneyland, with pockets of wonder and people full of bright ideas everywhere. But now, everything is measured with an ROI stick. How does she get her hands on a big bag of fairy dust?

2. Open Mind: What uncomfortable truth are you denying?

Joanne has every reason to blame her boss for not supporting her and setting her up for failure. She wishes that he'll stop raining criticisms down on her. She prays that he'll quit and finally leave her alone. She can pray for her boss to change, but it might be a very long time until change happens. It's not within her control. She has been working hard the last three years doing everything to please her boss and meet his absurdly high expectations. Now, she feels helpless and unappreciated. She does not like this aggressive feeling of powerlessness. *There is one thing that I have absolute control over, and that is my mindset. What am I here to do? How do I want to play this game?*

The team has been tackling the issues in a piecemeal fashion; checking off the boxes. Every issue carries the same weight, unless it comes from a loud HIPPO, then it goes straight to the top of the checklist. The team ends up plastering temporary solutions over symptoms, without addressing the root cause. As a result, instead of working hard to reduce the list, it only grows longer.

Joanne decides to step up and take charge. She goes through the list of over 50 improvement items and identifies three priority areas that have the highest impact *and* are easy to adopt. She seeks her boss's approval to focus on these three priorities. She puts up a budget to hire for these three priorities. She rallies the clients around the three priorities. She organizes the team to operationalize the three priorities. *Communicate, communicate, communicate.* Joanne repeats herself, again and again, to get everyone behind the three priorities. *Very lolly loh soh* (A mispronunciation of the Chinese phrase "*luo li luo suo*" (啰哩啰嗦), referring to people who tend to repeat themselves). Joanne is so bored of hearing her own voice repeating the three priorities over and over again. But that's what it takes to rally the organization.

3. Open Heart: What difficult emotions are you ignoring?

Joanne's boss will regularly call her in for a meeting. Once, he went on a tirade, peppered generously with expletives. Finally, the scolding ended; he ran out of steam. He plonked himself on the chair, and then he asked Joanne, "Do you want to grab a Coke?" Joanne realizes that this is his way of regulating his frustrations. He's not shouting and screaming *at* Joanne. It has nothing to do with Joanne. It's not personal. It's when he goes silent that you know you're in real trouble.

In a perfect world, all bosses will be nurturing and supportive all the time. But we're not there yet. When things are good, it's easy for bosses to be positive and polite. But when the stress hits, that's when the inner divas and despicable villains rear their ugly heads. Some bosses can be real tyrants. Joanne has had her share of working for despotic rulers in her gory but virtuous career. Most bosses aren't this explosive — this one is a real piece of art. I don't condone such behaviors, but these situations are *not* uncommon. They happen.

The villain here is denial. Like pretending that these situations never happen at work. Or that this behaviour is normal. The intimidation and snide remarks will slowly get to you. Every comment will feel like a personal attack. You will start to feel like a worm. It will make you want to throw your hands up and look to your boss for answers: *just tell me what you want me to do.* Psychologists call this learned helplessness. After a person has experienced a stressful situation repeatedly, they come to believe that they are unable to control or change the situation, so they do not try — even when opportunities for change become available.

Joanne does not deny the dysfunctional environment she works in, but she chooses to trust her boss. This doesn't mean that the verbal abuse is acceptable, but Joanne has to choose: either she trusts her boss or she has to leave. And more importantly, she chooses to trust herself. The mindset is the key here. With an open mindset, it doesn't matter whether you have a "good" or "bad" boss. You can even work with a tyrant and become a better leader.

When Joanne looks back at her career, she can see how working with these tough bosses brought out a strength that she never knew she had. She performs even when under pressure. She stays calm in a crisis. Joanne's boss is a business savant, even though his people skills may be lacking. At his feet, the world turns to gold. There were magical moments when Joanne's boss shone his Olympian gaze on her and painted a more dazzling version of her future than anything she could imagine. It makes her feel golden. Under his stoic stewardship, she rose through the leadership ranks like an enigmatic, golden star.

4. Open Will: What hard decision are you avoiding?

Joanne learns later that this client is a principal customer of her organization's parent company. This contract is just one of the smaller engagements the parent company has with this client and failing this project can jeopardize a much larger part of the business. The client is very well-connected with Joanne's senior executive team. It comes to her knowledge that her boss has been receiving his version of closed-door meetings from above, and he has been shielding her and the team from most of the fire.

Initially, Joanne's boss was resistant to relinquishing control. Joanne holds her ground, and he eventually relents. He steps back, and Joanne steps into that space. They work together as a team: the boss managing up, and Joanne managing down. They complement each other's strengths and correct each other's weaknesses. As a creative pair, they build a high-performing team.

With everyone rallying behind the same priorities, the team creates a few bright spots. *Things are working.* She scales the bright spots. *How do we do more of it?* The problems do not vanish overnight, but the bright spots set up the foundation for further success. Joanne sets up a cadence to scale the bright spots. This allows her to tackle the hard stuff, and that's when she starts making real change. Instead of moving an inch in a million directions, the team starts moving a mile in one direction. A lot of work is done in a very short amount of time.

5. New Mindset: Empowerment

Empowerment seems to have a bad reputation. Some even hate the word "empowerment." *I don't need to be given power. I have my own power.* The word "empowerment" makes them feel like some higher authority is minimizing their authority. I see it differently. To me, empowerment is about sourcing approval, control and security from within. The power comes from an inner authority. So, it's not a contradiction. We don't need to be given power. We have our own power. But sometimes, we forget that. We become disconnected, and we need someone to remind us of our power to reconnect to our natural state of being.

Sometimes there is no one around to remind us. That's when we can empower ourselves. We ask directly for the space to reconnect. We protect that space selfishly.

We can also empower our bosses. We can hold the space for our bosses to reconnect with their inner authority. When Joanne sits calmly through her boss's tirade without fear, blame or judgment, she is holding the space for her boss to reconnect. He calms down.

They work as a team. When he moves up the corporate ladder, he brings Joanne along. This is not happily ever after. He still has his temper. They still have their tiffs. The real test of a relationship is not how good the good times are, but how well you handle the bad times — and how quickly you recover from them together. Trust forms when you're able to be truthful to each other and provide constructive feedback when it's needed. In the process, Joanne grows. Her boss grows. The business grows. They go on to do some really big stuff together. Joanne knows she can count on her boss in times of difficulty. There's no hidden agenda. The only agenda is connection.

6. Practical tips

Communicate. We say that we don't receive enough management support. We say that we don't feel heard. *My boss never listens to me.* But sometimes, they don't listen because we're not speaking up. Your boss can't read your mind. Ask directly for what you want. If you're giving feedback to your boss, speak your truth clearly and quietly. You don't need to have the loudest voice in the room to be heard.

Emotions. Strong emotions flare up in difficult situations. Hold the space to avoid triggering your own panic monster. Meet the harsh criticisms without the usual fear, blame and judgment. Not blaming or judging someone for having an emotional outburst is a very active task — and a very generous one.

Validate their concerns. Try to understand their point of view. Promise to think about what they expressed and see what you can do. Schedule to meet and discuss the issue at a specific time in the future.

Don't argue. When your boss is having a tirade, don't try to reason with them. Don't contradict them. Don't defend yourself against accusations. And never, never make fun of anything. It won't do any good and only makes things worse. Wait for the right time, when things have cooled down, to bring up your point of view.

Proactive. If you wait for things to change, you may become overwhelmed and burn out before the change happens. Instead, ask your boss directly for the space to manage the situation. If you're giving feedback to your boss, center yourself before having the conversation. The feedback will come from the right place.

Face to face. Avoid sending, forwarding or replying to flame emails. It's difficult to communicate grievances in emails without looking like you're blaming your boss. It's also difficult for your boss to read grievances in emails without feeling like he's being blamed. Instead, speak to your boss face to face to resolve your differences.

Acknowledge. Acknowledge your bosses when they do something right. This surprises most people. But bosses need positive feedback too. Think of three things your boss is really good at and share them with your boss at the right time.

Rethink. When you're being asked to do the impossible, the typical reaction is to reject it. Instead, stop and think. Hold your initial objection. Give yourself time to process it. *What needs to be true for this to happen?* You might surprise yourself.

7. Related chapters

Chapter 14   Dealing with a Difficult Employee

Chapter 25   Transforming Your Culture

8

Dealing with Burnout

*"Go placidly amid the noise and the haste, and
remember what peace there may be in silence."*

— **Max Ehrmann**

irtual meetings pound Jacob wave upon wave non-stop from early
morning to late at night. That's how you talk to forty people in a
day. Jacob is the CEO of an Asian media tech startup with
operations across six countries. The company's two-year digital
transformation strategy became three insane weeks of pressure and slog.
Every day it's like a bomb has gone off somewhere in the business. In this
craziness, Jacob needs to make sure that everyone stays focused and on
point.

Jacob's sick of looking at people through laptop cameras and spending the
first five minutes talking about their home office décor. It's too personal.
Chats have negative vibes. Everyone wants a piece of him: employees,
leadership team, board members, even the press. Jacob checks himself not
to amplify the bad juju, but his knack for energizing people with fairy dust
is more like a dead cat bounce at the moment.

Never in Jacob's life has he been surrounded by so many people, yet felt so isolated. *No one understands me. No one appreciates how hard the job is. My Board doesn't care. My leadership team doesn't care. Even my wife doesn't care. No one is aware of the fact that I haven't got a clue what I'm doing. And if people figure it out, I will be kicked out onto the streets — homeless, penniless, and a pariah of the family.*

1. Old Mindset: Lonely at the top

The *Harvard Business Review* will have us believe that there is a standard formula for becoming a successful CEO. A model answer for CEO excellence. *The five things every CEO should know about leading an organization.* They make effective leadership look almost effortless. *Just add water, and ready to lead.*

They are all lies.

Sure, we've come across leaders who make effective leadership look natural, like they were born for it. They have that… *je ne sais quoi.* They look so effortlessly confident. They glide sleek in their power. The very air seems to give way where they walk. Working with them feels easy. They bring out the best in everyone, helping teams and organizations prosper. They're the dream bosses.

But that's not Jacob's reality. He works 70–80 hours a week. He drags himself from meeting to meeting, checking the boxes, until he can finally collapse on his sofa.

As a CEO, Jacob shoulders a lot of expectations from his stakeholders. The expectations are ridiculous, most of all the ones Jacob place on himself.

He looks to other startup companies for comparison, and all he sees are their bright and shiny PR: *We tripled our revenues last year and we're on track to gain unicorn status in three years.* Everything Jacob watches or reads online reflects something that is not his reality. All Jacob sees around him is the disaster that running a startup is. He feels like a fraud. He's worried that he will let everyone down. He can't share his fears with anyone, lest it causes mass hysteria. Or it makes him look weak. He's worried about being found out. He's meant to be this tech CEO wunderkind, dazzling the world with his show of boldness and charisma. But there's a disconnect. And inside that disconnect, Jacob feels that he's not normal or not good enough. *I'm never ever going to be like these CEOs.*

Jacob finds comfort in listening to podcasts like *How I Built This* with Guy Raz. Guy Raz gives his audience an honest behind-the-scenes perspective on how innovators and entrepreneurs of our time like Sara Blakely and Tony Hsieh built their empire. It's like therapy for Jacob. He gets to hear about other CEOs' disasters. He comes to a realization. *No one has all the answers.* For Jacob, this is the most liberating feeling. Here are other CEOs who state out loud what he knows deep down to be true — that being a CEO is exceedingly troublesome and pugnacious.

2. Open Mind: What uncomfortable truth are you denying?

Most leaders like to have full command over their destiny and where they are heading. But the world can be very disobedient, refusing to stay still and do as it's told. Things happen beyond their control, to their consternation. And so many things can change. Start a new line of business. End a line of business. Scale up the company. Downsize the company. To them, it feels like a loss of power, and that can be a blow to the ego.

The role of a CEO is like a circus act. As the CEO, Jacob has to be the first to adapt. It's basically a crisis of identity. It's a state change, like going from water to steam. One moment, Jacob is the high-growth CEO encouraging innovation and new thinking to capture emerging market opportunities. In the next instant, he's the austerity-CEO imposing financial discipline in an economic downturn. Jacob is balancing on a high-wire trapeze with no safety net. It is disorienting and schizophrenic.

Jacob moves too fast for his own good. When there's too much going on, his reaction is to move faster. We think that slowing down is unproductive.

When Jacob hits a roadblock, his automatic response is to push harder, *Grit your teeth. Just power through with sheer willpower.* That's just going through the motions. You're only drilling further into the wrong answers.

When things go wrong, Jacob's impulse is to fight stronger. He tries to problem-solve everything himself, and in doing so, he feels even more out of control. He worries excessively about the business as if the business will collapse if he takes his eyes off it for even one second. At his finest, he can come across like a military dictator.

When things get difficult, Jacob's reaction is to work faster, harder and stronger. Here's the thing. Leaders don't have a problem turning it on; their problem is turning it off. Your head is your prison, but sleep doesn't visit anymore. The best bridge between despair and hope is a good night's sleep.[1] Most of the time, the missing piece that you are looking for emerges out of nowhere after a good night's rest.

3. Open Heart: What difficult emotions are you ignoring?

Jacob is under a lot of pressure. There's always too much going on. His anxiety can get the better of him. He thinks he can function without sleep, food and exercise. Up to the point where his wife admonishes him: *Get into bed now!*

Jacob wants to trust his leadership team. But sometimes it's the most difficult thing for him to watch from the sidelines and not try to get involved. Jacob is careful that he's sharing the stress with his leadership team, and not putting additional stress on them in order to make himself feel better. It's a fine line.

Trust is a fragile thing. It doesn't happen overnight. You can't expect a group of independent, dominant, type-A strangers to trust each other immediately. Of course, there will be conflict initially. People jostle each other for power. Some of them challenge Jacob's authority directly. Others try to manipulate Jacob a lot more subtly. And Jacob has to keep them all on the straight and narrow. It is like herding cats.

All this require emotional intelligence. People think that emotional intelligence is fluffy and touchy-feely. There's nothing soft about it; it's absolutely foundational to leadership. When things get difficult, maintaining motivation at work becomes a challenge. It becomes way too easy to say, "I don't give a F." When you're not getting the external validation that you need, ask directly for it. Alternatively, you can dig deep to find that source of approval, control and security from within.

Jacob makes sure to stay away from doomsday preppers. Instead of bringing energy, they drag you deeper into the abyss with that dead cat bounce.

4. Open Will: What hard decision are you avoiding?

Jacob learnt to be ruthless when making decisions. Jacob believes in making decisions fast. Jacob's decisions may come fast, but they are not fast decisions. He strives to make better decisions *faster*. He doesn't wait until he has the "perfect" model answer before he acts. He absorbs as much information as he can. He solicits advice from trusted advisors. But finally, he makes the best decision he can based on his knowledge and experience of truth at that point in time. He develops prototypes to test ideas. That's how he sneaks up to the future.

When he makes mistakes, he allows himself one day to fume. Then he lets go and moves on. He realizes that the longer he fumes or sits on the decision, the longer he delays the organization from achieving what he wants. When Jacob can't decide, the organization can't proceed. Things get stuck and a backlog of work starts to accumulate. That's how things become overwhelming. There is also a multiplier effect. In Jacob's organization of 250 people, every day that Jacob sits on a decision is equivalent to a year's worth of loss in productivity.

If Jacob was not able to make hard decisions regarding unprofitable operations, the business would have failed earlier on. Hard decisions are… hard. These are really uncomfortable conversations. We prefer to ignore it altogether. The organizational debt mounts up — up to the point it can't. We'll be forced to make awkward decisions that we'd rather not make, and we'll say: *I had to do it. I had no choice.* The villain is denial. That certainty of making the *right* decision doesn't come immediately. Give it space. Wait for that moment when confusion turns into clarity. Let it emerge from the core of your being. It will feel obvious: *it's a no-*

brainer. It'll feel like it's something you can't NOT do. It will feel natural. *Au naturel.* This is how you accomplish more by doing less. It is the art of leadership, the *au naturel* way.

5. New Mindset: You are not alone

Jacob has something very special and unique. He has something worth saying. It can't be taken from him because it's essential to who he is. And he can lead people with that. He can build on that, whether it's a career, a leadership team, or a company. It guides better decision-making. It provides a framework to configure himself as an intentional trajectory through the shifting and ambiguous sands of running a business.

Jacob embarked on a quest and he has had his moments of truth. Through that journey, he learns who he is and what he's made of. It's the thing he believes he is uniquely positioned to do. The thing he fundamentally believes he is the best person in the world to do. This is his inner authority speaking. It doesn't speak in words, but Jacob knows, *intuitively*. He can feel it in his bones. It makes Jacob.... Jacob. At a very fundamental level, these are the things that he loves and knows to be true, where he feels compelled to act because it's the right thing to do, which makes him happy. No matter how difficult the situation is, it's something he can always return home to. It gives him his "edge." It's his secret sauce. It's his gift to the world.

Jacob will not be able to stay truthful to this inner authority every single day for every single decision. He will fail at it. But without this inner authority guiding him, Jacob can easily get lost in the circus. Because there is a lot of noise out there; Information overload, other people's expectations. He will get overwhelmed and lose that clarity of thought. Without understanding what he stands for, Jacob will try to do everything expected of him rather than stick to what's meaningful. That's how CEOs burn out. They focus on the what's and how's, forgetting why they wanted this in the first place.

Sometimes you must stand alone.

To say yes, even when people say, "It will never work." It always seems impossible until it becomes possible.

To say no, even if it makes you unpopular. In order to have one great idea, you have to say no to many good ones.

6. Practical tips

Self-care. Put on your oxygen mask first before assisting others. You are the CEO to yourself first, then your family & friends, then your business. When you are healthy, you are strong. Then you can do the superhuman things that every CEO needs to do.

Professional athlete. Your lifestyle is as disciplined as a professional sports athlete's. You have eight hours of sleep every day. Sleep is a weapon. You run every morning. You eat a mainly plant-based diet. You stay away from alcohol. You meditate. You have a team of nutritionists, sports coaches, physiotherapists and stylists to keep you in your best shape. The alternative is waking up one day at the back of an ambulance, siren wailing, experiencing a sharp pain in your chest.

Switch off. The biggest challenge for leaders is not switching on; it's switching off. You are so used to being ON! ON! ON! Ruthlessly guard the blank hours in your calendar. This is your thinking time. Otherwise, when will you have the time to dream? Productivity falls sharply after a 50-hour work-week and falls off a cliff after 55 hours — so much so that someone who puts in 70 hours produces nothing more with those extra 15 hours.[2]

Support. Build a support structure to keep you from going over the edge, whether it is an empathetic board member, some sort of peer network, or even a friend who's on a similar roller coaster.

Prioritize. Start your day by prioritizing what tasks need to be done that day. Prioritizing takes up a lot of brainpower. It's better to do it when you have your peak energy.

Perfectionist. High performers have obsessive, compulsive, perfectionist tendencies. Sometimes, it's better to complete all tasks well enough. Other times, it's better to complete one task brilliantly.

Communicate. It's okay for your team to know when you're feeling burnt out. Acknowledging how we feel unlocks a megatonne of energy. Denying it just makes it worse.

7. Related chapters

Chapter 29   Define Your Leadership Brand

Chapter 35   Uncomfortable Conversations

9

Climbing the Corporate Ladder

"The one thing that you have that nobody else has is you. Your voice, your mind, your story, your vision. So write and draw and build and play and dance and live as only you can."

— Neil Gaiman

May is attending a reunion with her ex-colleagues whom she has not seen for more than a decade. Back then, May was the R&D (research & development) Director leading engineering teams across Europe and Asia Pacific. May tells her ex-colleagues that she's now working in Sales for a systems integrator. May's ex-colleagues give her a withering look of pity. Out loud, they say, "Good for you!" But their faces say it all. *Poor you. How far the mighty angel has fallen.*

Ten years ago, the software company that May was working for was acquired. As part of the acquisition, the R&D function was pulled back to the US. May was offered a role in the US, but she didn't want to relocate. Instead, she took up a regional sales engineer role and remained in Asia. She was stripped of the Director title and relegated to a Manager. What followed were more drastic adjustments. May subsequently moved from Sales Engineering into Sales, at the country level. And the final nail in the coffin, she left the technology vendor for a systems integrator. May went to the dark side.

Back at the reunion party, May feels her ex-colleagues' sympathy for her. They think it has been one career disaster after another, going from bad to worse. But May thinks differently. She understands why they think that way. Once upon a time, she was just like them. Talked like them. Thought like them. But now, May looks at them like they are relics from the dot. com boom of the 1990s. Sheltered in their bubble, they still haven't got a clue. They are still stuck in La La Land. *God, that could have been me.* May shudders at the thought if she had not taken that extraordinary and fatal leap of faith.

1. Old Mindset: Climb the corporate ladder

Whenever you hear a plan for developing your career, you'll likely find some kind of backward math: if I'm going to become a CEO by 40 years old, then I need to be a VP by 35, which means I need to get my MBA before I turn 30.

And if they don't have such a career plan for themselves, their employers will provide one for them. It usually goes in alphabetical or numerical order. For example, IC1 to IC6, or job bands A, B, C to H. Like you're back in kindergarten.

When people first start out, they think that their careers will be on a one-way street to the top. It never crosses their minds that they need to orchestrate their career development. They assume that everything is planned for them. Confidential files locked in the HR department with their names on them, created by the warm and fuzzy HR mama bear who looks after everyone's careers and gives out hugs when they are feeling down.

Sometimes these career expectations are met. Sometimes not. But often, people come to a crossroad in their careers where they feel like they are missing something they imagined they would have by now. Most of the time, they can't even articulate what that thing is. And for people who have worked hard and done everything right, this feeling can be destabilizing.

During my recruitment days, I would start an interview with this question: "So, what do you want to do?" I'm met with silence.

They might say:
"I can do anything."
I didn't ask what you can do. I asked what you want to do.

"Anything, except what I'm doing now."
I didn't ask what you don't want to do. I asked what you want to do.

"I'm open, if they pay more."
I didn't ask how much you want to be paid. I asked what you want to do.

"I'm not looking. I just want to know what's available in the market."
In other words, you don't know.

The truth is... most people don't know what they want to do. That's the bare naked truth for more than half of us.[1] That's an exciting place to be; it's an open question mark that holds delightful possibilities. But most don't see it that way. The question mark can be so uncomfortable that some rush to do their $100,000 MBA, only to find themselves upon graduation exactly where they left off.

2. Open Mind: What uncomfortable truth are you denying?

May has been fascinated with technology since young. She was that kid who was into computers before they became ubiquitous. May was wearing the Casio Databank CD-40 calculator watch before "wearable technology" was a buzzword. Basically, she was a tech geek before it became geek chic.

It was a no-brainer that May ended up as an R&D engineer at an innovative technology company after university. May gets her adrenaline kick riding at the bleeding edge of R&D, supporting rapid innovation and developing the next Gmail and Windows for the enterprise technology industry.

Talented engineers are treated like rockstars in the tech world. And R&D engineers are the cherry on top of the cake — the creme de la creme. The R&D engineers take great pride in their inventions. They don't really see the need for Sales: *the product is so good, it sells by itself.* Salespeople are just good for bringing clients out for long boozy lunches and taking their orders at the end of it.

But working for Sales is not the lowest in the pyramid. If you're working for a technology vendor, you're still doing okay. Because right at the bottom of the food chain is working for the systems integrators. They are like a supermarket hawking other people's wares, selling anything they can get their hands on. Their tactics are that of a used car salesman, synonymous with sleazy, pushy, crooked sales over karaoke. People working for systems integrators see the technology vendor as the promised land. Career progression means crossing the Red Sea to join a technology vendor, and never the other way around.

In the sales engineer role, May acted as the middleman between the systems integrator and the R&D team in the US. Whenever there was a problem with the technology during implementation, the systems integrator would bring the problem to her attention, and she would consult her R&D team.

The R&D team would revert. It's a 1D-10T error. A very common error. Also known as IDIOT error. Or PICNIC error. *Problem in chair, not in computer.* Or IBM error. *Idiot behind machine.* The tech is a piece of engineering marvel, designed to deliver advanced and sophisticated functionalities, worthy of a Nobel Prize for computing. Obviously, the fault is on the user's side. Clearly, it's a lack of computer savvy, which can only be fixed on the user side.

May would bring the feedback to the systems integrator. They disagree. Obviously, the technology doesn't work. Clearly, it's a software design error, which can only be fixed on the R&D side.

And May would go back and forth. Back and forth. She would feel strait-jacketed in the role. Stuck. Caught in the middle. Unhappy customers on one side and stubborn engineers on the other. She'd be caught in a stalemate. What else could she do?

3. Open Heart: What difficult emotions are you ignoring?

Of course, there was the option of simply doing nothing. It's the wait-and-see game, playing the postman, passing the buck around. This is how the game is played, has *always* been played. Everyone knows the rules of the game, and May just has to play by the rules.

And by the way, May's life was fantastic. She was a PPS member jetting around the region in Business Class. She was earning a generous salary. She just had to keep her mouth shut, collect the paycheck and watch her bank account grow every month. On the surface, May's life looks fantastic. Yet, deep down, she was not. There was a niggling feeling of dissatisfaction. And she was embarrassed for thinking like that. *My life is perfect. What right do I have to complain? I should be grateful.*

No, it's better to keep your head down. Continue your supposedly awesome life. Invest your energy into climbing the corporate ladder, pretending to be happier, more successful and more in control than you feel.

But who will I become?
Will I like who I will become?

This was a moment of truth. The questions had been brewing in May's head for a long time. She kept putting it off, thinking she still has time.

May has always been driven by an internal mission. She has always been hungry to do something big and excel in it. She wants to make a real impact for real people, run a real business making real money, and not just be a paper pusher.

Being stuck in the middle doing nothing was simply not an option.

4. Open Will: What hard decision are you avoiding?

May decided that she wants to move closer to the customers. That's when she moved into a Sales position. Subsequently, she jumped ship to the dark side — joining a system integrator.

That's when May struck oil.

May realized that customers are dealing with over-complicated legacy enterprise systems, layered on top of old systems, amidst a complex business environment where technology is increasingly being held up as the messiah that will save the company. "Install cloud" seems to be the mantra. *And you will be the Uber of your industry, disrupting the whole business model, and wiping out all your competitors.*

On top of that, May realized that many technology products prioritize sophisticated functionalities over ease-of-use and intuitive design. Complex user interfaces meant that the customers themselves cannot make minor adjustments or updates to their own IT systems without calling in the systems integrator and paying their fees. The cost of the technology may not be prohibitive, but the cost of integrating and maintaining it can be.

All this calls for a trusted systems integrator that can make the technology work in the customers' environment.

5. New Mindset: Find your personal path

There is a calmness that follows May into a room. There's something about her dignified mannerism and impeccable British accent that hint at her respectable education and prestigious heritage. Even the most skeptical CTO opens up to May, which allows her to get to the core of their issues and create custom-fit solutions leveraging multiple technologies. May develops real solutions to solve real pain for real users. This is true R&D.

May found her purpose — the Work. And she's only just beginning.

Let's be clear here. Moving from Engineering to Sales is NOT natural. It goes against the grain of our kindergarten system of numbers and alphabets, which is so logical, so precise, so chronological.

But career progression is not a linear path, especially if you are working in tech. Technology advances so rapidly that our computers and mobile phones become obsolete practically the moment they are launched. There is always something newer, faster, better coming our way. The rapid pace of change means that a mobile phone from a decade ago now looks positively alien. The Motorola brick phone is obscenely dated by today's standards. You could say the same thing for jobs in tech.

The early techies used to bill clients for half a day's work just to connect the printer to the computer. Today, there is a tidal wave of young punks who can out-code and out-program them. And technology is constantly simplifying to the point where even your grandmother can plug the printer into the computer. Expecting a promotion or salary increase just to do the same thing each year is not just daydreaming. It's a death trap.

So it might look like May was taking a huge risk moving from Engineering to Sales. After all, she was at the top of her game, Director title and all. She was winning. But maybe she was the conservative one. By taking that moonshot, May pushed herself out of the sandbox that she was playing in. She let go of beliefs that held her in the past and adopted new beliefs that were better fitted for the present situation. That's how May secured her future and stayed immune from obsolescence.

As May stops running away from the big question mark and faces it, the horizon opens up in front of her, and it dawns on her: *Oh, I'm only just beginning.* It is exhilarating to be at the top of your game and feel like you've only now just learned your craft. The Work. From the vantage point of this larger worldview, May realizes that she was not aspiring to the caliber of performance she's capable of. And that's what's incredible about life and challenging yourself. It's a constant reinvention, constantly learning and growing, and it just gets better. You're never done. Career development is not a bunch of alphabets and numbers. Find your personal path. It is a series of fights. You got this.

6. Practical tips

Self-discovery. Know yourself first. When you know what you want, you may discover your dream job is right under your nose. It may not look like your dream job initially, but the potential is there, and it requires your commitment and creativity to tailor it to fit your needs.

Be proactive. Initiate that conversation with your boss. Don't assume your boss knows what you want. Don't leave your career development to HR. Take charge of your own career.

Learning. When you switch careers, there is a steep learning curve. Go out and connect with a diverse range of people. Read voraciously. Listen to podcasts. Leave no stone unturned. For elements you can address, put a plan together. For those you can't, at least be aware of it. As time progresses, you'll develop mastery in several areas, not just one. This makes you a rare talent in the market.

Steal with your eyes. Take on new and challenging assignments outside your work scope. Understand different departments within the organization. Learn the roles of others. Walk in the shoes of your customer or business partner for a day.

Get a mentor. Mentors let you stand on their shoulders to help you get a perspective on the market that you can never otherwise have. They give you an insider's view of the industry ecosystem. They share the loopholes and booby traps that lie hidden within the organization. The best mentor-mentee relationship is never contrived. It's often sparkling, thought-provoking conversations over a glass of wine.

Journey. Career development is not a destination you must arrive at in order to be happy. It's the journey that matters. It's okay not to have 100% certainty about your dream job. It's also okay if you change your mind. With experience, you'll discover what's important to you. Like a good bowl of Cantonese soup, it's all about boiling it down to its essence. Every step is a discovery. Even if you make a wrong turn, it's not a mistake — you learned what to avoid.

7. Related chapters

Chapter 19   Scaling Your Business

Chapter 24   Reducing Employee Turnover

Chapter 26   Learning at the Speed of Business

10

Job Hopping

"Games are life distilled into programmable parameters.

And life is a game where everyone is still learning the parameters."

— Anonymous

Thomas is a Sales and Marketing professional, and he has been switching roles quite often. Seven roles in 10 years, to be exact. A two-year stint here, another two-year stint there. And then there was that dead cat bounce of 10 months he prefers not to talk about. He has tried many different things. However, he hasn't quite found his groove yet.

Are you a hob-jobber?

hob-jobber (noun), British dialect

- a man or boy walking the streets on the lookout for small jobs

Thomas goes all sentimental talking about his first job: running multi-million-dollar marketing campaigns for some of the hottest electronic gadgets. But there was one problem... the pay sucked. All that marketing budget had to come from somewhere.

So, after 2 years of doing charity, Thomas bounces and lands in another A-lister tech company, running multi-million-dollar marketing campaigns for sexy gaming products, with better pay. However, as time goes by, he realizes what justifies the higher pay: the boss is an insane workaholic megalomaniac.

After 2 years, Thomas had enough, and by the way, another exciting opportunity has come along, and he bounces. And bounces. And bounces. Thomas decides to leave Marketing and dabbles in various Sales roles.

1. Old Mindset: Finding the perfect job

Thomas searches, and searches, but he can't seem to find that perfect job. From the outside, the job looks like a dream. But within a few months on the job, some problem or another will crop up. The job becomes a nightmare, and he has to leave.

Paid peanuts for your work? There's a better paying job out there.

Hate your boss's guts? There's a better boss out there.

Every time Thomas changes his job, he thinks he has fixed his problem. It may seem like Thomas has solved the crazy boss problem by replacing him with a new one. But what's happening here is that Thomas has successfully rid his life of this insane megalomaniac, but he has not gotten rid of his real problem: Thomas still feels miserable. Every time Thomas makes a change, he thinks: *This is it. My woes are over.* But inevitably, a new problem will crop up, and he's back to feeling miserable again.

Seven roles, and 10 years later, Thomas is having those familiar thoughts again. But this time, there's a twitch of worry. It feels like he's gone down one too many rabbit holes. Same old problem, just a different day. He doesn't want to go down that short dead-end rabbit hole again. He doesn't want to run away from his problem anymore. He wants a real solution.

2. Open Mind: What uncomfortable truth you are denying?

This is the thing… Deep down, Thomas knows he's born for greatness. *I'M DIFFERENT.* He can feel it in his bones. Even if he doesn't have the words for it yet.

Thomas was a precocious child growing up, questioning everything. His mind is like a sponge hungry for knowledge. He's a walking encyclopedia of random factoids. He has a million brilliant creative ideas swimming in his head. He picks up new skills very quickly. That's why he can bounce from job to job with ease.

Thomas resists being forced into a mold. He's self-aware and he knows what he wants, but sometimes it comes into conflict with the job. He puffs up with self-righteous indignation when he's threatened for not meeting the unreasonable sales targets: "Bring in the numbers, or else." Conformity riles him because it's so boring, and his mind switches off. This is a slippery slope. When you don't love what you do and you're doing it just for the money, it becomes a job that pays the bills. There's no spark. The work quality deteriorates. Relationships suffer. And to Thomas, that's plain stupid and a complete waste of potential.

Thomas doesn't take things for granted. He believes that the highest authority is his own experience of truth. He needs to test things himself to see whether it works. He's been experimenting and looking for ways to make things more efficient and logical. After 10 years, the experimentation is stabilizing. The experiences of his youthful enterprises have granted him the depth to be truly wise about life.

3. Open Heart: What difficult emotions you are ignoring?

Thomas feels like he's been going round in circles. He has a sinking feeling that he may have been complicit in creating this situation. He has been running away from the real problem. He thinks the boss is the problem, so he changes his boss. But whatever new job he goes to, the problem follows him like a shadow. He's still miserable. He just can't shake it off. He has nothing to show for it, except for the nettle scars he collected along the way.

Thomas figures this is the time for change, a radical one. He has been chasing the wrong tail. This time, he aims directly at the source of the problem. He wants to cut through the delusion he has been telling himself that has kept him playing small. This time, he wants to set himself up for long-term success.

Thomas has been so focused on running away from his "problems." Problem is the territory where things go wrong. Salary problems. Boss problems. He's been so busy running away from his problems that he lost sight of the destination: setting his vision. Vision is about your direction, where you are heading, and why you are heading there. Put simply, running *away* from your problems does not necessarily move you *towards* your vision. Running away from your problems only prevents misery; taking bold action towards your vision leads to greatness.

Most of us were brainwashed since young to pursue a job that pays the bills and a career that moves us as quickly as possible to the top of the corporate ladder. We push aside ideas about finding our calling until we've paid off the mortgage, sent the kids to college and built a nest egg for retirement.

You don't have to wait till retirement to daydream about your calling. Thomas experimented with many different roles and took the unconventional path. When he reflects on his personal experience, he realizes that when he is doing work that he loves, when the job allows him to stay true to himself, he is a source of positive energy. It has a tremendous impact on the people who work around him. He produces award-winning work. He knows from direct experience that he is not interested in jobs that perpetuate the safe and familiar. He prefers jobs that allow him to explore what is unsettling and strange.

To others, Thomas looks like a hotchpotch of uncoordinated talents and expertise. Where others focus on sharpening their skills in one discipline, Thomas mastered several, and he brings these skills together to create something extraordinary. Because of his versatility, Thomas sees possibilities where others see none. And that makes what he has very valuable.

4. Open Will: What hard decision are you avoiding?

Through his personal experience, Thomas realizes that there's no perfect job *out there* that will make him happy. No job is 100% aligned with who you are and what you want to do. Instead of trying to shoehorn himself into another job, Thomas finds creative ways to tailor the job to take advantage of his unique strengths. He brings an X-factor to the role because of how he thinks: *I don't do Sales; I do relationships.* In his new role, Thomas is not just a Director leading a sales team across APAC. He's Lilith leading the Crimson Raiders into battle in *Borderlands 3*. To Thomas, life is like a game. And there are so many different types of games to play: games where you need to use all ten fingers and ten toes. And then there are the one-swipe games. *Candy Crush* your life!

5. New Mindset: Crafting the perfect job

Thomas has a tremendous amount of power to lead change. The key to unleashing his full potential is to be bold and articulate his vision. Thomas is an experimental learner. He needs to try something to understand it better. He does not take people's opinions for granted. Thomas knows what energizes him and what doesn't because he has tried it all. He knows this through his direct and personal experience, not intellectually through a personality profiling test.

It's misleading to think that jobs are a lifetime commitment. Things change. Disruption happens. When Thomas was in a role, he was fulfilling its purpose. When he has fulfilled his purpose professionally, he moves on. When Thomas couldn't fulfill his purpose professionally, when he was not loving his work, he also moved on. Build and maintain relationships, as you never know when those will come in handy in the future.

Crafting the perfect job is a continuous evolving process. Pack your bags. There's a much bigger game to be played.

6. Practical tips

Vision. It's difficult to speak up when you are not sure who you are and what you're here to do. The inner work has to be done upfront. Craft your leadership brand. Tell your authentic story — what you are uniquely positioned to do.

Big picture. Always keep the big picture in mind. Don't let the extraneous details distract you from your big and audacious goal.

Moonlighting. Try on the suit before you buy it. Drive a Grab car during the weekends. Sell your old camera gear on Carousel. Become an Instagram influencer. It gives you first-hand experience about the job, company or industry.

Informational interviews. Connect with industry insiders. Ask them to share their stories about their jobs and the industry. What does a typical day look like? What do they enjoy about their work? What challenges do they face?

Be direct. Be direct about what you want. Don't beat around the bush, trying to be coy. Don't wait for people to second-guess what you want. Or hoodwink you into a role that you later regret.

Guilt. People still hold dysfunctional beliefs around lifetime employment. They think that just because you've been job-hopping, that means there is something wrong with you. Shift the guilt, don't bottle it up. Surround yourself with people who are more open-minded and supportive.

8. Related chapters

Chapter 19   Scaling Your Business

Chapter 24   Reducing Employee Turnover

11

Being Let Go

"When the Lord closes a door, somewhere he
opens a window."

— **Fraulein Maria in the movie** *Sound of Music*

R obert is a fund manager with a large real estate development company. It's Thursday, Robert is already looking forward to the weekend; it has been a hell of a week. He sees an email from his boss titled: URGENT. His boss wants to see him at 5.30 p.m. He doesn't mention why.

Robert is filled with dread. He has a nauseous feeling in his stomach. The relationship with his boss has been deteriorating over the last few months. They do not see eye-to-eye on certain things. There's been an undercurrent of aggression. Small matters get blown out of proportion, the proverbial storm in a teacup, culminating in a messy nuclear blow-up earlier in the week.

At 5.30 p.m., Robert enters the boss's office. When Robert closes the door, his boss lays down his cards, "Your under-performance can no longer be tolerated. You are now put on the pip." That dreaded word: "pip." For the uninitiated, that stands for Performance Improvement Plan. Maybe once upon a time, the term meant what it says: performance improvement. Today, it's more like a witch hunt to prove the employee's incompetence, lest the incompetence is pinned on the manager. Then Robert's boss reveals his hand: "Or you can quit voluntarily."

Before Robert can take a resuscitating breath, his boss goes in for the kill: "You have to decide by tonight. If you choose to quit, you have to tender your resignation by the end of today. Otherwise, you automatically go on the 'pip' tomorrow."

And then Robert's boss delivers the sinker that drags Robert into the abyss. "If you don't resign by tonight, you are not going to get a good reference from me. The industry is very small, and I know people," browbeating Robert into abject submission.

WHOA!

And that's how Robert is told his life in this company is finished. It hits him like a tonne of bricks. This is what you get after five years of 12-hour days and six-day weeks.

YOU'RE OUT! You've been kicked out onto the streets.

1. Old Mindset: It's just business. It's not personal.

When Robert first joined the company five years ago, he was all bright-eyed and bushy-tailed. He thought he found his dream job. But this current situation is not happily ever after. This is a slap in the face. Robert's face burns up like a fever. So *diu lian* (the literal translation from Chinese is "lose face"). It feels like he's been disowned by his own family.

Robert crawls out of the room with as much dignity as he can muster. And once in the privacy of the fire escape staircase, the fiery violent ego acts up like a severe case of allergy. It really does not appreciate the brush-off. *How dare they! Don't they know who I am?!*

Robert has never been fired in his life. He constantly sees people suddenly disappear around him. It's something people don't talk much about, but it happens — all the time. *Yeah, yeah, these things happen. BUT NOT TO ME.* Robert has always been the high-flying executive, the blue-eyed boy of the Chairman.

All this talk about one family, one team, one dream. ALL LIES!!! Robert feels naive, cheated. He was stupid enough to believe the lies. He put in the hours. He forsook his life and real family, skipping birthdays and weddings. *Do it for the team.* And this is how he is repaid. He feels used, discarded, like a piece of used tissue paper.

What was I thinking?! I was just a hired help. The relationship was purely transactional. *It's just business. It's not personal.* Employees jump ship for an extra $1,000. Companies hire and fire. It sounds like the oldest profession in the world.

prostitution (noun)

- the unworthy or corrupt use of one's talents for personal or financial gain

2. Open Mind: What uncomfortable truth are you denying?

It seems even CEOs are not immune to being let go. CEOs' median tenure at large-cap (S&P 500) companies is five years.[1] Most of these departures were classified as "resignations." Executives are rarely officially "terminated," even when they leave under duress following scandals, as we've seen with Goldman Sachs' Southeast Asia chairman Tim Leissner and his involvement with Jho Low and his multi-billion-dollar money-laundering scheme. Thrown under the bus to save the prestige of the firm. Collateral damage.

The way that Robert's boss behaved is not uncommon. Nobody discusses it openly, but everyone knows that it happens. We sweep it under the carpet. It's an open secret that if brought into the light will cause morbid anxiety.

Robert feels the urge to slink quietly into oblivion, terrorized by the thought of facing the horror vacui of Chinese whispers in the office. But that's how Robert's boss wants it. The "You will never work in this town again" threat is pure balderdash. It's the quintessential Jeffrey Epstein bully tactic to shame their victims into silence. It's a blow below the belt, and it says more about his childish tyrannical pettiness than it reflects on Robert.

3. Open Heart: What difficult emotions are you ignoring?

The next 12 hours is one roller coaster ride of emotions.

First comes the shock: *what should I do? Do I quit or not? I really don't know....*

Then slowly, denial creeps in. *This can't be happening. He's an incompetent buffoon. Who's going to do all the work? He needs me. Wait a minute... That ass-licking new hire who joined two weeks ago. That's my replacement!*

Now anger starts to rear its head. *What happened to loyalty and commitment? What does he think he's doing?!! He can't do this to me! It's illegal!*

Followed by guilt. *This is my fault. If only I did as I was told and kept my mouth shut, this wouldn't be happening. All you had to do was shut your mouth and collect your paycheck, and you couldn't even do that.*

Past the guilt trip and around the corner, the roller coaster opens up into sheer panic. *What am I going to do now? We're in the middle of a pandemic. I won't be able to find another job!*

Finally, depression sets in. *I just don't have the energy to fight this anymore.* And Robert slips into a zombie-like comatose state.

It's a very isolating situation. It crushes his confidence. It's a punch in the face. Robert was knocked off his pedestal. These emotions are especially troubling for Robert because he's such a cool and composed person. Nothing ever fazes him. He's THE SPECIAL. He's always been the one who has it all figured out.

Robert does not want to feel all those strange and intolerable emotions. But ignoring those icky emotions won't get Robert anywhere. Paradoxically, the more he tries to ignore those difficult emotions, the tighter he holds on to them. Ignoring his emotions actually keeps him stuck in the past.

Robert thinks he has "got over it" in 12 hours — the emotional roller coaster ride. Dusted his hands. *It's over and done with. I've moved on.*

Well... think again.

That's not moving on. Robert's only burying the stinky rubbish truck of angsty emotions. Whether Robert likes it or not, those angsty emotions are still churning underground, and it will come back to haunt him in the future, at the most inconvenient time. Those wild, indefinable emotions are seeking expression. Constantly. It lies in wait for that perfect moment, when the stakes are high, and Robert's guard is down. And he'll be completely blindsided.

Robert will go for interviews for several exciting roles. The conversations will go smooth as silk, up to the final interview. It'll come down to the last two candidates — it's either going to be Robert or the other person. And Robert'll lose out. It happens again. And again. And again. Robert will try to figure out why, he will ask around, but he won't get a straight answer.

This is a standard interview question: "So, why did you leave your last company?"

My boss was an incompetent buffoon.

The company did not value loyalty and commitment.

It was purely transactional.

Obviously, Robert will never say it aloud. Our wonderfully vile ego is much more subtle than that. But people can sense the buried angst. Even if they can't put their finger on it. In recruitment lingo, we used to term these "red flags." On paper, the candidate looks like the perfect match for the job, a potentially excellent hire, but he is rejected in the end. Why? "It's a "red flag." Like a niggling doubt that refuses to go away. You'll never get straight answers. And the more you try to explain, the more it confuses people. So… "red flag."

Emotions are running all the time, whether you like it or not. You can pay attention to it and make it be your superpower. Or you can ignore it and have it be your kryptonite. Either way, it's running.

4. Open Will: What hard decision are you avoiding?

So, Robert gave it his best shot. He dedicated a significant part of his life to the company. But the reality is… not every boss is going to be a charm. Robert didn't do anything wrong, so why give the boss the satisfaction of hurting him and making him miserable?

Plus, failure can often lead to something better. This could be one of the best things that happens to Robert. He just doesn't know it yet.

If Tony Fernandes hadn't taken the severance package from Warner, there would be no AirAsia.

If Jack Ma hadn't gotten rejected by KFC, there would be no Alibaba.

We think that successful entrepreneurs like Tony and Jack are "destined" to build companies that change the world. We say this with the benefit of hindsight wisdom. I'm sure being rejected by KFC doesn't quite have a "destined" quality about it. The same thing can be happening for Robert right now. If the Universe didn't give Robert a kick in the bum, he will wake up at the age of 80 regretting a lifetime of playing small. Face it, if the company had said to Robert, "We have another job for you" such as setting up the Mongolian office, Robert would have done it in a second. Robert likes the organization, and he would have been happy to stay in the "family."

So, Robert faces a dilemma: *Leave or stay? Even if you're not welcome?*

It might be a timely question. Impeccable timing.

Robert has shot through the upper echelons of the organization, driven by his desire to keep moving up the ladder. This is not just another job to get a paycheck. He loves what he does. Robert has ambitions to grow the Asian market, but his boss has not been supportive. His effort to capture the technological shift in the industry butted head-to-head with the bumbling bureaucracy of a big corporation. It has been extremely frustrating for Robert. He's losing interest in his job. He doesn't feel the same adrenaline rush he felt at the beginning of his career. That fiery passion has been waning. And his performance has started to falter because of it. His career has stalled. The writing is on the wall. It's time. Time to let go of the past. And allow the future to emerge.

5. New Mindset: It's not just business. It's also personal.

Maybe, deep down in his murky subconscious brain, Robert has been wanting out. And the Universe delivered what Robert unwittingly wished for. This is happening for him.

Of course, this is much easier to appreciate once Robert is on the other side of the journey. But right this moment, it requires a leap of faith... a

CRAZY leap of faith. It requires Robert to accept his situation fully, and then ask: *How is this happening FOR me?*

When Robert does that, he gives permission to that quiet, creative voice within to wonder. *Yeah, how is this happening for me?*

Robert starts to loosen his tight-fisted grip. His eyes begin to open. He keeps his ears peeled to the ground. He starts looking outwards, towards the vast open ocean of exciting opportunities. It's looking for Robert to show up. It's inviting him to dance on the edge of greatness. Robert feels he's not ready because he's been so focused on the little things.

Maybe Robert will realize what he really wants is a six-month paid sabbatical (or angel investor funding to start his next thing). And what his boss really wants are automatons, and he's willing to pay good money to keep Robert quiet and not tarnish his reputation. So, the organization pays out a sizable compensation, and Robert gets his funding. That's a win–win.

Here's an alternative scenario. Maybe Robert wants to remain in the organization. That means going on the "pip." Robert must be willing to change and shift his mindset. I don't say this lightly. If Robert really wants this to work, he has to connect with his boss. To truly connect with people, you have to agree with them. Let me put this simply. Robert has to convince himself, "My boss is right." This is a big mental job because agreeing with his boss challenges Robert's identity: *I might become my boss.* This is the uncomfortable truth that Robert must confront. It'll be meaningless to stay and pretend everything is fine. Robert will just be kicking the can down the road. The good news is if Robert makes this mindset shift, everything else after that becomes easier. Robert will naturally be committed to engage with "pip." He will be proactive and takes ownership. He will create support structures to hold himself accountable.

Robert decides to leave. He gracefully holds the space for his boss to be accountable. Hold your boss to a higher standard, and they will rise to meet it. Don't give their frail ego even a minutiae of a chance to sink into thuggish behavior.

Robert wants to look back at this moment with pride. Lead with your values. Don't be a jerk. But also don't be a doormat. And *always always* do it in style.

On Robert's last day of work, he puts in his regular 12 hours. He leaves the office and makes his way to Orchard Road to pick up his made-to-measure Zegna suit. It fits perfectly. Robert looks like a million bucks. He's delighted. He heads off to dinner. His wife joins him. Robert pops open a bottle of Dom Perignon. For tomorrow he begins his new life. Robert is starting a fintech company. He's embarking on a completely different path. Afterwards, Robert won't look back over his shoulder. He won't hang around wondering what is happening back at the old company. He won't go back and visit. He moves on. In style. On his terms.

It will take a bit of work, a bit of practice, a bit of courage. But you got this.

6. Practical tips

Emotions. Label the emotions. Being asked to leave hurts. It's okay to feel all those rubbish emotions. The villain is denial. Simply acknowledging the emotions actually changes the brain, and can make all the difference.

Blame. Don't play the blame game. Finger-pointing has never helped resolve the situation. No one is fully responsible, everyone is complicit in creating the situation that nobody wants. Robert plays the most significant role in his own performance, but it's not all his fault. The processes and infrastructure play an important role, but it's not all his boss's fault.

Support. Reach out to your support network. Seek out someone who has solved your problem. Look outside your organization. Look within your organization. Seek advice from your HR and Legal Department. Seek out the opinion of your mentor, even if he's the Chairman. You'll be surprised at how much people are willing to help.

Negotiate. To negotiate for a win–win, you need to be clear about what you and the other party want. Either/or dilemmas like "Should I quit or not?" are restrictive. Instead, ask open-ended questions. *What do I really want, and what are the best options to get it? What am I here to do, and how do I want to spend my precious time? I really love this company, it's just this hiccup of a boss. He's not an evil person, what's really happening here? Why is he behaving like this? What does he really want?*

Gratitude. Be grateful. Count your blessings and express gratitude to your boss and organization. *But they have done NOTHING to help me!* Expressing gratitude may taste a bit salty right now, but there's always *something* to be grateful for. *It was character-defining. I learnt what NOT to do as a boss. The company paid for my Maserati.* This is as much for you as it is for them. There's no better way to placate the disturbing inner demons than to hold a genuine sense of appreciation for your life.

Blessing in disguise. Ask yourself: *How is this happening FOR me?* Maybe this is the Universe's way of getting you to let go of the past. A better future is waiting for you to show up.

7. Related chapters

Chapter 16   Letting People Go

Chapter 20   Restructuring Your Business

Chapter 23   Restructuring Without Talent Loss

Part 3
People Leadership

12

Becoming a New Manager

*"If you want to go fast, go alone. If you want to go
far, go together."*
— **African proverb**

ichard started his career as a one-man IT (Information Technology) department for the New Zealand office of a multinational organization, responsible for making sure everyone's laptops and emails work 24/7. He would write long emails to the Asia Pacific regional boss based in Singapore, articulating potential problems and proposing new service improvements. Some of them must have been half-decent because they were actually implemented, like the helpdesk ticketing system. One of Richard's email tirades must have titillated his boss's curiosity. Richard's boss offers him a job in his regional team and relocate to Singapore to roll out his idea on a much larger scale across Asia Pacific. This is a huge jump in responsibility. Richard is going from an independent contributor role to a manager role leading 30 people with three direct reports.

1. Old Mindset: This is how we've always done it

So here is Richard, fresh off the boat in Singapore, and immediately he's confronted with a very closed service culture within the IT services team. The team literally sits behind a wall with a tiny service window where people hand over their laptops. Richard sees a long queue snaking around the corner with people waiting impatiently to get their laptops fixed so that they can get back to work. Now he understands why his boss brought him to Singapore. Richard has a very different perspective on IT. He envisions IT as a business enabler, and not just a back-office support function. At the moment, IT is more like an IT fortress with its closed service culture; blocking the business from being agile. He wants to transform IT from an inward-focused functional silo into a customer-centric center of excellence. Richard has grand plans to implement world-class processes and infrastructure to keep up with the organization's mercurial business growth. He feels like a superhero swooping in to save the day. The work is cut out for him. It's a clear-cut case. *This will be easier than I expected.*

2. Open Mind: What uncomfortable truth are you denying?

The first item on the agenda: change the mindset of the team. For Richard to have a shot at achieving his goal within 12 months, he needs everyone on board within two months. Richard organizes a *kumbaya* teambuilding workshop. Richard wants to motivate the team. He tells them how they can have more open interactions with their internal customers, more opportunities for learning and growth, and always... service with a smile. Richard expected people to jump on their feet, wave their hands in the air, and be energized: *Everything is awesome!*

Instead, it goes down like a cold cup of sick. One of Richard's senior direct reports was resolutely combative against the new philosophy. Richard will find out later that he was the one who built the IT fortress to keep customers *out*, not welcome them in.

Back in the office, things grow worse between Richard and the senior direct report. Every initiative Richard tries to implement, the senior direct report blocks. The senior direct report manages a team, and he puts up a firewall between Richard and his team so that the changes don't get implemented. Richard has many awkward little "differences of opinion" conversations with him. During a rather testy exchange, without warning, the senior direct report swivels his chair, turning his back to Richard, and starts typing on his computer. The silence is deafening. *This conversation is over.*

3. Open Heart: What difficult emotions are you ignoring?

Richard experiences an existential crisis. He feels like a forlorn and ignorant stranger in a strange land. Richard misses his family and friends back in New Zealand. He also feels like a rather green rookie. Half of the team are older than him. Some of them, like this senior direct report who has made Richard his arch-nemesis, can almost be his father. He likes to remind Richard that he was working for the company when Richard was still in diapers. Richard feels unwelcome and ostracized by the very team that he should be leading.

Richard is unsure about himself. *Am I fit to lead?*

Richard checks in with his boss, "Am I on the right path?" Richard's boss assures him that he is on the right track. But Richard's boss never steps in. Never makes his stand publicly. Richard is left to fend for himself.

Shortly after, the senior direct report resigns. Without a qualified person to take his place, Richard has to take over his role and manage his team. Soon, half of them leave as well, taking with them their knowledge and relationships with suppliers and customers. Richard is left stranded to meet demanding customer needs, but with half the capacity to deliver. Richard thinks this will make him look like a still pale and shaky leader in front of his boss and HR. *You have failed.* Richard feels like he's just been exposed as a fraud.

4. Open Will: What hard decision are you avoiding?

Richard feels the bitter bile of regret rising in his throat about leaving New Zealand, about leaving his family and friends, giving up a life he loved. Right at the edge of despair, a memory bubble arises.

Richard remembers a business trip he took to Bangkok three years ago, his first time in Asia. He can still remember walking down the streets of Sukhumvit, all bright-eyed and bushy-tailed, not believing his eyes how different things were from home: cooking and eating on the streets, the noise, everyone speaking a language he didn't understand at all, the manic pace of everything. *We're not in Auckland anymore.* At that moment, Richard knew he had to be a part of this. Asia beckoned.

Richard quickly put together a hiring plan. He starts rebuilding his team. Richard is careful about hiring people who share his vision of an open client-centric service culture. Richard is intentional about building a diverse team to engage better with the customers and encourage different ways of thinking. Good ideas can come from anywhere. People are so accustomed to hearing only the dominant voices, cancelling out the rest. Richard wants to bring out the more silent voices to balance the conversation. They are precious and need to be protected.

Richard's team tears down the wall, literally. No more IT fortress. They launch new services, like a centralized phone helpdesk supporting Asia. They start providing critical onsite service support, meeting customers where they are. No more long queues. Service levels soar, customers are happy.

Richard's boss brought him in at the exact opportune time. The organization's headcount was expanding rapidly, and the incumbent closed service culture would have created a lot of frustrations for many people and slowed the business down. With the new services Richard's team implemented, they could provide responsive IT services to support the growth.

Richard will always suspect that his boss had intended all along to wield him like a sledgehammer to break down the walls. Introduce him as a trouble-maker in a hierarchical pyramid based on traditional management thinking, where ideas only flow one way, top down.

5. New Mindset: Pack your bags. There's a bigger game to play here.

When you change the leadership of a team, the whole team also goes through a change. The team needs to be reboarded before they can move as a united entity towards a common goal. Just as you can't expect a new team to perform well when it first comes together, there is an adjustment period when the team re-establishes boundaries with the new leader.

Initially, people were positive and polite when Richard first arrived. But as Richard implements the change in direction, the team moves into the storming phase, where people push against the boundaries, and there is conflict among people's working styles. Gradually, the team moves into the norming stage where people start to resolve their differences, appreciate each other's strengths, and respect Richard's authority as a leader.

Many teams fail in the storming phase. There is nothing good or bad. It's part of the learning process that teams go through. As a new manager, you can help your team to become effective more quickly when you accept this as part of the process of building a high-performance team.

6. Practical tips

Authority. As the leader, you'll need to provide some structure and guidance, which can involve making tough decisions. Take back control by taking action.

Accept. Appreciate that not everyone will welcome your leadership. No amount of cajoling will change their minds. Getting angry only makes matters worse. Take a deep breath and let it go.

Reboarding. Whenever there is a change in the leadership, the whole team falls back to storming, even if they were high-performing before. Thus, every time you change the leader, not only the leader goes through onboarding, but the whole team also needs to go through reboarding. There will be tension between the old and new. *There's deep blue, and there's new blue.* Hold the space for the reintegration to happen. *Whether we're deep blue or new blue, we're all blue.*

Learn, unlearn, relearn. In a rapidly changing world, the ability to unlearn and relearn might matter more than ever. We need to *actively* stop thinking one way — the dominant thought — before another train of thought can arrive. It's not about adding to your suitcase of skills; it's about letting go.

Social energy. Create space to connect as a team. There's no agenda, except to have fun.

Be personal. Take an active interest in people. Be curious about the human being behind the job title. Learn about their motivations, likes and dislikes, talents.

7. Related chapters

Chapter 6   Starting a New Role

Chapter 26   Learning at the Speed of Business

13

Leading People
Through Change

*"Never doubt that a small group of thoughtful,
committed citizens can change the world; indeed,
it's the only thing that ever has."*

— Margaret Mead

S am leads the e-commerce business for a global computer
manufacturer. His management team has seen the explosive growth
of e-commerce sales and tasked Sam to set up this new channel
business and bring the organization into the future.

It's a significant investment: the plan is to hire 60 people within a six-month
timezone. For the first time, Sam feels insecure: *what if I fail?* Sam reacts
to that nervousness and insecurity by trying to do everything. It leads to
some pretty ordinary habits: controlling the flow of information, playing
politics with people, talking behind people's backs. There is one new person
in particular whom Sam simply can't get along with. He comes with strong

technical knowledge on building e-commerce infrastructure, and Sam is intimidated. Sam has many testy conversations with him. The office starts reeking of bad juju. Sam catches the wafts of Chinese whispers: "He is uncaring," "He is power-hungry," "He is arrogant," "He is a babe in the woods — ignorant."

1. Old Mindset: Chipping away at the tip of the iceberg

When faced with new challenges, most leaders' typical reaction is to work harder. They'll knuckle down, get in the weeds and try to micro-manage everything. And everyone. They don't have the time or resources to try to deal with what each individual employee may be concerned about or need. They assume people will adjust. *Just get on with it.*

Sam is having a beef with this new person. First, he tries to cajole him, encourage him, do whatever it takes to win him over. When that doesn't work, the inner tyrant emerges. Sam is direct and honest with him: *You are not on the bus, and you are holding us back.* Sam feels that he has to explain the consequences if he does not change. It leaves Sam with no choice but to replace him. *It's my way or the highway.*

Sam is only playing the small game in the drama triangle. Sam can continue to rely on being the loudest person in the room — or the person with the biggest stick — to get what he wants. But that will only be a bloody and gory race to the bottom to win the prize of being the biggest victim. Employees work in fear. They pour their most imaginative creativity and gritty perseverance into avoiding risk or responsibility altogether. Lest they are blamed for failing to prevent a mistake. That's how the wheels start coming off the bus. Everyone is burnt out, and no one wins.

At the end of the day, Sam is exhausted, prickly, over-sensitive and prone to violent outbursts of anger. Erratic and volatile. Generally, not a nice person to hang out with. *Nice Guy, But...*

2. Open Mind: What uncomfortable truth are you denying?

Nobody likes uncertainty, and corporations rarely tolerate it at all. Just like how the Great Wall of China was built organically across different times, modern corporations are built in response to business challenges, which are plastered on layer upon layer over time. Inconsistencies are swept under the carpet, adding complications to how work is done. Things work smoothly, up to the point when there is a change, and a lot of things go wrong. Theoretical models and strategic plans all serve to add a sheen of certainty to what is, in its glorious truth, a monolithic organization that is increasingly unwieldy and ungovernable. In this situation, if you try to mitigate everything that might go wrong, you end up in paralysis analysis.

Sam is building the e-commerce business within this monolithic organization and he needs to do it within six months. The scale of what needs to be achieved within such a short time is outrageously ambitious. They have to build the e-commerce infrastructure. They have to figure out what products to merchandise. They have to find and sell to customers. They have to figure out how they will be paid.

Sam slowly wakes up to the fact that the new e-commerce business will never happen with the neat top-down hierarchical organization structure.

Especially not in six months. In this "cross-matrix" organization with its confusing maze of solid-line/dotted-line reporting and conflicting priorities, if Sam thinks he can get things done "by mandate", then he is truly delusional. Traditional management thinking, where the leader sets the goals, creates the standards and tells people exactly what to do, will only end in cataclysmic disaster.

Sam realizes that this situation requires a radically different approach. Sam envisions a culture of innovation where *everyone* in the team is accountable for driving change. Everyone is responsible for creating and delivering innovative solutions that are centered around customer needs. Sam believes that the truly disruptive thinking will come from the ground — the collective subject matter expertise gained from interacting directly with real customers, and not just from someone from the top telling them what to do.

3. Open Heart: What difficult emotions are you ignoring?

Many leaders struggle with relinquishing control. Why? Maybe because they want to play the hero — they can't bear to see others feel bad, and they swoop in to save the day. Or they can't bear to lower their impeccably high standards. *This work is unacceptable. Move aside, I'll fix it. I can do it twice as good as you and in half the time.* And they pop other people's work into their backpacks. These leaders think they are the best person in the room to fix the problem. And they're not wrong. But this creates learned helplessness in their team. Their employees become dependent on them. People are afraid to act without their permission. People come to believe that they are unable to control or change the situation without the boss's intervention, so they do not even try — even when opportunities for change become available.

As these leaders fuss obsessively over communicating the details of WHAT needs to be done by WHEN, they fail to contextualize the WHY for the change. To their employees, it will seem like yet another hyped-up, random, top-down management initiative. Sam has to explain how this e-commerce platform fits into the broader vision of the company. It helps people understand where the change is coming from and why it's important. Sam repeats himself, again and again, to get everyone behind the strategy. *Very lolly loh soh*. But absolutely necessary. Sending them to a mind-reading course would be the alternative. Sam thinks that people don't listen. People will tell him that this is the first time they are hearing about it. *Oh… I've explained it many times to myself… but not to them*. It packs an emotional wallop.

Sam wants to play the bigger game. He grants people plenty of freedom within their areas of responsibility to develop innovative and unique solutions. He expects everyone to be a subject matter expert and bring a point of view relevant to the e-commerce charter. He doesn't put boundaries on where they think they can go. He makes sure they have what they need, like staffing up their teams. Sam acknowledges their creativity by conveying excitement and enthusiasm for their ideas.

Sam consciously reminds himself to glide *on* top of the business, instead of drowning *in* the details of the business. Everything is moving so fast, and if Sam instinctively tries to manage every minute detail, he'll feel even more out of control. He loosens his obsessive-compulsive grip and let things run their course.

Very quickly, Sam sees the results of the change. People enjoy the autonomy. People take responsibility for their ideas and turn them into reality. There is nothing dictatorial about it.

Not everyone will adapt to this new way of working. Leaders are so accustomed to dictating orders top-down, and people have gotten so used to being told what to do. They have built their success on guessing what their bosses want and meeting their expectations. *Now the boss wants me to come up with my own solution?* Some people do not know how to deal with that uncertainty. They no longer know what it takes to succeed — this scares them. They will eventually leave the team on their own accord.

4. Open Will: What hard decision are you avoiding?

Every day there is a crisis that needs solving. You do not need to go looking for challenges; the challenges find you. There is a palpable feeling of fear of making mistakes. Sam feels that everyone is working against this invisible force that pressures them to be less innovative than they need to be.

Sam encourages the team to welcome these challenges. When update meetings feel too contrived, Sam will ask, "Where are the problems?" Everyone prefers to avoid these "awkward" conversations. It's pure self-defence. Nobody wants to be the harbinger of doom. The villain is denial. The problem with denial is that the challenges can't be dealt with until it is acknowledged. You can't solve a problem you're not willing to have. Ignoring them won't make them go away.

If things are not failing, then we're not innovating enough. Sam works hard to help people be more open about failed initiatives. The value is not in the failure itself, but the courage it takes and the valuable lessons that come out of it.

This open decentralized way of working allows for the dynamism and flexibility that is required to support the business' mercurial growth. People communicate, organize themselves and coordinate activities in totally unique and powerful ways. Sam is democratizing innovation. He holds the space for people to innovate rapidly, deliver results faster, engage people better and stay closer to the mission.

5. New Mindset: Diving to the bottom of the iceberg

What Sam has here is a highly empowered team. It's every leader's dream: to have an elite squad that can take an idea — any idea — and make it great. You can throw any challenge at them, and they will self-manage. You do not need to intervene or micro-manage. You don't get dragged into doing your employees' jobs. This liberates you to focus on actually doing the job that's stated on your business card. When this acentric way of working becomes a "thing" in your organization, people will say that your organization has a great culture. This is an agile organization that can spin on a dime.

When it comes to leading change, you can do almost anything with just five people. When it is just you, and you have to do everything, it is hard, almost impossible. But when you join up with four other highly committed people who are completely aligned to the mission at hand — they have their hearts in it — you suddenly have a force to contend with. As they align around the mission and it goes out into the world, it creates a force field of positivity and excitement around them that attracts other people and opportunities, and makes doors open up that were closed before. That's the essence of creativity and innovation.

It is incredible what a small group of people can do when their hearts are in it. They may even change the world.

6. Practical tips

Blind spots. Don't sit in your ivory tower. Actively seek out the disconnects and blind spots. Open your ears for the voices that are not being heard. Conduct skip level meetings.

Communicate. When things go wrong, managers blame it on employee resistance. They say that their employees are resistant to change. But sometimes, people resist change because they simply did not receive the memo. People don't know that they have to change. Your employees can't read your mind. Communicate regularly, even at the risk of sounding like a broken record.

Clarity. Problems occur when people are not clear about what you expect from them. Keep it simple. Explain the purpose and what success looks like.

Contextualize. People look to you to provide the direction. Don't assume that the same message will be effective for all 1,000 employees. Help people understand what is happening and how it impacts them. This provides meaning to the ambiguity and uncertainty.

Trust. Most people want to do a great job. Nobody shows up to work to suck at it. The more open you are to trust others, the more likely this trust will be returned, respected and rewarded. Trust, inspire, encourage and motivate your people.

Avoid gravity problems. Make sure that your team is taking on tasks that are actionable. If you try to solve gravity problems, you'll only end up stuck, because gravity problems are not actionable.

Space. You paid top dollars for the smartest talents. Now give them the space to think and make their own decisions. The last thing top talents want is for someone else to tell them how to do their jobs.

7. Related chapters

Chapter 5   Find Your Calling

Chapter 18   Becoming an Intrapreneur

Chapter 21   Managing Complexity in Your Organization

14

Dealing with
a Difficult Employee

"From caring comes courage."

— Lao Tzu

Jacqueline is a client lead for a large advertising company. She recently won a new business, and it's a lucrative one, accounting for 20% of the company's sales quota for the year. In other words, they are a very important client, and Jacqueline can't afford to lose the account. But already the client has a beef with Jacqueline's project team. Missing deadlines. Shoddy work. The only thing that's consistent about the project team is delivering too little, too late. What alarms Jacqueline most is their feedback about the project manager. The project manager has been firing off rude emails to the client at 2 a.m. The client has tried to give him feedback directly, but he dismisses it. The project manager has a habit of talking down at the client and not taking their inputs seriously. Turns it into a joke, dripping with sarcasm, and then laughs it off as if the conversation never happened. Blissfully unaware that his behavior irritated people.

Internally, Jacqueline can understand why the project manager is acting up. The clients are no angels themselves. It's a challenging account with super-demanding expectations and impossible deadlines. The project team is overwhelmed, understaffed, and there is tremendous pressure to deliver.

Still, the project manager's behavior is unacceptable. This is not the first time Jacqueline has had this issue with him. She has spoken to him many times about taking his work more seriously. He can't just sweep his problems under the carpet and hope no one will notice. He's no longer a junior staff. He's now leading the team. In the past, he might have been able to get away with it. But he can't now.

Jacqueline is quite direct and honest with her feedback to the project manager so that he understands the situation. She makes clear to him that his behavior needs to change. He needs to step up his game. He needs to be more responsible. Jacqueline clearly lays out what's expected of him and the kind of behavior she wishes to see. She sets the metrics. Jacqueline wants to support him, so she schedules to catch up with him every week, squeezing water out of a stone of a calendar.

It's not Jacqueline's intention to give the project manager a hard time, but he isn't driving the project like he needs to. She also feels that she must explain the consequences if he doesn't change. If the client still has problems with him, it leaves Jacqueline no choice but to replace him. She really wants to support him. However, if the client loses trust in him, that means the client loses trust in the whole company. So, this is his last chance. If he doesn't change, the next step is putting him on the "pip" — Performance Improvement Plan — which inevitably means being given the boot.

One day, Jacqueline is in a taxi rushing to the client's office when she receives a call from the office.

Office: Come back now.
Jacqueline: Why? What happened?
Office: Just come back now.

Jacqueline trudges back to the office, grumpy for the interruption. When she arrives, she finds out that the project manager has taken his own life. Everyone in the office is in shock. He was the joker in the office, always making people laugh. No one saw it coming.

It is a numbing experience. The next few days, Jacqueline packs up the project manager's belongings in the office. It's painful packing up a dead man's things. Jacqueline finds out from his line manager that he was depressed, going through a hard time personally. But the line manager didn't feel it was right to share it with anyone else. Jacqueline was giving him grief without realizing the impact. Suddenly the deadlines and tasks are not so urgent anymore. Had she known he was going through a difficult patch, she would have supported him differently.

1. Old Mindset: Command and control

If you google "How to manage difficult employees," you will get the standard manager response, not unlike the above. *Critique behavior, not people. Document problematic behavior. Set specific consequences. Recognize a hopeless situation.* This is straight out of the manager handbook. This is how managers are supposed to behave. That's how our managers dealt with us in the halcyon days of our youth — classic management 101.

Traditional management literature carries a hidden assumption: that people are not fit to do their job and need to be "empowered" to get the job done. The experts tell us to "delegate authority." Managers tell employees exactly what they need to do. They put in place OKRs (objectives and key results), in addition to the existing 400 KPI's (key performance indicators). They schedule weekly "special project" meetings, on top of the regular departmental, cross-departmental, local, regional, global meetings. To motivate their employees, they dangle the carrot and stick. They give inspirational pep talks, "You can do it!"

That is not empowerment. That is command-and-control, dressed up as empowerment. What these managers are really saying is, "You are free to do what you think is best, as long as you do it my way." And the managers expect their employees to comply without asking "difficult" questions.

When we've worked in a corporate environment for so long, we become trained experts at command-and-control. This command-and-control habit is such an inherent part of us that we don't even realize that we're doing it.

Economists say that we are evolving from the knowledge economy to the human economy, moving towards a more inclusive and human-centered future. Businesses say that they invest in the most important part of the future of work — human beings. Leaders say that people are our greatest assets.

All this sounds good. It makes the leader look good. But here's the rub. We command and control people. This is how we learned how to manage people. With our carrot and stick (mostly stick). We dismiss leaders who show vulnerability as not tough enough to lead others. We think that leaders can't make hard decisions if they are feeling for all the people who will be affected. We mistake candor about feelings for wimpiness, and fail to recognize the humility it actually takes to recognize our own ignorance and the courage needed to acknowledge our own shortcomings.

2. Open Mind: What uncomfortable truth are you denying?

From my experience, I have found organizations to be large idea factories, where people, "our greatest assets," are fed into one end, and finished ideas come out the other. Idea factories that squeeze the creative juices out of people, machined by strict unrealistic parameters and wrapped into fancy presentation decks with a pink ribbon. Just to drive profitability.

Corporations have created this whole "cross-matrix organization" thing, setting up convoluted dotted-line/solid-line reporting structures where people are busy swimming in unaccountability. Congrats, we have succeeded in finding the most complicated way of doing simple things. And in the smoke and mirrors, who even notices the frantic minions working till 3 a.m. to deliver work that doesn't really matter?

There is something morally sick about the modern corporation. "Corporate" is almost like a bad word. We might conclude: *It's not personal. It's just business.* But it's simply not true. We make it personal.

We see this at work every day. When something goes wrong — a customer complains about bad service — the manager responds by firing off an angry group email that pins the blame on one or more employees: "This is unacceptable!"

Feeling attacked, the employee lashes back in response, "This is your fault!!!", adding more heavyweights onto the cc list. They proceed to play the blame game. *Tag, you're it.* Everyone is dragged into the drama of finger-pointing and backbiting, leading managers to think their employees are difficult, and employees to think their managers are difficult. The result is a dysfunctional workplace in which both management and employees believe they are dealing with difficult people.

This dysfunctional behavior is nothing new. Psychologist Lee Ross calls it the "fundamental attribution error." When someone else makes a mistake, we tend to attribute the mistake to internal characteristics. *He is so lazy. He is so stubborn. He has a known morale problem.* We launch a "fact-finding" investigation, more like a witch-hunt, until we get to the "root" of the problem: the employee. *I'll remove every excuse you can come up with until there is only one left... you.*

Reminds me of Dr Evil's conference room and the small red buttons that mechanically launch his out-of-favor employees from their high-backed conference chairs into roaring pits of fire. *Fundamental attribution error.* We make it personal.

At the same time, when we make a mistake, we are more likely to attribute our own behavior to external rather than internal factors. *The market shifted. The client keeps changing their mind.* We let ourselves off the hook.

We blame others in part because we lack full knowledge of the person's experiences and decision-making processes. All we can see are their undesirable behaviors, which is just the tip of the iceberg, and we label them as "difficult." We fail to give them the same benefit of the doubt that we give ourselves when things go wrong.

3. Open Heart: What difficult emotions are you avoiding?

It seems there is not a word in management literature that is as divisive and controversial as the word "empowerment." It confuses people. And no wonder. Because it is a very fine line between sharing the stress and stressing others to make ourselves feel better.

Empowerment begins with appreciating that people are a powerful force for positive change. When people encounter hardships, it's easy for them to forget this. And all they need is someone to remind them of their power. When you give someone love and support in the way they can best receive it, they will find that power within themselves.

As humans, we are born with an empathy gene. We have this innate capacity to feel what another person is feeling, not merely through observing or judging, but by *experiencing* similar feelings within us. You don't just *see* a person struggling; you *feel* like you are struggling. Now, how we respond to that experience is another matter altogether.

When we see someone in difficulty, our inner hero wants to get the person out of trouble. But it's more accurate to say that we are trying to get *us* out of trouble and make *us* feel better. In other words, we're not rescuing them, we're rescuing us. In the bid for self-preservation, we may take matters into our own hands and make hasty decisions about things we have little understanding about, resulting in a messier situation and more distress for everyone involved. We end up stressing others to make ourselves feel better.

On top of that, we are weighed down each time we stuff other people's problems into our backpacks. We ignore our basic needs, such as sleep, food, exercise and socializing with family and friends. Slowly we become numb inside, moving into a space of helplessness and emotional shutdown. *I feel flat and grey inside.* We become overwhelmed and we burn out. *I just don't care anymore.* Or we become more impulsive, impatient and blind to other people's points of view. Secretly, we start to resent our employees. *What is this?!! A kindergarten?!!*

This is the bane of every leader. What is your tolerance for casualty? For making tough calls? For cutting losses? Can you stare adversity in the face without flinching? Because zero tolerance is simply not an option. That means not being completely exhausted and repulsed by people's vicious egos as they come under incredible pressure. Instead, you are willing to stifle your gag reflex and clean up after them.

Are you sensitive enough to pick up the quiet but potentially fatal distress signals? To simply bear witness to their Joker-like neurosis, allowing it to bother you and overcrowd you without recoiling in disgust. To just be there and listen. To be patient, and not feel rushed, inconvenienced or angry.

Now, that's sharing the stress.

4. Open Will: What hard decision are you avoiding?

Bearing witness like this without the usual blame or resentment provides people with the experience of being seen and understood, like the Na'vi greeting in Avatar: *Oel ngati kameie. I see you.* The effect on the other person can be truly transforming. The other person feels seen. *Phew, I am not alone.* Their usual sense of confidence and composure return.

When people meet Jacqueline today, she radiates an other-worldly sense of calm and positivity even in the deepest crisis. Just being in her presence makes people feel comfortable. She's highly sensitive to her employees' emotional state. When Jacqueline sees someone facing difficulties at work, she reaches out a gentle hand. *You're not alone.* The person opens up about their problems. She then shines the light of her experience on the situation they are facing. Instead of telling them what to do, she asks questions to get them thinking. She sees the cool wave of insight wash over them. They start building their own ideas on how to fix their problems. They come up with their own solution. They own the solution. They're motivated to fix the problem and they hold themselves accountable.

The willingness to patiently witness someone's drama queen antics and imperious power trips without resentment, blame, or other fear-based reactive behaviors may be the necessary means to discover how best you can help the person. When you hold the space for them to process their thoughts and emotions, something magical happens; they transform. It's not that you're directly changing the person. Instead, you are inviting the person to rise to the occasion of changing. Transformation is self-liberating. You are helping them to help themselves. And that is absolutely empowering for the other person.

5. New Mindset: Empowerment

As a manager, you have the authority to make decisions and direct the behaviors of your employees. The authority granted to you is a kind of legitimate power. Your employees are expected to follow your orders because their positions demand it irrespective of how they may feel about you or your orders. Your words carry the power of decree. This positional power flows one way — downhill. Even Number Two does not get his own panel of red buttons. Only Dr Evil does. This is external authority; not everyone has this authority. And that gives you an advantage over others.

There is nothing enlightened about being ashamed of this. It does not cost you anything to acknowledge the power you hold over others, and doing so does not discredit the hard work you have put in to get to where you are today.

Most people struggle to acknowledge this privilege. Why? Because with this privilege comes great responsibility. I'm not talking about an obligation that weighs down on your shoulders, but something that brings great meaning to your work.

As leaders, we want to help our employees reach their full potential, but we don't know what they are capable of. So how do we help them? By giving them the space to make their own decisions. By allowing them to learn from making mistakes, quietly witnessing them come under tremendous temperature and pressure without flinching ourselves. Everyone handles stress differently. Some erupt in a volcano of expletives, resentment and blame. Some retreat inwards and go quiet. As the pressure mounts, the loud gets louder, the quiet goes quieter. And you witness it all with the benevolence of a Zen master.

But there's also a limit to how much stress people can take. If there's too much, you end up with ash. It's a delicate balance. It requires great care and skill to keep the balance. You're, literally, dancing on the edge of greatness. You have to be alert. You can't be numb. Empathy is your sensing tool.

There is a certain weight that comes with such responsibility. But it's also an incredible opportunity. It's a privilege to lead. This is not something you have to do. It is not a rule you must abide by in the fear of being punished or stripped of your power. This is an invitation, and all you can do is allow yourself to rise to it. Learn to wield your superpowers skillfully. Recognize the leader that already exists within.

If you have the space to listen to someone, listen.
If you have the wisdom and knowledge to share, share.
You have the power to make someone's life better.
Leadership is a privilege.

6. Practical tips

Emotions. Strong emotions flare up in difficult situations. You can't control the person's emotions. Trying to control their emotions makes them feel judged. Instead, keep enough distance to avoid triggering your own emotions. This keeps you from making matters worse.

Don't argue. When someone is acting out and out-of-character, don't argue. Don't try to reason with them. Don't contradict them. Don't defend yourself against accusations. And never, never make fun of anything. It won't do any good and only makes things worse. Wait for the right time, when things have cooled down, to bring up your point of view.

Don't blame. Instead of blaming people, try to understand the situation that's creating the conflict. Turn on the lights. You can't solve what you don't understand.

Validate their concerns. Try to understand their point of view. Promise to think about what they expressed and see what you can do. Schedule to meet and discuss the issue at a specific time in the future.

Emails. Avoid firing off emails when you are angry, even if you believe it's justified. I have never heard of emails resolving conflicts; only of making it worse. Try speaking with the person face to face.

Don't give advice. Avoid giving advice, even if they ask for it. Instead, try asking powerful questions to get them thinking. When they come up with their own solutions, they are more likely to act on them.

Clear the space. Don't go into the conversation tense and uptight. Schedule time to reconnect with yourself before having a difficult conversation. With an open mindset, it is more likely that the conversation will be empowering.

Acknowledge. Pay more flattering attention to people. We are such grouchy misers when it comes to giving praises. Acknowledge people when they do something right. It makes people feel seen and heard.

Rethink. When your employee asks for something which sounds unreasonable, the typical reaction is to reject it. Instead, stop and think. Hold your initial objection. Give yourself time to process it. *What needs to be true for this to happen?* You might surprise yourself.

Non-performers. No one shows up to work to suck at their jobs. The person may be a great talent, but it's the wrong job fit. Letting them go gives them a chance to find a job where they can thrive, rather than waste their time doing something that doesn't align with them. Don't delay the agony.

7. Related chapters

Chapter 7   Dealing with a Difficult Boss

Chapter 25   Transforming Your Culture

15

Avoiding NATO Summits and TWOT Meetings

"In many ways, the work of a critic is easy. We risk very little, yet enjoy a position over those who offer up their work and their selves to our judgment. We thrive on negative criticism, which is fun to write and to read. But the bitter truth we critics must face is that in the grand scheme of things, the average piece of junk is probably more meaningful than our criticism designating it so."

— Anton Ego, from *Ratatouille*

Cindy's workday is filled with back-to-back meetings with employees and business partners. After a while, the string of meetings becomes one big blur. *Same, same, but different.* People sharing their pressing problems, venting their frustrations and blaming the world for their misfortunes. They shower Cindy with a million reasons why something can't or shouldn't be done until she is practically choking from their suffocating insecurities.

During group meetings, Cindy silently laments the lack of substance behind the intense theatrical presentations given by people. At leadership meetings, she secretly rolls her eyes when the CEO goes on a long diatribe about how great the business is doing, filled with details and pontifications. She's amazed at how well her peers mimic the CEO's opinions, offering their own long, rambling and shallow version to everyone who is forced to listen.

1. Old Mindset: Chipping away at the tip of the iceberg

Virtual meetings pound Cindy wave upon wave, non-stop from early morning to late at night. Everyone wants a piece of her — employees, clients, leadership team, board members and business partners. She can't find enough time in a day, but yet she must accommodate everybody, so she squeezes water out of a stone of a calendar.

Cindy's appointments are scheduled back-to-back. She leaves no gap in between the meetings to prepare or decompress. Meetings will inevitably drag, which stresses her because she abhors being late. And she arrives late for the next meeting anyway, harried and disheveled from the stress.

With her calendar completely booked with meetings, it leaves zero time for Cindy to do her *actual* work. To alleviate this problem, Cindy tries to catch up with her work on those slower Zoom calls. She's grateful that her computer screen does not have a camera function, so no one notices that her attention is somewhere else.

We have all attended meetings where the only output is fluff. We have also committed these unnameable and unforgivable crimes ourselves. These are the habitual conversations that comprise most of our days: the venting, the griping, the snarky remarks, the TWOT meetings (total waste of time) and the NATO summits (no action, talk only).

2. Open Mind: What uncomfortable truth are you denying?

In an ideal world, Cindy's calendar will be neatly laid out in a bunch of different colored blocks, reflecting different areas of her work. There will be a buffer of 30 minutes before each meeting. There will be open spaces in her calendar when she can meditate, read or reflect, and she'll show up at the next meeting as the poster child of enlightened leadership. She'll be a paragon of virtue, exercising godly patience and divine wisdom. Her mere presence will elevate the habitual conversations into something profound and sublime.

But that's not reality. In modern corporate life, with its impossible targets and ridiculous timelines, Cindy is constantly rushing from one meeting to another, solving one crisis after another. It never stops. It never slows down. In fact, it's only gotten faster. Cindy thinks that she must go fast to get things done fast. *Grit your teeth. Just get it over and done with. Chop chop lollipop.* These meetings are something to rush through or tolerate until she reaches the end of the day. Just another tick in a long list of meaningless meetings. Her body might be in this meeting, but her mind is already racing to the next one. Likewise her speech. She brings the same rat-tat-tat machine gun energy into every meeting — whether it's about fixing a technical bug or brainstorming on a marketing campaign. And she's not the only one. Everyone takes turn to talk fast. People are talking a lot, but not saying much. The conversations stay superficial. One leg in the past, one leg in the present, pissing down on the present. Every meeting becomes a crushing waste of time.

It may seem like a contradiction, but in order to get things done fast, you need to go slow. Management literature tells us that active listening is one of the most important leadership skills. Active listening supports better decision making, smarter problem solving, and more innovative solution creation. But we always fail to take note that *active* listening is a very *active* task. Active listening requires us to slow way down. The problem is: we don't like slowing down. Slowing down feels like death. *Just get it over and down with. Chop chop lollipop.* We are more comfortable rattling random facts and figures at a hundred miles an hour towards a destination we have not yet determined, rather than tolerating the deathly silence.

3. Open Heart: What difficult emotions are you avoiding?

Cindy prides herself as a problem solver. She fixes people's problems. She asks questions to try to solve the problem for the other person, then tells people exactly what to do.

In the short run, it may seem more time-efficient for Cindy to solve the problem for them. But in the long run, Cindy is only encouraging learned helplessness. People come to believe that they are unable to control or change the situation, so they do not try — even when opportunities for change become available. This is how leaders gridlock themselves in a Gordian knot where people are still frustrated and venting, no one grows, some regress, and we're overwhelmed.

We are very familiar with this mode of existence.

We are strangers to empowering conversations. That's when everyone brings their full attention to the meeting. You take in the whole person in front of you: verbal, physical, mental and emotional. You hold the space for people to process their thoughts and emotions. You ask thoughtful questions; you help them articulate their deeper thinking. You do this patiently, again and again, without bringing out your inner critic to judge and criticize people's ideas.

We find these empowering conversations very alarming, just because it's so unfamiliar. *Are you on drugs or smoking something special?* Instead, we are highly trained assassins with our AK-47s, sniping down people's ideas. We are more familiar with providing rat-tat-tat "constructive feedback", where we poke holes at people's ideas, thinking we are doing them a huge favor.

Empowering conversations provide people with the experience of being heard and understood. They feel acknowledged and valued. The effect on them can be truly transforming. They come out of the grip. You see their usual sense of confidence and composure return. It gives them space to bring their ideas to somewhere new. You're not trying to change the person. Instead, you are inviting the person to rise to the occasion of changing. And that is absolutely empowering for the other person.

4. Open Will: What hard decision are you avoiding?

Typically, at a brainstorming session, there will be a lot of talk, a lot of slides and spreadsheets, and a voluminous and incandescent cloud of Post-its stuck to the board. Lots of ideas. Lots of options. Lots of suggestions.

But no decision.

This is a reflection of our too-noisy mind, pontificating at us at 300–500 words per minute, spewing facts and figures, spinning up as many ideas as possible. We can be suffering a pandemic attack of too many ideas. Having many ideas is good, but if it triggers analysis paralysis, then, in reality, you have no idea at all. Ideas only become valuable when they are committed to and executed on.

Creative breakthroughs arrive at their own time. It requires us to shut down the inner speedy commentary. You need to give it space. It can't be rushed. Our wisdom is made available to us emotionally and intestinally. They do not communicate in words. Only when we quieten down the noise can we hear the quiet intuition that helps us make better decisions.

5. New Mindset: Diving to the bottom of the iceberg

This kind of leadership presence forces a kind of full-bodied awareness. You're held in rapture by the everchanging spectacle of every passing meeting. In this sublime state, you see everything with crystalline clarity. You are sensitive to every thought and gesture. You can then respond appropriately and proportionately to the situation unfolding in front of you. It can *feel* like you're on the edge. You're in control, but you're that close to losing it. But that's exactly where you feel it. Only then, you're asserting your *human*-ness.

Every moment presents a breakthrough if you're paying attention.

When you bring your full leadership presence, the conversation transforms. The conversation deepens. It becomes more creative and generative. People sense an opportunity to bring about profound change. They will leave the conversation feeling more confident, empowered and energized for action.

We're more familiar with working like a machine: all IQ and no EQ. This way of communicating takes time. But with practice, it also gives time back. It gives you back your life — every moment of it.

6. Practical tips

Listen. Pay attention to people as if they are the most important thing in your life at that moment. To listen actively, you must *stop* talking. Control that compulsive demonic chatter in your head. Active listening is a very *active* task.

Ask questions: Remind yourself that your role here is to help people think better, not to tell them what to do. This prevents learned helplessness.

Stretch. Avoid finger-pointing. Instead, ask more vision-type questions and stretch the person to come up with their own solutions to the problem. Happy people do great work, so support them to be in a confident and motivated state.

Defer judgment. Bring down the Great Wall of innovation. Hold the space to allow for crazy ideas because beyond the Great Wall is a plethora of strange and mad ideas, promising tantalizing and ingenious possibilities, one of which could be the BIG IDEA that would be really exciting for your organization.

Freestyling. Build off each other's ideas. The best ideas emerge from the collective creativity of the group.

16

Letting People Go

T his is Anne's first day of work as the Asia Pacific Managing Director of a global advertising agency. She's having mixed feelings. On the one hand, she's excited because she'll be responsible for steering the company forward in a dynamic industry that is changing fast. On the other hand, the company has not been doing well financially the last few years. Anne is not sure what she's getting herself into. She was told during the interview that she will be starting on a clean slate. The previous Managing Director, whom she is now replacing, had already gone through one round of retrenchment.

As the first order of business, Anne dives straight into the belly of the corporate beast. She pores through the agency's client roster, organization structure and financial statements. She scrutinizes every account and every role. And she comes to a sobering realization. Even with the organization still hobbling from its freshly hacked off limb, it will run out of cash in six months.

The previous Managing Director had already done an incredible job cutting costs, reaching into every nook and cranny within the organization.

But the cut was not deep enough. They still can't afford this office. Anne needs to go through another round of layoffs.

The decision to go through another round of layoffs makes Anne extremely unpopular. Chinese whispers in the corridor:
We have to let go of more people just to pay her salary.
The previous CEO was already a b*tch, now here comes a bigger b*tch.

Anne's Chief Creative Officer resigns within days.

Anne's early days are met with a mixed bag of being hated and being questioned about her fundamental existence. Anne can understand the hostility towards her. They are old-time buddies. Some of them have been in the company for many years. They had gone through the trenches together during the hedonistic days before the advent of the Internet. Anne was expecting to at least get some sympathy from the Board of Directors for committing the grisly act. Or at least a small sign of appreciation.

She'll receive none.

1. Old Mindset: It's just business. It's not personal.

Logically, Anne knows what she must do. It's a no-brainer. The business is not profitable, and it does not have a war chest. The company is bleeding cash. And if it continues like this, the company will bleed to death before it even smells the black.

Anne must face other hard truths, too. Advertising in the post-pandemic world looks completely different from what it was before, and the agency must evolve accordingly. This is not just an economic blip where things go back to normal after the crisis. There is a fundamental shift in the industry and significant challenges lie ahead.

In today's corporate world, letting people go has become a fact of life for every leader. If you manage people, you will have to deal with letting people go. We live in very different times from our parents. They experienced double digit growth year on year. Lifelong employment is a given. Iron rice bowl. Growth is less certain now. Expectations are much higher. When a company is not doing well financially, it must cut headcount. The board of directors expects it. The stock market expects it. It's the unspoken part of running an organization. It's not something you put in the job description. But don't be mistaken: corporate restructuring comes with the job.

Sometimes you are given the autonomy to make that decision. The board of directors leaves it to your discretion. But other times it is foisted upon you. Like Bob. As a welcome gift to Bob on his first day of work in his new organization, he was asked to lay off 30% of the team he was supposed to be leading. He did not even get a chance to know these people. Instead, he was forced to look at them as named entries on an Excel spreadsheet.

Hand them their letter. Escort them out. Check. Who's next?
Hand them their letter. Escort them out. Check. Who's next?
Check. Who's next?
Check. Who's next?

Just checking the boxes. Until he reaches the end of the list. After a while, you become numb to the entire experience. *It's just business; it's not personal.*

This is not how Bob imagined his first day of work will be. In fact, he can't think of a worse way to start.

2. Open Mind: What uncomfortable truth are you denying?

When people find out Anne was responsible for the decision to let people go, they blame her for being heartless. Quickly, she becomes very unpopular. The people who leave hate her. The people who stay also hate her because she got rid of their friends. Anne is public enemy number one.

Anne doesn't like letting people go. She doesn't want to do it. She prefers not to do it. The easy way out would be to pretend that everything is hunky-dory. But she can't deny the hard truth. If she doesn't do anything, the company will run out of money in six months. The company will have to shut down, and people will lose their jobs anyway. And that's assuming Anne doesn't lose her job first. Anne can sweep the problem under the carpet for now, but she's only kicking the can down the road.

It's a messy and sticky situation with no model answers. Anne is stuck between a rock and a hard place. Letting people go is hard. But not taking action and regretting the decision six months too late feels worse. Regret is a cruel and brutal tormentor. By the time you regret it, it's too late. You're left with no other option. You can't do anything. So, whatever Anne does, there will be repercussions. Whichever way it goes, she still ends up the bad guy. She just can't win.

Most people think that the biggest dilemma leaders face is whether to cut headcount or not. That's not exactly it. The real dilemma is: *how deep do you cut?*

Not many people are courageous enough to make a cut deep enough. They try to delay the inevitable. Or worse, they carry out a half-hearted attempt, out of shortsighted compassion. Inadvertently, it leads to recurring rounds of layoffs, dragging out the agony on employee morale with every cut they make. Instead of a clean bullet to the head, they put five in the chest and the victim bleeds to a slow death.

Letting people go requires skill. Like a neurosurgeon carrying out brain surgery, you need to make a clean precise cut. Anne has enough experience to understand the business financials well enough to decide how deep to cut, and she does it unapologetically in one fell swoop. Her singular focus is on making the organization agile enough to compete in the market, and she swallows the cost of doing so.

3. Open Heart: What difficult emotions are you ignoring?

Letting people go makes people very uncomfortable. So uncomfortable that they make up polite names like "resource action" and "right-sizing" to mask the grisliness of the act. When you've worked in a corporate structure this long, you learn how to give legalistic mumbo jumbo responses. You use PR-speak and "spin" the truth. You don't talk straight. You beat around the bush. You hide behind corporate jargon to protect yourself from the ugliness of it all. You build a wall to protect your fragile heart.

That's how we drift into the gray zone. We become numb. *Just get on with it*. In the foggy exhausted state, leaders forget that they are dealing with humans. The humans become faceless representatives of a "redundant workforce." Merely names on an Excel spreadsheet.

Leaders think they must shield people from the harsh reality. They think they must put up a positive front. They think they must project this hero image: *We have everything under control. We have it all figured out.* As if raising doubts will make them look weak. People are not dumb. They *know* the company is not doing well. But at the same time, they are too scared to do anything. Externally, they play along with your false bravado. But internally, they are just waiting for the axe to fall. The lamest thing leaders can do: reassure their employees, then lay them off a few weeks later.

The villain here is denial. On the contrary, when leaders stop denying the truth, they miraculously find this inner reservoir of clarity and courage previously untapped. It's those simple moments where we confidently open ourselves to difficult emotions — rather than feel rushed, inconvenienced or anxious — that can make all the difference.

Leaders get no acknowledgement for doing this work. One HR person told this business leader who just laid off 10% of his team, "You got off easy. Other departments had to make much deeper cuts than you." Let's be clear here — it's *never* easy.

4. Open Will: What hard decision are you avoiding?

Anne quickly assembles a new leadership team, replacing the leaders who walked out. As a team, they pitch to death. They work days and nights. They invest all their time, energy and commitment. Things start to fall into place.

From a loss-making position, the agency breaks even within 18 months. The agency even makes a profit the next year. Bonus for everyone!

Anne will move on to turn around other advertising agencies in Beijing, New York and other countries. Her reputation will precede her. She will come to be known amongst industry insiders as the business turnaround maven, the miracle worker of business turnarounds, the diabolist with the Midas touch. The people who stick with her through thick and thin will become more than just people she worked with. They will become like family. She knows she can depend on them, come what may.

5. New Mindset: It's not just business. It's also personal.

As unpleasant as it is, being told that you must let go of an arbitrary percentage of your team is not uncommon. It happens. There's no point arguing with management's decision; it's already been made. You can't unscramble scrambled eggs. It's better to focus on restructuring the business so that NO ONE has to go through this again.

It's not the actual headcount cut that riles people so much. It's the failure of the people in power to appreciate that feeling of personal loss, to understand what it feels like for the person being let go, that upsets people the most. That is often the biggest cause of resentment, for the people leaving and the people remaining. This resentment can drag out long after the actual restructuring has taken place.

Leaders shy away from feeling the personal loss. They think that if they become personal, they will *lose* their edge, they will turn into an emotional puddle, they will look weak. They live under this fear every day. They are living at the edge of despair. But this is also the edge of greatness if your heart is in the right place and you have the right mindset. Denying those feelings don't make it go away. They just go underground and resurface at the most inconvenient time.

Leadership from an open heart does not actually drain us. It unlocks an insane amount of energy that makes our responsibilities come alive and becomes a source of inner resolve, instead of feeling like a death sentence. This magical effect isn't confined to us. We radiate this calmness and quiet strength to the people around us. We are the fountainhead.

6. Practical tips

Back to fundamentals. Get back to what really matters. In a crisis, you are forced to strip right down to the essentials. Sharpen your focus to get back to your roots, back to the basics, back to what is truly special about your organization. This is also the perfect time to realign everyone's commitment to the vision. Be upfront with people that the path ahead is not going to be easy. But easy is not the goal; greatness is.

Acknowledge the challenges. Be clear and direct in your communication.[1] Personalize your communication to the different stakeholders — what it means for them. Don't hide behind legalistic mumbo jumbo. Our instinct is to shield people from the truth. The villain here is denial. Nature abhors an empty space. Rumors fill it up marvelously.

Transition. Offer support to help people transition into new roles. This includes a redundancy/severance package, extended health insurance coverage, job support, and even keeping their laptops. Even if it makes a temporary dent in your profit & loss.

Hope. Encourage those who are staying. Change is a process. It will require extreme effort and relentless creativity. Hold on to the belief that the company will recover.

Resilience. Initially, you will struggle just to survive. Letting people go IS difficult. But as you become more familiar with the situation, you will learn how to manage. And soon, you will be thriving. Just remember: you got this.

7. Related chapters

Chapter 11   Being Let Go

Chapter 20   Restructuring Your Business

Chapter 23   Restructuring Without Talent Loss

Part 4
Organization Leadership

17

Becoming an Entrepreneur

"A business is an idea that's going to make lives
better. That's all a business is."

— **Richard Branson**

After building a career in investment banking in the US, Ben arrives in Singapore to do his MBA. For ease of convenience, he lives close to the campus and gets his groceries at the supermarket nearby. It has a pitifully limited product range. What's more, Ben has to lug the bags of groceries home. He is not used to this manual labor — and the sweaty polo tee is not a good look on him. Back in New York, Ben's groceries would magically appear on his doorstep, which is a godsend for a busy professional like him. Ben is perplexed. Singapore is one of the most tech-savvy cities in the world, but they lack this one basic lifeline. Online grocery shopping is a necessity, just like water, electricity and internet. This is an emergency!

Ben does some research. Fair enough, online grocery shopping is not new to Singapore. The Singapore grocery business is dominated by two large players, and one of them started an online service more than 10 years ago. He checks their website — it *looks* like it's from 10 years ago. And the actual shopping experience leaves a lot to be desired.

Someone else in Ben's shoes will moan and complain ceaselessly about the backwater state of grocery shopping in this bustling metropolis — whilst continuing to lug their groceries home. But how does a former investment banker fresh out of business school respond to this malady?

Let's put on our investment banker thinking hat, shall we? The grocery business in Singapore generates $4.2 billion in sales annually, with double-digit growth forecasted annually. This lucrative industry is monopolized by two giant incumbents who, despite their size, have shown little innovation in decades. That's the situation on the supply side. On the demand side, there is a rising generation of busy and tech-savvy people who love to shop online, and it's just starting.

Any self-respecting former investment banker fresh out of business school will tell you: *This industry is ripe for disruption.*

1. Old Mindset: This is how we've always done it

Together with his MBA classmate, Ben begins to put his expensive education to work. They estimate the market size, conduct focus groups, evaluate the business from a strategic, marketing and operations angle, and develop a business plan. In theory, the business plan looks perfect — if they have a spare million dollars or so conveniently lying around.

Also, there is a significant barrier to entry. The competition is not another online grocer. The *real* competition is the highly developed network of traditional brick-and-mortar grocery stores across the island. The two incumbents have the whole country mapped out. Grocery is easily accessible physically. There is a grocery store — sometimes even two competing ones — at almost every corner of Singapore.

Furthermore, grocery is a volume and scale kind of business — you need to be big to make it big. This is an extremely lopsided boxing match. Here you have two former investment bankers with zero tech and retail experience, going up against two large well-established retailers who have been serving Singapore before Ben was even born. It's like a rookie fighting Mike Tyson in his prime.

We'll disrupt the whole industry. Change the business model. The Machiavellian scheme starts to take shape.

2. Open Mind: What uncomfortable truth are you denying?

Ben comes up with an ingenious idea.

Uber is the world's largest taxi company. It owns no vehicles.

Facebook is the world's largest media owner. It creates no content.

And he will build Asia's largest supermarket. It will have no inventory.

Ben won't go head-to-head against the incumbents and become an online grocery retailer. That's too old-school. No, he's going to build a multi-sided platform. The platform will allow consumer goods companies to bypass the traditional retailers and go directly to consumers. It will be the eBay for everything a home needs, from instant noodles to baby diapers. *Now, that's a radical thought.* This way, the start-up can stay agile and nimble. It can be asset-free and start without needing millions of dollars.

The genius plan is to hold no inventory — the Uber model. They will only purchase the products when the customers have ordered. The products will then be delivered just-in-time from the manufacturers and dispatched to the customers with marginal handling and storage time. The plan looks great on paper. But it's not reality. Ben will soon learn that the suppliers' delivery timings are not always reliable.

The genius plan is to outsource delivery and avoid the hassle of managing it themselves. They try out a few delivery services. Ben will soon learn that delivery services are also not always reliable — deliveries get messed up, or groceries mysteriously go missing.

Ben will soon learn that you only get one chance with customers. You may have the fanciest website and provide a great online experience, but if the customers have a terrible experience with their first delivery, they won't use it again. Worse, they will tell everyone else how terrible the service is. Ben would have spent all that time, effort and money to acquire the customer just for it to flop in the end.

It is a steep learning curve.

3. Open Heart: What difficult emotions are you ignoring?

When Ben first steps into the ring, he is the rookie going against Mike Tyson in his prime. The punches come in fast and strong. Things get crystal clear very quickly. The bliss of ignorance pops. He falls from the peak of Mount Stupid into the Valley of Despair.

As the rookie in the ring, Ben is knocked down many times. Statistics show that nine out of ten startups fail. I don't say this to discourage entrepreneurs;

just the opposite. Here is a piece of statistic that states out loud what seasoned entrepreneurs already know through their own visceral experience: Things *WILL* go wrong. It's not a reflection of their intelligence or ability. Failure happens to every entrepreneur. It's OKAY to make mistakes. Isn't that the most liberating statement for a budding entrepreneur?

Every day, it's like a bomb has gone off somewhere in the business. *We're f*cked! It's over!* This is the classic WFIO moment[1] when the entrepreneur is certain his startup is dead. A typical entrepreneur will experience three of these per week. It can feel like the edge of despair. But this is also the edge of greatness if you hold the space and not freak out.

Of course failing sucks. It feels unpleasant. We'd rather avoid it. This is the exact point where most entrepreneurs give up. When you are punched to the ground, people are laughing at you, saying, "I told you so," what do you choose to do? Do you stay down for the count? Or do you get up? This is the moment that separates the entrepreneurs who succeed from the ones who don't.

4. Open Will: What hard decision are you avoiding?

Ben pivots the genius plan and starts holding inventory. Ben learns from his personal experience that if he wants to provide a great experience, he has to control the supply chain himself.

Ben starts managing deliveries himself. He learns from his personal experience that convenience is the differentiating factor for people to purchase groceries online versus physically going to the store. Also, delivery is the only physical touchpoint with the customer. There is something magical when customers receive their groceries at their doors.

It's like receiving a present in the post box. This is the exact moment when the brand promise is fulfilled. Get that wrong, and the promise is broken. *It's just another fancy collage of pictures on a website.*

Ben starts raising tens of millions of dollars. He learns that just-in-time delivery looks perfect on paper but doesn't work in reality. To grow the business, they have to increase capacity before the orders come in. That means investing in software, automation, warehousing and fleet management.

Many things will go wrong when you first start your business. If you try and fix everything that's going wrong, you will be overwhelmed. Instead, Ben zooms in on the bright spots, the areas where things *are working*, and scales it. The business plan does not stay frozen. It changes as new knowledge emerges. Ben doesn't go down for the count. He learns how to roll with the punches.

5. New Mindset: Pack your bags. There's a bigger game to play here.

This is the surprising truth about building the next blockbuster product: you have to be willing to work with your hands at the beginning. By day, Ben is the CEO, CFO and CIO all rolled into one. By night, he is the warehouse packer and delivery man all rolled into one. People think it is crazy to see the founder at their doors delivering groceries. Ben gave up his comfortable, air-conditioned job for manual labor (and he still doesn't look good in a sweaty polo tee). It's painstaking work, and only bearable when you believe in what you're doing. *Think big, act small, and you'll grow bigger.*

For the first few months, it was just Ben and his co-founder working out of his home. There is no office, no team. Just two guys and their laptops. It's the greatest feeling in the world. There's no pressure when you're unknown. You can do whatever you want. Do things for the fun of it. When you're an unknown, there's no PR to manage. No investors to report to. No emails from your employees. You'll never get that freedom back once your startup takes off.

Up to this point, Ben had always been working for big brands and big companies. He felt it was the right time for him to branch out and do something more "adventurous." He always had the entrepreneurial bug in him. Even at the big companies, he always found himself launching new products, entering new markets or building new divisions. Now, he's doing it *for real.*

Many things will change: extend product lines, kill off product lines, rebrand the business, change industries, even tear down the business to start over again. You'll make mistakes. That's part of the entrepreneurship journey. You roll with the punches. The more agile you can be, the more likely you will succeed. You start to find yourself going toe-to-toe with Mike. You find yourself winning — on a bigger stage.

6. Practical tips

Founder-market fit. Don't incorporate the company until you have found the founder-market fit — you deeply understand the market you are entering and the customers you are serving. You personally believe that you are the best person in the world to do this thing, where you have a unique proposition given your story, to solve that problem.

Bootstrap. Strip off your crisp business shirt and don the humble t-shirt. Exercise extreme simplicity and laser-sharp focus on executing the big idea. Before making any decision, ask, "How does this make the product better?"

Use the tech. Even your kid can create beautiful designer-quality social media graphics and presentations using online tools like Canva. For non-product-related tasks, for example, CRM, use the tech, don't try and build your own Salesforce.

Learn, unlearn, relearn. Theoretical models don't survive first contact with reality. It's about experimentation. Learn by making mistakes. Let go and try again. Be open to the future that is emerging. You don't know what will finally emerge, but you are committed to holding the space.

7. Related chapters

Chapter 5   Find Your Calling

Chapter 19   Scaling Your Business

18

Becoming an Intrapreneur

"It doesn't matter how many times you fail. You
only have to be right once and then everyone can
tell you that you are an overnight success."

— **Mark Cuban**

S am leads the e-commerce business for a global computer manufacturer. His management team has seen the explosive growth of e-commerce sales and tasked Sam to set up this new channel business and bring the organization into the future. Some people question the mandate. Is there really a need for this new channel? Will it cannibalize the existing businesses? Business looks better than ever. Revenues are growing, clients are rolling in every day, and everyone is extremely busy. *If it ain't broken, why fix it?*

But Sam knows better. This is a little red riding hood moment. He can see a cliff coming for the business. The way people buy computers in five years time will be completely different from how they buy them today. Digital presence is the key. If the organization doesn't start laying the foundations right now, it'll be too late.

Sam is excited to lead this new venture. He has always wanted to flex his entrepreneurial muscle. He wants to get his hands dirty, solve a big pain point, and drive the whole industry forward. It feels like the right time in his life to take some risk, try something a bit more adventurous, and see how things play out.

1. Old Mindset: This is how we've always done it

From day one, Sam meets with internal resistance from the rest of the organization like Finance, Legal, HR and Marketing. The e-commerce business might be growing exponentially, but it's growing from a small base. The actual revenue size today is small in comparison to the core business. This e-commerce business is just not worth their time. They are already very busy, and this tiny business is clearly not a priority.

But the frustration doesn't stop there. So, the rest of the organization may not have the bandwidth to support Sam's business. They refuse to support Sam's business, yet they want veto power over what he's doing. Sam is launching a mega-campaign in one week, and the Marketing Department wants to embargo his ads because the logo is the wrong shade of blue. *It's corporate policy.* Not only are they unwilling to support Sam's business, but they also try to stop Sam from taking things into his own hands.

Because the e-commerce organization is too insignificant to warrant the Marketing Department's attention, Sam looks to external vendors to support his business. Procurement tells him that he's only allowed to use the Agency of Record that is appointed by the global headquarters on a global scale, according to the service level agreement (SLA) stated in the global contract. *It's corporate policy.* Sam gives the agency a try. He briefs the agency on an online banner that needs to launch tomorrow. The agency tells Sam that they will deliver the online banner in two weeks, as per the SLA. Maybe the agency didn't hear him correctly. The online banner needs to launch tomorrow, and Sam needs it in two hours.

Sam is being held to ransom by these global advertising agencies, amongst the largest in the world. He is forced to pay premium prices, but he does not get the premium service. *They are delivering too little, too late.*

E-commerce moves very fast, but Sam can't keep up because of the bumbling corporate bureaucracy. Sam is blocked from executing his online marketing campaigns on time and to the required standard. He experiences roadblock upon roadblock internally. It's as if the business is set up to fail. It's not external competitors that are knocking them down. The blows are coming from within.

This is what the corporate bureaucracy says:

This is how we've always done it, and you must comply.

Your business is like a blip on our radar. We have much larger things to focus on. Do us a favor and disappear.

Even if you succeed in growing revenues by 100%, in the bigger scheme of things, it's a drop in the ocean. Don't waste my time.

To them, this e-commerce business is a mere sideshow: cute, interesting, fluffy, the CEO's pet project.

2. Open Mind: What uncomfortable truth are you denying?

Sam sees it differently. He envisions a completely different organization. He sees a future where the organization creates and delivers innovative solutions centered around customer needs, rather than pushing boxes through traditional sales channels. This new e-commerce business unit threatens to cannibalize business from the traditional sales models which have made the organization very successful in the last 30 years.

The world is changing and the organization needs to adapt if it wants to stay relevant. It can't be "business as usual." Sam knows that this e-commerce charter will not thrive organically in the current environment. The organization talks about innovation. But make no mistake. The few people who actually innovate move against the institutional grain in a way that makes the rest of the organization twitch with nervous anxiety. The modern corporation was built for profit maximization and efficiency. It excels at optimizing within known parameters. Big problems are broken into smaller and smaller pieces and then assigned to departments that only do that one thing (and do it really well). This works so long as things are *within* the working parameters. Anything that falls *outside* the parameters disrupts the efficiency, and thus are sought out and pulverized by the swarm of corporate sentinels.

"Digital transformation" is such a buzzword today. Everyone has a "digital transformation" KPI in their balanced scorecard. But with this "optimizing" mindset, you'll only be spending your millions on digitizing old ways of working. That's how organizations burn lots of cash to take a giant leap... into the past. Innovation emerges from truly disruptive thinking from a collective of subject matter experts across different disciplines working together. Innovation is going to come from investigating, experimenting and doing things differently, and not from blindly complying with traditional ways of doing business.

Sam rallies the team: "We're going on a journey. I don't have all the answers, but I believe the innovation required by the organization resides within each of *you*. Join me."

3. Open Heart: What difficult emotions are you ignoring?

Sam is an intrapreneur — an employee with an entrepreneurial mindset developing innovative ideas and products within an organization. You would expect applause and handshakes for his ingenuity and courage. You would expect Sam to be treated like a hero by his organization. Instead, he is seen as a pariah, a terrorist, even.

Innovation sounds cool on paper. In reality, it clashes with the highly self-preserving corporate bureaucracy. The bureaucracy is there for a reason: to protect efficiency and generate a lot of money. It seeks out anomalies and destroys them so that the cash-generating machine can go back to generating cash.

What Sam does is very unnatural. He moves fast and breaks things. Breaking things is not appreciated by the core business. Every day, Sam lives under the fear of getting fired. To the corporate bureaucracy, he is seen as the hustler cajoling and coaxing people to give him resources. Other times, he is seen as the pesky nuisance that nobody wants to have around. At worst, he is seen as the saboteur who stabs people in the back.

Life for an intrapreneur can be alienating. You're made to feel unwanted and unwelcome like you don't belong. There is nothing right or wrong about it, noble or immoral. That's the very essence of innovation — of bringing something new into the world. It rattles the status quo. The villain here is denial. Every intrapreneur will feel this way at some point. This is part of life for an intrapreneur. It can be the most liberating thing to know that you are not alone in feeling this way. Put on your thick face. Protect your vision from the ordinary opinions of others. Do not accept the limitations that others try to impose on you. This frees you to be flexible and relentless. Go back to the joy of jumping in with both feet when inspiration strikes. By your absolute self-confidence, you will instill confidence in others.

4. Open Will: What hard decision are you avoiding?

Sam's e-commerce business unit identifies several opportunities for delivering a more compelling customer experience. They use data-driven approaches to test new business models. They launch small proofs-of-concepts to learn about the customers and what adds value to them. They double down wherever they see customer delight. They evangelize best practices across all regions.

These data-driven customer insights give Sam the courage to break rules that add no value to the customers and push the boundaries of how things can be done. He restructures the workstream and builds new in-house competencies to be more agile and responsive to the market. This enables the business unit to have the agility of a startup backed by the might of a multinational company.

5. New Mindset: Pack your bags. There's a bigger game to play here.

Sam is bringing innovation into a large bureaucratic multinational company. But it doesn't happen on its own. It's a fight to unleash it. Failure is synonymous with innovation. You can't have innovation without failure. But celebrating failure is a far departure from the norm for most organizations. It's just not part of their DNA. There is still a stigma around failure. People are pressured to be less innovative than they need to be. The good news is, you can try and fail many times, but you only need to get it right once.

The organization's intention to innovate must be backed by mechanisms to promote innovation. Intrapreneurs take a huge personal risk. Internal innovation can be a career-limiting move. People have to take a step away from the corporate ladder and do something completely different. Regardless of how much innovation is prioritized in the corporate agenda, the traditional performance metrics are formulated based on "business as usual," which does not reflect the contributions made. But this can change. There is already a groundswell of ideas. The potential for innovation is already within the organization. You just have to create the space to unleash it.

6. Practical tips

Iterate. Instead of thinking of a singular and miraculous win, think about a consistent stream of small wins that builds momentum towards a great victory. Deliver consistent results for a broad range of stakeholders.

Storytelling. It's not enough to have the support of the leadership team. They can't be there with you at every meeting. You have to evangelize, too.

Build a credible image for yourself and your program. It's a communication game. It's about selling a vision of the future that's compelling for your most important stakeholders.

Remuneration. It may not be fair to assess your contribution using traditional performance metrics. Discuss a hybrid arrangement with your boss. You are personally committed, and your organization should reward you likewise, for example, by providing commercially blatant amounts of stock-based employee compensation. As the CEO, you should be delighted to grant stocks as much as the employees are to receive them.

Doomsday prep. Do not use the "We are standing on a burning platform" analogy. That's using fear to drive change. It backfires on you. Fear drives very ordinary behaviors like tunnel vision and turf mentality. The fight-or-flight response kicks in. People work harder doing what they've always done in the past. You end up very busy digging your own grave.

7. Related chapters

Chapter 5   Find Your Calling

Chapter 13   Leading People Through Change

Chapter 26   Learning at the Speed of Business

19

Scaling Your Business

"Your job as a leader is not to drive the
performance but to actually care enough about
the institution and the system so that the
performance comes naturally."
— Gianpiero Petriglieri

E ric started his own creative agency two years ago with a small team of five people to serve one client. They were like a roving in-house creative agency flying across Southeast Asia to support the in-country product teams to deliver award-winning localized marketing projects. Like the SEAL Team Six, they would dive-bomb into the country for a month to launch the campaign, and then evacuate.

The team worked on anything from illustrations to website design and events. Eric was fastidious about delivering on his promises. As a result, one project turned into two and continued to grow. Today, the creative agency is 150-people strong and growing. Eric put in place a leadership team and skeletal processes to support the workload, but he's reaching a point where he's finding it unmanageable. The organization is growing faster than its people. It's tempting to put in more processes to increase the efficiency, but great ideas don't just roll off a mass production line. That will just produce confused and disingenuous work void of any soul. That would be Eric's worst nightmare. The process of delivering authentic creative solutions is emotional and complex. Eric does not want to compromise the quality. There needs to be creative control, but there is only one Eric.

Eric is stuck in a dilemma. He feels pressured to scale the company, but he's afraid the quality will deteriorate. As the workload increases, Eric's becoming overwhelmed. He can keep denying it, but that will only push him over the edge and burn out.

So how does Eric deliver authentic creative solutions at scale? How do you scale creativity? How do you scale something that is inherently not scalable?

1. Old Mindset: People are replaceable

Eric did not grow up dreaming of becoming an entrepreneur. Instead, his entrepreneurial journey was born out of frustration with how big advertising agencies work. He should know. He used to work for one.

Big advertising agencies take a production line approach to scaling creativity. It's all about efficiency, cost-cutting and profit maximization. The creative process is compartmentalized and standardized to fit a neat workflow: account management, creative, planning & strategy, production & creative services, social media community management, just to name a few. Client jobs are fed into the assembly line and go through a linear and procedural process to produce a creative output. These big advertising agencies have very sophisticated billing software and complicated reporting processes to monitor the efficiency of the assembly line and maximize profits.

The production line approach makes it easier to replace employees. Agencies no longer need "craftsmen" — employees with multiple talents and skills — to carry out the jobs. With the assembly line approach, if an employee is not working out, the agency can replace that position with another person. The advertising agency is no longer beholden to their employees. The production line becomes the most important thing. Everyone else is replaceable.

The assembly line approach is extremely effective if you need to make a lot of the same thing. For example, if you need to make more cars, you can optimize the efficiency of the existing assembly line, or add a new assembly line. Manufacturing is a bounded process. It's linear, it's procedural, there are no variations.

Having fixed boundaries with absolutely no variation is the antithesis of creativity.

Every organization talks about the need for creativity. Creativity is about generating new ideas, concepts and perspectives. It's about coming up with something new. Yet what we have today are heavy bureaucratic conglomerates applying Fordism large-scale mechanized mass production methods, and expecting to create the wow factor of a Ferrari. As for the big creative agencies, in their pursuit of commercializing creativity, they inevitably corrupted it.

2. Open Mind: What uncomfortable truth are you denying?

The industrialized world rewards specialization, but specialization comes at a cost. You learn more and more about less and less until you know everything about nothing. That's how you end up with a team of 100 specialists — lots of ideas, yet nothing gets done.

When Eric worked for a big agency, he saw a lot of strong business opportunities fade away just because his agency couldn't react fast enough. Every new opportunity had to be approved by three directors who were all based in London.

To justify the exorbitant retainer charge to the client, Eric and his colleagues were told to pad out their timesheets. A piece of work that took an hour to design, Eric had to bill for three hours. It felt dishonest. Also, it made Eric look inefficient, which provoked a lot of questions from the client's procurement team. This put additional pressure and burden on him, on top of his "regular job," the creative work.

There were budget discussions before any project can commence. When a client briefed the agency, the creative team would only see the brief two months later. Most of that time was spent disputing budgets or costs.

Trying to collaborate with his own colleagues was also a nightmare. The so-called "specialists" were reluctant to engage with "junior" clients. Meeting anyone less senior than a Director was seen as not worthy of their time. *They are not senior enough. They are not decision-makers.*

Eric grew increasingly frustrated by the agency's inability to do what's best for the client. During drinks with a long-standing client, Eric's frustrations boiled over. It was a culmination of 15 years of frustration coming to the surface: agencies applying the same mundane factory parameters again and again, and bastardizing the creative process. Eric shared his vision of how things could be done better if he was put in charge. He pointed out the inefficiencies and how to change them.

That impromptu rant eventually turned into something more. Within six months, Eric found himself in charge of setting up a new agency to support this one long-standing client.

With the mandate in hand, Eric got to work. This new agency would be different. It would be set up as a retained resource. No more approvals needed from London. No more tedious budget discussions. No more filling overinflated timesheets. No more black holes between the client and the creative team.

Because they were a retained resource, they were seen as a free resource. So the briefs poured in. Eric actually enjoyed being seen as a free resource. With the corporate bureaucracy, Eric would have to spend two months disputing the budget on a new brief. With the new terms of engagement, Eric could spend that two months on actual creative work. Previously, it was like driving with the handbrakes on. With the handbrakes removed, the squad of five people can deliver a lot of work in a very short time.

3. Open Heart: What difficult emotions are you ignoring?

During the startup phase, Eric needed to be hands-on to *build* the agency. He had to get his hands dirty. He had to do everything. That's how you win one championship.

But now that Eric found the proverbial product-market fit, he needs to shift his focus to *scale* the business. He's no longer trying to win one championship. He's aiming to win four championships at the same time.

To scale the agency, Eric has to step away and become the General. Delegate to accelerate.

Eric has to consciously shift away from being the hands-on CEO to a strategic planner and decision-maker. This is a huge identity shift. It's like changing state: from water to steam. It takes a lot for Eric to loosen his grip on the reins of control and hold the space for his people to get work done. He has to be extremely mindful to move away from being the Chief Everything Officer and lean into the "executive" part of the job. He has to resist his naturally competitive impulse to run onto the field to score the goal and be the manager coaching the team from the sidelines.

There will be tremendous pressure to hire. It can be tempting to lower the bar on talent just to put bums on seats. This is a slippery slope. When you drop the bar on standards, you need stricter processes to ensure quality control. That's how promising startups stifle their exuberant vitality and put on the heavy pounds of corporate bureaucracy.

4. Open Will: What hard decision are you avoiding?

Traditionally, large organizations are organized in functional departments. Each department operate in their silos, optimized for their own specialization. You end up with this "cross-matrix organization" thing, with convoluted solid-line/dotted-line reporting structures.

Instead, Eric forms teams around a shared passion for a brand. He has an intuition for people's energy and he brings together a collective of people who amplify the shared love for the brand. The team members come with an eclectic mix of skills. Their work is not confined to their specialization.

For example, the same person can be working on the planning, copy and art for a banner ad. They work more like Hollywood movie production teams, with people coming together to tackle projects, then disbanding and moving on to new assignments once the project is complete. Instead of a traditional top-down hierarchy, the organization structure is built upon a network of highly empowered teams working on specific projects and challenges.

Organizing teams this way is a lot more agile and flexible. But it is unfamiliar to most people. People who first work with Eric and his agency feel like a lost person. Eric spends a lot of his time familiarizing new employees and clients with this new way of working. He wants people to understand why there is a need for this new way of working, and he does it through his founder story. He narrates his frustration of working for a big soulless agency which gave him the imperative to do things differently. He maps out and introduces simple processes which help people collaborate better within and across teams, and reduce duplicate work. This way of working empowers people to start leading their own areas within the common frame.

Eric encourages cross-breeding of ideas. He nudges people to be open and supportive of each other's ideas. It's not about whose ideas are the best. Instead, when people build upon each other's ideas, they end up with a truly original concept that they would never have come up on their own. This generates a collective force of energy and creativity, and when they channel that energy into a campaign, whether it's a website or an EDM, it creates a WOW factor. It puts a smile on people's faces. A smile has an infectious quality. And it begins with a smile from within the creative process. This is the secret sauce to creativity. When the team is smiling, it sparks motivational energy and collaboration, both key ingredients for creativity.

Eric is always on the lookout for creators and originators. He works hard to keep them. He creates a safe space where they can be creative. This is a deliberate move. Because it's much easier to be a critic than a creator. If you don't hold the space where creators and originators can get things going, you won't have any new ideas.

5. New Mindset: People are your ONLY competitive advantage

Creativity is not about coming up with another idea. It's about coming up with a better idea.

To Eric, advertising is not about selling another product. It's about increasing awareness about something that brings meaning to people's lives. Not just for one or two people, but for millions of people.

This is a huge responsibility. It means that every ad that Eric's agency creates has to move people. Every product, every piece of communication, has to evoke an emotion. If it doesn't, it does not go out. Not everyone understands this responsibility. It may even seem perfectionistic or obsessive compulsive to some. *Why bother? It's just a web banner. It doesn't really matter.* But for people like Eric, it matters. A lot. It's deeply personal. Eric hires people who share the same values — people who *get it*. To them, it's the right thing to do. They can't *not* do it.

This is how Eric envisions the future of the advertising industry. This is the kind of advertising agency Eric wants to build. It is powered by multi-talented and agile creatives. The agency was born out of frustration with the dysfunctional assembly line approach to creativity. The digital revolution has changed everything. Now anyone can pick up Photoshop skills on the internet. With intuitive point-and-click apps, even a complete beginner can become a decent graphic designer instantly. You can learn almost anything on the internet today. It's disrupting the way we work. It's also disrupting how whole industries work.

6. Practical tips

Product-market fit. Do not scale until you have the product-market fit. Handcraft the user experience until it works, then start thinking about automating it.

Growth. Stop trying to do *everything* to show growth. Instead, be ruthlessly strategic about what your startup is here to do — its purpose. Growth is the outcome of holding this intention. Say a thousand little no's in order to say one big yes.

Learn, unlearn, relearn. With new and better apps coming onto the market every day, the ability to unlearn and relearn matters more than ever. It can give your startup a competitive edge. Invest in learning for your team. Don't stop learning, be curious, to stay relevant.

Recruit. Screen for job candidates who share the same values. Look for individuals who have been involved in the design or scaling of something completely new, or who bring inventive ideas to the table when you talk to them.

Process creep. Be wary of process creep. It's a discipline to keep a tight, lean set of processes — just enough to get maximum results.

7. Related chapters

Chapter 10   Job Hopping

Chapter 24   Reducing Employee Turnover

20

Restructuring Your Business

"Everyone fails at who they're supposed to be.
A measure of a person, of a hero, is how well they
succeed at being who they are."

— **Frigga,** *Avengers: Endgame*

Alex oversees the Asia Pacific business for a global logistics company. A year ago, the organization decided to merge two of its largest business units to become the number one global superpower of the logistics industry. Alex's mandate? To turn that vision into reality. Scale matters in this industry, and the competitive advantage can make the difference between making negative and double-digit margins. The winner takes all, and his organization is determined to capture the dominant market position.

The lofty vision is to become a fourth-party logistics (4PL) company, providing end-to-end integrated supply chain solutions to customers. Essentially, the 4PL company takes control of all logistical operations for the customer, from picking up the goods from their manufacturing facility all the way to delivering them to the doorsteps of the consumers, overseeing the complex web of warehouses, shipping companies, freight forwarders and agents in between.

Alex and his leadership team are building the future of the logistics industry. They conceptualize new products and services. They identify new capabilities and hire a whole bunch of people. The organization makes substantial capital investments to build brand-spanking-new warehouse facilities. They launch the service into the market with big fanfare, fancy brochures and big promises. The market loves it, and four manufacturers sign up.

In a typical case study, this is where the story ends: happily ever after. But this is reality, and the story is just beginning.

1. Old Mindset: It's just business. It's not personal.

In the next year, container shipping rates decline steadily due to overcapacity. Unfortunately, Alex's organization is locked into long-term block space agreements with the carriers at a much higher rate. To take advantage of the lower rates, their customers start dealing with the carriers directly, bypassing them as the middleman. To keep their customers, the organization has to operate at a loss.

The organization experiences serious negative margins very quickly, losing money on every dollar billed. They are losing money every month. After a year, the new products and services are not delivering value fast enough for customers. On the surface, the business looks healthy. Revenue is going up and up. But the business is making significant losses. Under further pressure of high debt, the organization decides to cut costs. The strategy is simple enough. They will remove the entire regional layer of the freight forwarding business. The logic behind it? Freight forwarding is a global business, so it can be managed globally, and regional control is unnecessary.

2. Open Mind: What uncomfortable truth are you denying?

No theoretical model survives first contact with reality. The cut looks simple conceptually, but it triggers a cataclysmic meltdown. The cut leaves a large gaping wound in the regional leadership ranks, like a head severed from its body. The global leadership team is in the ivory tower, and the local country teams are left to fend for themselves. People have to run with half-sized teams, broken processes and outdated systems. Things stop working. Customers start screaming. Partners start distancing themselves.

Alex lost his regional role and takes on a new role leading the Singapore local market team. Immediately Alex gets caught in a tight spot, pushed from the back by his business partners, shoved from the front by his customers, and squeezed from the top by the global bosses.

If Alex tries to fix everything that is going wrong in the complex web of customers, warehouses, shipping companies, freight forwarders and agents, he will quickly be overwhelmed. Instead of trying to do everything, Alex decides to focus on their key existing customers. He invites them into the conversation. Alex learns that their biggest customers in terms of volume prefer to negotiate preferential rates for individual services rather than relying on a single provider for everything. Alex also learns that the integrated approach only makes sense for very specialized applications like managing complex chain-of-custody requirements and delivery schedules for a medical device company. Their supply chain requirements are fixed and bounded, and not as complex to manage.

By focusing on the real needs of his customers, Alex gains clarity on exactly where he needs to enhance the existing system and invest in new systems.

The plan is so practical it gets an instant sign-off from the company president.

3. Open Heart: What difficult emotions are you ignoring?

Logistics is a network type of business. It is a highly fragmented and complex system on a global scale. Moving cargo around the planet is a complex job, often consisting of multiple stops and handoffs along the way. Running the behemoth is a complex ecosystem of salespeople, freight stations, carriers, airliners and customers spread across the globe. On paper, it looked logical to remove the regional leaders. However, under the hood, these regional leaders were playing a pivotal role in allowing communication to flow in the network and keep the whole business going. It's like a beehive, and the regional leaders were like the mother bees keeping the entire hive alive.

This is a typical problem: leaders in the ivory tower making cost-cutting decisions without having a fundamental understanding of how the business actually runs. Orders are issued, the axe falls from the top, and heads start rolling down like a coin-operated machine. With the regional layer removed, operations literally came to a standstill.

Alex had to reconnect the severed network. One Friday at 5 p.m., Alex is winding down for the week over drinks at the bar when he gets a phone call from a client in Perth. They need to ship two generators from Singapore to Perth as soon as possible. This is mission impossible. He doesn't have information on the freight availability. It's the end of the workweek. The office is closed for the weekend. The port is closed for the weekend.

Most people will give up at this point. *It can't be done. Nothing you can do.* Followed by a shoulder shrug.

Alex doesn't want to give up. He doesn't know what he doesn't know. So he makes a few phone calls. Before he knows it, he is liaising with a colleague in Shanghai who happens to be having drinks in the same bar as a shipping partner. Over a series of phone calls to various parties on both sides, the Shanghai colleague strikes a deal right at the bar. He calls Alex and provides him with the email address of an officer who works in the Singapore port authority. He instructs Alex to send the documentation to this officer. This officer will arrange to allow the two generators into the port on Saturday. The Shanghai colleague ends the call by telling Alex exactly where to park the two generators so that they can be picked up by the container ship that is now going to stop by Singapore. All this flurry of activities happens over a glass of martini. Mission impossible made possible, like a James Bond movie. This is the magic of the hive network.

The excitement starts coming back to Alex's organization. Everyone can't wait to move ahead. People start feeling empowered and take accountability to drive their sub-functions forward. The team is committed to the new path, which creates better chemistry. With support from customers and partners, the organization makes substantial progress. The Singapore business goes from loss-making to the highest profitability in Asia Pacific.

4. Open Will: What hard decision are you avoiding?

When things go wrong, it's easy to blame people. Employees blame it on the lack of management support. Managers blame it on employee resistance. Everyone forgets that "simple" things like reducing handling time, deploying work-share processes and harmonizing track events involve a lot of coordination and many rounds of process re-engineering. The devil is in the details. A lot of the details are not known upfront.

When Alex signed the 4PL deal with one of the manufacturers, he thought they do their manufacturing in Singapore. He'll find out later that they outsource it to contract manufacturers like Foxconn all across China. Alex's team had to figure out where their factories are located and how to consolidate the orders and the shipment trajectories.

Because of the ambiguity, Alex needed people to be agile and creative at problem-solving. On one occasion, the warehouse received more shipments than they could process, leaving hundreds of pallets of expensive electronics lined up outside the warehouse. A guy had to be stationed outside just to check the sky for rain.

There were many sleepless nights for Alex and his team; scary days of going down to the warehouse in the middle of the night to clear the backlog. But by having the courage to make those mistakes, Alex's team learns very quickly what works, and does more of it. That's how they begin to transform.

5. New Mindset: It's not just business. It's also personal.

Things change. Disruption happens. As they should. But we deny the changing reality. We fight reality. The logistics industry was shifting. And the organization thought removing the regional layer was going to solve their problem. Accepting reality can feel like the edge of despair for us.

It packs an emotional wallop. But this is also the edge of greatness. When Alex engaged in a generative conversation with his customers, things got real fast, which allowed him to create real impact in a very short time.

Gone are the good old days of making double-digit margins in the dark. It used to be a mystery how a parcel from the US ends up in Asia within a day. It's like magic. Everything happened in a black box. And it was very profitable. It was also rather mysterious how a handful of people at the top earned half a million dollars on the backs of dispatchers and warehouse stockers earning slightly above minimum wage.

But all that is changing. Most of the new entrants to the logistics sector are start-ups, and many of these are looking to use new technology to enter the industry. These new entrants are starting to shine the light around the black box, looking to carve out the more lucrative elements of the value chain and exploit them using digital technology or new "sharing" business models. They are agile. They are not weighed down by asset-heavy balance sheets or cumbersome existing systems.

And they thought removing the regional layer would solve their problem.

As a transformational leader, you are at your innovative best when you are put in situations where you can make a difference, no matter how impossible it might seem. It's like the challenge brings out the innovator in you. There's a fearlessness about you. You keep your calm in a crisis. In the chaos, you forge a path, you bring people with you, and you always emerge victorious. It's not just business as usual for you. It's also personal.

6. Practical tips

Insider knowledge. Lean more on insider knowledge than external consultants. They have deep knowledge about how change will affect customer experience. They also understand the legacy problems that are unique to your organization. They can develop real solutions much faster and the solutions can be more finely executed.

Engage. Engage all your stakeholders in a collaborative conversation. Employees, business partners, customers. Past and present. Imagine what a better future looks like for everyone. When you engage with real situations and real people, the solutions that emerge from *within* the complexity are inherently realistic and sustainable.

WFIO. There will be WFIO moments. It will be tough. People will be let go. People will have to deal with broken processes. There will be difficult emotions. Hold the space for these difficult emotions without the usual fear, resentment and blame. The villain here is denial.

7. Related chapters

Chapter 11   Being Let Go

Chapter 16   Letting People Go

Chapter 23   Restructuring Without Talent Loss

21

Managing Complexity in Your Organization

"Simplicity is not an end in art, but we usually arrive at simplicity as we approach the true sense of things."

— **Constantin Brâncuși**

Anne is the Asia Pacific Managing Director of a global advertising agency. The agency is closing the financial year of 2020, and Anne already knows there will be hell to pay. The coronavirus pandemic has led to an immediate and drastic drop in advertising spending. All media buyers and brands paused spending as quarantine took effect, with travel and retail media taking the brunt of the hit. As a result, Anne's organization made significant losses. Anne knows what is coming up. Anne knows the drill. At the close of the year, when business has not been good, there's housekeeping to be done. A cost-cutting exercise, which usually means laying off people. This is not a peculiarity confined only to Anne's organization. In fact, the entire industry goes through a round of musical chairs. We don't raise an eyebrow. *It's just business. It's standard operating procedure.* We all know the game. We've been playing by its rules for a very long time.

But is there another way?

Being the wily old fox of the industry, all this comes as no surprise to Anne. The writing has been on the wall for quite some time. The crisis only exacerbated the situation, throwing the deep underlying problems into stark relief. The company's growth has hit a wall for a while. Consumer behavior, and correspondingly advertising spending, has shifted significantly since the advent of the digital age. Advertising has become more complicated. Externally, Anne's advertising clients are more demanding than ever. They want bigger value for smaller prices. They want a single face to the company rather than working with ten different business units unaware of each other. Internally, these business units compete against each other like sworn enemies. Employees are frustrated with confusing messages from leadership. Externally, they are supposed to show one united face. But internally, they fight and backstab each other.

1. Old Mindset: Chipping away at the tip of the iceberg

Anne is dealing with a lot of complexity. She's supposed to oversee more than 20 advertising and media brands, but with no standard method for tracking, reporting, or analyzing results. The organization's lack of cohesion is the unintended consequence of an enormously successful growth strategy which involved acquiring other agencies, from boutiques to conglomerates, and then allowing them to operate relatively autonomously. This has conspired to add layer upon layer of complexity to how the businesses are structured and managed. Responses to new business challenges — globalization, emerging technologies, and regulations like personal data protection, to name a few — are plastered on like a band-aid, layer upon layer. Inconsistencies are swept under the carpet. This is how complexity is created right under their noses — the by-product of organizational changes, big and small, cemented layer upon layer over the years, surreptitiously weaving complications into how work is done. The unintended result? A monolithic organization that is increasingly ungovernable, unwieldy and underperforming. More energy is devoted to navigating the labyrinth rather than achieving results. Accountability is unclear, decision rights are muddy, and data are sliced and diced, again and again, frequently with no clear idea of how the information will be used.

When a crisis hits, the fragmented organization's lack of standard systems, data, and processes makes it impossible to respond to the challenges in an agile manner. How well can she assess the relative brand or business unit performance? How well can she evaluate individual performance without micro-managing? How well does she know where to place her bets?

This will cause the most severe case of heebie-jeebies for any sane CEO. But this is not peculiar to Anne. It seems everyone across the marketing industry is stressed out, angry and afraid. When people are too stressed to think big thoughts, ideas become smaller and more disposable, worth barely two seconds of attention. In all that noise, their advertising can't break through. How does Anne get everyone back into the game of creativity and stop this tanking?

Of course, Anne can continue to ignore this obvious problem that *no one* wants to talk about. She can deny it, but she's getting uncomfortably close to the edge. There is a bigger game to play, but Anne can't do it herself.

It requires a different playbook. The internal rules and regulations need updating. It can't be another round of musical chairs. Childish games no longer interest her.

2. Open Mind: What uncomfortable truth are you denying?

The simple idea is brilliant. From the Danish hygge lifestyle concept to the KonMari Method anti-clutter campaign, simplicity appears to be gaining a lot of traction. Not only has the simplicity idea caught on in the lifestyle section, but it's also spilling into business.

But simplifying business would appear to be rather like the myth of Sisyphus, condemned to the eternal punishment of forever rolling a boulder up a hill just to have it roll back down. Global headquarters have been rolling out slogans and propaganda to simplify, but then they force everyone to implement ever more bureaucracy and convoluted systems. As soon as one set of rules are taken down, they are replaced with two more.

This is another common one. The organization embarks on a one-off effort to simplify processes through implementing large-scale enterprise software systems... without addressing the underlying fundamental issues. *Here we go again; another random (and expensive) top-down management initiative.* They implement the latest whizbang software, holding it as the panacea to all their problems. Unwieldy organizational structure, lack of standard systems and processes, confusing product offerings and conflicting priorities... Poof. Gone. Like magic. But eventually, they are disappointed when they don't achieve the results that they hoped for. Instead, a new layer of complexity has been slapped on, interrupting established relationships, introducing unanticipated roadblocks and triggering confusion over decision rights.

Isn't Simple Business perhaps the biggest oxymoron?

3. Open Heart: What difficult emotions are you ignoring?

In the effort to drive growth for the business, Anne's global executive team paid half a million dollars to management consultants to tell them how to simplify their business — condensed in a 35-page presentation slide deck. They spent another million dollars on a new CRM enterprise system to drive customer-centricity.

They have the best strategy. They have the latest CRM system. But they don't see the results. Why? Because people's behaviors have not changed. Whatever dollars they have left after paying the management consultants and software companies — we're scraping the bottom of the barrel here — they spend it on training. People always come last. Why?

Because it's the hardest.

The global heads want quick wins. They need to show the Board of Directors that they are making fast progress. It needs to be swift. It needs to be at the forefront of technology. And it needs to be *very* visible. The global heads compete against each other to see who has the most bombastic and revolutionary projects. The bigger, the better. To justify their own massive existence. And Anne's team on the ground has to deal with implementing 10 high-profile "transformation" projects at one time.

In the best-case scenario, the ten transformation projects are implemented successfully. Everyone celebrates. It is very visible. But they are only chipping away at the bits and pieces at the tip of the iceberg. Yes, Anne has a new CRM system, but the underlying fundamental issues have not changed.

If you want a different result, then people need to behave differently — that means changing people's mindsets. Changing mindsets lies at the bottom of the iceberg. It takes time, a luxury that leaders can't afford in this instant gratification "I want to see results NOW" world that we work in. Anne may not have the seat long enough to see the changes through. Even CEOs are not immune to the vagaries of job insecurity.

The idea that Anne can *eliminate* the complexities in the business in six months by implementing a whizbang software is not rational. But the idea that she can *manage* the complexity by focusing on shifting people's mindsets to fundamentally change the system is a compelling one. There's more leverage on the system if Anne can understand the dysfunctional habits, thinking and processes that are keeping the organization stuck in the past. Chipping at bits and pieces of ice at the top of the iceberg just creates more busy work for everyone.

4. Open Will: What hard decision are you avoiding?

The year 2020 was a transformational year, albeit not according to what Anne thought was best. In 2020, the year of the onslaught of the coronavirus pandemic, Anne's organization *experienced* being agile. People had to deal with uncertainty. Things got real… fast. The situation was changing every day, and people adapted. People stood up and took ownership of the change. People came together and collaborated. They embraced the constraints and made things happen. They learnt to make do with whatever resource they had, asking, "What can we do with what we have right now?" They went through the crucible moment together. 2020 indeed was a transformational year. They didn't study it, wish it, or pontificate about it. It wasn't an academic or intellectual exercise. In 2020, they actually did it.

It's not that people resist to change; people change all the time. What they resist is change imposed on them; with no reason given for the need for change. In 2020, people busted old habits, old processes and old thinking that kept the organization stuck in the past.

People didn't think they could be as productive working from home.

People didn't think customers would buy online.

People didn't think corporate policies could be overridden.

People didn't think it was possible to implement the "digital transformation plan" in four weeks.

In the past, people would have said: "No, it will never work."

Now, they know better. And the organization has transformed. It's no longer the same organization as before. It's more agile, focused and creative.

5. New Mindset: Diving to the bottom of the iceberg

It's not that the pandemic changed the advertising industry. The industry has been *talking* about disruption for a very long time. What happened with the pandemic is that people can no longer deny that things have changed. The traditional boundaries in the advertising world are blurring. The Googles of the world are working directly with the P&Gs. The P&Gs are building their own Ogilvys in-house. The Ogilvys are starting to look like the Accentures. And the Accentures are trying to be the next Google. No wonder everyone is confused.

Businesses may have prioritized survival when the quarantine initially came into force, but a fundamental shift is afoot. People are more open-minded and not as resistant to change. You know that saying: what doesn't kill you makes you stronger. You're going to see people finding ways to push for real transformation. There's never been a better time to pitch ideas that involve real transformation to tackle the fundamental issues that lie at the bottom of the iceberg. With a more open mindset across the organization, pushing for "simple business" will face radically less resistance than before the pandemic.

The last gravy train left the station a long time ago. A new one has just arrived, and it's time to hop on.

Gravy train (Noun)

- Used to refer to a situation in which someone can make a lot of money for very little effort. Originally railroad slang for a short haul that paid well.

Things change. Disruption happens. As they do. Great companies learn to adapt and become better. The organization can stay numb to change, and 2020 will feel like it was full of drama, chaos and bad ju-ju, mandating for everyone to get back into the office like "normal" pre-pandemic days. Or you can embrace change and look back at 2020 with a sense of excitement and déjà vu. *Wow, all that happened FOR us. We've emerged stronger and closer than before. We're a completely different organization — ready to take on the next wave of our transformational growth.*

The future of work will be fundamentally different than before. It can feel like the edge of despair. But it is also the edge of greatness if you hold the space for the new to emerge. Holding on tightly to a past that no longer exist is the alternative. This will be a heartbreaking loss now that everyone has had a tantalizing taste of thriving in a volatile environment.

6. Practical tips

Acknowledge the complexities. Give information face-to-face in large groups regularly, with opportunities for discussion and questions. Tell people how they can offer comments, concerns and suggestions, with a clear time frame for doing so.

Context. Help people make sense of the complexity. Give the logic behind any changes, including alternatives you considered, with the pros and cons, and invite feedback. Show people how to break down the problem into its parts and then map out the actions they need to take to resolve it.

Strategy. State organizational goals, time frames and plans clearly. Set checkpoints at which progress and direction will be evaluated and midcourse corrections will be made.

Reporting. Understandably, leaders need information to make decisions. What seems to you like a simple request can set off a cascade of reporting work for everyone else, which often keeps being added to over time, like the new OKRs on top of the existing 400 KPIs. Simply keeping this waterfall effect in mind when you request for information makes a difference.

7. Related chapters

Chapter 13   Leading People Through Change

Chapter 26   Learning At The Speed Of Business

Chapter 36   Culture of Innovation

Part 5

Culture

22

Why We Hate HR

"As a HR person, you're bringing me answers to questions I don't have. But I have a lot of questions and issues that I need your help on as a HR practitioner, to help me find new and innovative answers."

— Anonymous

S am is a business leader working for a global computer manufacturer. Sam does not have the best impression of Human Resources (HR).

HR only sides the business, not the people.
HR doesn't know the inner workings of the business, but they think they do.
HR = administrivia.

As if HR is somehow out to get people in trouble, and therefore, perceived as a threat and enemy. An excerpt from *Fast Company* article, "Why We Hate HR,"[1] sums it all:

"The human-resources trade long ago proved itself, at best, a necessary evil — and at worst, a dark bureaucratic force that blindly enforces nonsensical rules, resists creativity, and impedes constructive change."

1. Old Mindset: HR is a gatekeeper

No one likes being told how they should behave, especially not dominant type-A personality type leaders. But no other group in the organization has the kind of diabolical power to boss people around like HR does.

HR thinks they know how to do people's jobs better than they do. HR communicates in an alien corporate jargon language. HR forces people to perform odious tasks that they prefer not to do, like ranking their employees from first to last and completing time-consuming and useless forms. HR prevents leaders from doing what they want, such as hiring the unicorn employee that they absolutely must have. HR's rulings impact everybody, from the bottom to the top, every single day. No one is spared.

HR is an imperious discipline master who takes the fun out of everything, throws a wrench into people's plans and serve as a bureaucratic speed bump to the success of the business. The bureaucrat HR abhors exceptions. Instead, they pursue standardization and uniformity in the face of a workforce that is heterogeneous and complex. HR benchmarks salaries, function by function and job by job, and keeps pay strictly within a narrow band, without compromise. The bureaucrat's greatest fear: Make one exception, and the floodgates will open. Exceptions are time-consuming and expensive to manage. They expect people to comply with the one-size-fits-all solutions.

When we think like this, it's no wonder that we hate HR.

2. Open Mind: What uncomfortable truth are you denying?

Sam is having a scheduled one-on-one introductory meeting with the new HR Business Partner (HRBP). The HRBP starts rattling off his responsibilities: organization design, reorganization design, fair employment practices, occupational health and safety, and so on. Leaving space to take in one quick breath, the HRBP then launches into his expectations on how they should work together. Put bluntly: These are "corporate policies," some are even regulated by law, and Sam is expected to comply.

Whatever enthusiasm Sam had at the beginning of the meeting, out of pure courtesy and proper manners, dropped to zero. Sam observes the mercurial shift as the HRBP goes from the nice, enthusiastic guy-next-door into the formal bureaucrat who thinks he knows exactly what everyone in the organization needs to do.

Sam feels disconnected. He asks the HRBP about the conversations he had with the other managers. Sam is silently hoping that the other managers would have told the HRBP what he felt he couldn't — being the perfect gentleman that he is. "Oh, they had no comment," he replies.

The HRBP is not deliberately trying to be difficult. In the last decade, the HR function has become incredibly complex. The way people work is changing, driven by technological advancements. There is a huge war for talent. Governments have created a thicket of employment regulations and practices: Fair Employment Practices, Workplace Safety and Health, Work-Life Strategies. These are complex issues requiring technical and specialized expertise. Some of these carry serious consequences for the organization if the rules are flouted. They can get lost in translation when communicated beyond the HR sphere. Thus, the need for a HRBP. But this puts whoever in that role in the unenviable position of playing the bad cop.

3. Open Heart: What difficult emotions are you ignoring?

Sam sees himself standing at the edge. He knows he must take a leap of faith to make a difference. But an incredible inner gravity holds him back. Sam's inner villain goads him, "Tell him why what he's doing is useless." The inner challenger whispers, "Be open. Be vulnerable. Use this opportunity to learn and grow together."

Sam knows that by being open, he can be inviting any number of responses — anger, accusations, future inconveniences. Maybe even a big red cross on his impeccably clean report card. He decides to take the leap, choosing to be vulnerable and open to feedback, no matter what it may cost him. "As a corporate person, you're bringing me solutions to problems I don't have. But I have a lot of problems that I need your help on as an HR practitioner, to help me find new and innovative solutions."

Silence. You can hear a pin drop. But the silence is pure energy. Sam hears a very deep sigh from the HRBP. Then he speaks up, "That's not the worst thing people have said to me since I started here. I've heard worse."

In that moment, the whole conversation shifts.

4. Open Will: What hard decision are you avoiding?

Sam watches as the HRBP's mind starts freewheeling. After a long silence, he asks Sam, "So how do you see my job? How can I support you?"

No more expecting blind compliance to pedantic guidelines and dogmatic corporate policies. No more hiding behind "spin the truth" corporate jargon. No more bargaining over pre-prepared plans and trying to convince the other person to your side of the table. Both Sam and the HRBP are seated on the *same side* of the table. It's a creative pair. The HRBP brings his strong technical expertise in recruiting, managing and motivating people, and Sam provides the point of view about the future of the business, how the organization is going to change, and how people will adapt.

Shortly after the conversation, people will approach Sam and say, "We've heard about your amazing relationship with HR. You built a lot of trust. How did you do that?"

5. New Mindset: HR is a business enabler

In the knowledge economy, organizations with the best talents win. Business leaders are collaborating with HR to find the best hires, nurture the stars, weed out the bad behaviors and foster a thriving work environment where people can do their best work. HR's role is, and has always been, to be strategic — the consultant to the CEO and the business leaders on all matters related to talent.

As organizations continue to farm out the administrivia to contractors and HR automation, HR is liberated to focus on the more important strategic role of raising the reputational and intellectual capital of the organization. There is a learning curve — the administrivia tend to be what HR has traditionally been good at, and how business leaders traditionally box them in. Business leaders need to let go of that old mentality and seek innovative ways to engage HR. *They are the experts.*

Use them! See the broad possibilities and take a more open-minded approach. This is the opportunity for HR and the business to elevate to the next level of performance.

6. Practical tips

Resistance. Some managers are resistant to approach HR for help. They worry that asking for help makes them look weak, that HR will see them as incompetent. So, they sweep their problems under the carpet. Painting HR as the villain is not going to solve your problems. Instead, see HR as the business enabler with the expertise to get you what you need.

Be strategic. HR is your weapon of choice. HR helps you to find the best hires, nurture the stars, weed out the bad behaviors and foster a thriving work environment where people can do their best work. In other words, HR helps to set you up for success.

Take ownership. It can be easy for managers to not manage and push it to HR. They make HR play the bad cop. Be aware when you're falling into the victim trap of expecting someone else to do your dirty work.

23

Restructuring Without Talent Loss

"If you are going to kill a man, it cost nothing to be polite."

— **Winston Churchill**

Bob recently accepted a new regional role to head the Asia Pacific cloud services business for a big global technology company. He is excited to be driving the growth mandate for Asia Pacific, the fastest-growing region for the organization.

As a welcome gift on the first day of work, Bob is told that he is laying off 30% of his team. Even though the Asia Pacific region is growing, growth is coming from the new cloud services, and growth has been stagnating for the traditional network equipment business, which is where the cut is being made. Bob has not even met the team yet. Instead, he is forced to look at people as named entries on an Excel spreadsheet. Bob is led into a small room to start the proceedings.

The first agenda on the hit list: the Regional Head of Sales for Asia Pacific. The man is a longtime employee, 15 years in the organization, a pioneer who helped build the Asia Pacific business from scratch when it first entered the region. He has an excellent track record and is 100% reliable. Unfortunately, the entire network equipment business is being retired, and his services, along with the services of 10 other people, are no longer needed.

When Bob meets with the Regional Sales Head to review his separation benefits and severance package, he is clearly distracted and impatient. "Just read me the letter, and let me be on my way," he says in a brusque tone.

On the one hand, this person is making Bob's job easier. For one, Bob does not enjoy firing anyone, and the shorter such an experience, the better. Just like so many other unpleasant circumstances at work, keeping employees and their dilemmas at a distance appear to be the preferred way to go. Yet Bob can tell that he wants to move on from the conversation for a reason that is not clear to him. His gut tells him that something is missing, but he does not know for sure what it is.

Should I try to find out?

No. Get it over and done with. Don't delay the agony.

But what if there's something important here?

You're only inviting trouble, anger, accusations. Worse… tears. Don't open that can of worms.

Something within Bob urges him not to run away from the moment. He abandons his desire to rush through the conversation, and instead gently asks, "I know you want to get out of here, and I appreciate that, but I can't help but feel that I'm missing something. Can you help me here? What am I missing?"

Bob doesn't know what to expect. He reminds himself to be mindful and not defensive. *Be prepared. Remain resolutely open to whatever he has to say. Don't even try to defend yourself.*

"You're not missing anything," the Regional Sales Head quickly responds. "For me, it's all very straightforward. For the past 15 years, I've been leading a double life. I am on the road 50% of the time. I've missed children's birthdays and school graduations. I've given my life to the organization. When the company needs to cut costs, they let people go. I've survived in this cut-throat environment for 15 years now, and I will do it again, albeit not in this organization. Nothing in this little letter is going to get in my way. So don't worry — you're not missing a thing."

Bob is genuinely touched that the Regional Sales Head chose to be honest with him. But Bob also feels a bit overwhelmed by what he just heard. Bob is unsure how the Regional Sales Head sees himself as he stood there, but what Bob sees is a tremendously loyal and brave professional. Bob feels he made the right choice taking the time to open up mindfully rather than rush past the discomfort. This person is teaching him a profoundly valuable lesson and inspires him to re-examine a critical but often overlooked aspect of employee layoffs: their emotional well-being.

1. Old Mindset: It's just business. It's not personal.

Organizational restructuring is a complex process, fraught with statutory, regulatory and operational challenges. Change management is a huge challenge for organizations, especially when it involves multiple countries.

It starts with senior management going through rounds of number-crunching and planning. There are contingency plans. Then there are contingency plans for the contingency plans. There are so many parties at stake at a time of instability dealing with highly sensitive material. Everyone is walking on eggshells. Whatever you say or not say, do or not do, can very easily end up in a legal dispute with an aggrieved employee.

In an ideal world, the organization and its custodians will be given enough time and resources to do a proper job. But this is reality. They don't get the space and time. Everything needs to be done and dusted yesterday. In this high-pressured and highly volatile environment, it is not difficult to go over the edge and become numb.

The restructuring then becomes a top-down exercise like a coin-operated machine. Robot sentinels swarm down the organization command chain onto people like Bob in a public execution style, axes swinging swiftly and mechanically, going purely by the numbers in a nightmarish state of hallucination caused by extreme sleep deprivation. With managers down the line flailing to shield themselves from the inescapable and inexorable hacking from above, they will miss small but vital clues. Like how one person Bob is about to cut — because he only achieved 20% of his numbers *this year* — was the top biller *last year*. The committee in the ivory tower can't possibly foresee how this person will later join the competition and steal customers away from the organization.

The organization expects those who remain to go back to their usual working lives as if nothing happened. They can't fathom how the departures will trigger a downward spiral on employee morale. Employees read between the lines: *You are only as good as your last quarter's performance.* A general malaise creeps across the organization.

2. Open Mind: What uncomfortable truth are you denying?

Bob is a high-flying executive with 20 years of experience under his belt. It has been an incredible journey, but it's not all a sweet-smelling bed of roses. He has had to eliminate many jobs, displace many employees, and advise others that they must seek employment elsewhere. It's the least pleasant part of his job. It's the hardest part of the job, and also the most compassionate. Letting people go is difficult, but he is acutely aware that it's equally difficult for the person who is being let go. Someone who is made redundant — even if they are the Michael Jordan of a blue-chip Silicon Valley tech company — will take it hard.

This is my fault! I should have kept my mouth shut.
Why is this happening to me?
Why not the guy sitting next to me? Why me?

This internal torment can go on in their heads for a while, even after they are long gone. When they are not given a valid reason for being let go (or they refuse to accept it as a valid reason), confusion arises. There is a cognitive dissonance. First, they will blame the organization. When they can't blame the organization, they will blame themselves. *There must be something wrong with me.*

I'm too old.
I'm too expensive.
I'm not local.
I'm not Chinese (the majority ethnicity in Singapore).

People will contrive stories. Stories upon stories. It spreads like Chinese whispers leading people to believe and spread the gossip. *The company is only retaining the young employees because they are cheaper.* It's bad juju that floats around the office like a vengeful spirit.

3. Open Heart: What difficult emotions are you ignoring?

Letting people go is a distasteful part of management that most people fear. Managers are given nicknames like "The Executioner." Some managers fear it so much they push the responsibility to HR. When people ask for the basis of the layoff, they will say: "It was HR's decision." HR fills the role of the office bad guy.

Some managers are narcissistic enough to like the bad-guy image. But being the bad guy is hard for Bob who has a healthy dose of empathy. People scream in his face. They stop talking to him. They storm out of the office when he is mid-sentence. Bob will encounter all sorts of negative emotions from others: anger, tears, accusations, even hatred. It can feel like the edge of despair. It is reasonable to want to avoid situations like this. It's human instinct to protect our sanity, to give "corporate" responses to avoid legal disputes and cut conversations short to avert emotional puddles. But this is also the edge of greatness if you hold the space to manage your emotions. You maintain your dignity. It also creates the space for the other person to leave with their dignity intact.

Leading from an open heart does not drain us. Simply opening yourself to the discomfort, anger, tears, anxiety and accusations, rather than feeling rushed, inconvenienced or anxious, can make all the difference. For yourself and the other person. Your tender heart is what makes you human. Hide it, and you hide what's superhuman about you.

Letting people go is the hardest part of the job, and it is also the most compassionate, for yourself and others. Create the space and time to center yourself. We think that taking the time to take care of ourselves and respecting our boundaries is selfish. It's not true. Like the pre-flight safety briefing, you put on your oxygen mask first, before attending to others. ∎

4. Open Will: What hard decision are you avoiding?

Organizational restructuring is a complex process. It helps when you're not doing it alone. Having an open-hearted HR makes all the difference.

HR works with Bob to craft a heartfelt announcement for the layoff. We are more familiar with announcements that are done in a heartless way, with a disingenuous apology, and pinning the blame on a scapegoat without addressing the real issue. They usually reek of corporate-speak and half-truths.

With the help of HR, Bob chooses to state the obvious and tackle the mission statement head-on. He explains the decision-making process behind the restructuring. Leaders think they must be positive and be seen to be in full control of the situation, as if raising doubts will sink the ship. On the contrary, when leaders are transparent and speak the truth authentically, people's confidence in them will increase. Bob clearly defines the ambiguities: what he knows and what he doesn't. He articulates clearly the issues the organization is facing, the corresponding risks and possible rewards. Bob provides a structure to help employees navigate the ambiguity. Bob makes it clear to employees that this wasn't their fault. It has nothing to do with their performance. Their skills are not being questioned.

5. New Mindset: It's not just business. It's also personal.

Normal times are like formal social situations: we smile politely, we say the right things, we are a paragon of virtue. But when we're in a crisis, it's the opposite. Stuck between a rock and a hard place, our executive brain does not perform as well. Our brain's braking system is impaired; we get triggered easily and make knee-jerk reactions to minor inconveniences.

During a recession, the mission statement is often forgotten. Instead, it is replaced by graphs of revenues going down, justifying the number of employees to be laid off going up. People become numbers on a spreadsheet.

By putting the mission statement right, front and center, you remember what you stand for and why you are doing this in the first place. It's your measuring stick to use in every decision you make. Rally those who are remaining behind the mission statement. Honor those who are leaving, their work will live on through the mission statement.

And remember, you don't have to do this alone. Having an HR partner whose values align with yours can make all the difference.

6. Practical tips

Be creative. One of the main obstacles is the time constraint. Even with constraints, there are still ways to treat people fairly. This means that you must be creative to do things that you may not have done before, like pivoting your recruitment resources to provide in-house outplacement and transition support.

WFIO. There will be WFIO moments. It will be tough. People will be let go. People will have to deal with broken processes. There will be difficult emotions. Hold the space for it without the usual fear, resentment and blame. The villain here is denial.

Communicate. Be clear and direct in your communication.[1] Personalize your communication to the different stakeholders — what it means for them. Don't hide behind legalistic mumbo jumbo. Our instinct is to shield people from the truth. The villain here is denial. Nature abhors an empty space. Rumors fill it up marvelously.

7. Related chapters

Chapter 11   Being Let Go

Chapter 16   Letting People Go

Chapter 20   Restructuring Your Business

24

Reducing Employee
Turnover

*"Real leadership is when everyone else feels
in charge."*

— **Bono**

Jack heads the digital business unit in a global advertising company. His business unit is the meteoric rising star of his organization. Its rapid growth far outstrips the growth of its people, requiring a continual flow of talent with very specialized technical skills. It has been frustrating for Jack trying to fill all the roles, especially the senior ones because of the talent shortage in the market. Jack currently has four Client Leaders in the team, but he doesn't think they are good enough.

Jack tells his HR business partner to start looking for talents externally. His HR business partner sends him a few candidate profiles — they are supposed to be the best in the industry. Jack thinks none of them is good enough.

Within the next two months, two Client Leaders resign, and one is put on the "pip." All three of them barely lasted a year in the organization. This leaves the business unit in a lurch. Jack has no one to look after his largest and most important customers. The last remaining Client Leader looks like a flight risk who might resign at any moment. He was recently reassigned to focus on client acquisition. He has his hands full focusing on acquiring new business. What little time he has left, he spends on supporting the role he just moved out of. Essentially, he is doing two jobs.

1. Old Mindset: People are replaceable

Let's paint a picture of what "good enough" entails for Jack. This person needs to be a senior performance marketing manager fluent in the best new techniques in data-driven online advertising systems. This person needs to manage a project team of twenty. Essentially, this person needs to have the strategic mindset of a McKinsey consultant, the commercial savvy of a CFO and the execution power of a COO.

Jack is not looking for a Client Leader. Jack is looking for a unicorn — some magical creature who swoops in, sprinkles magic dust and solves all his problems. The problem is: Outside of cartoons and cute pencil boxes, unicorns don't exist.

Jack thinks that the Client Leaders are the problem. *He is incompetent. She has an attitude problem.* Jack thinks that he has solved his problem by getting rid of one Client Leader and bringing in another. Jack may have rid his life of the previous Client Leader, but he has not gotten rid of his problem. Jack is disappointed again when the new unicorn can't deliver fast enough to fill the bottomless pit. Obscene growth is a ravenous beast.

Jack comes back to the same problem of "not good enough." Jack goes on his search for unicorns again.

The hunt for the mystical unicorn never ends.

2. Open Mind: What uncomfortable truth are you denying?

Jack can keep changing Client Leaders, but the deeper problem remains unaddressed: market demand for this new service far outstrips the talent supply. The industry is growing faster than it can develop people. Organizations look externally to fill their roles; competing for the same limited talent pool.

Jack doesn't want to run away from his problem anymore. He does not want superficial changes. He no longer wants to chip away at the tip of the iceberg. He wants a *real* solution. He knows he needs to dig deeper. He's been avoiding the elephant in the room. His HR Business Partner has been suggesting for him to look at redesigning the team structure. But it's not that simple. This is a complex business. The current structure has worked successfully in the past. This is how they've always done it. Changing the team structure will raise some eyebrows among the leadership ranks. There's a lot at stake here, including his own job.

This is a moment of truth for Jack. *This way is no longer working.* Jack decides to take a risk and do something controversial. He realizes that the Client Leader role is the bottleneck. It's like the Client Leader is expected to be on top of *everything*. With the HR Business Partner, Jack redesigns the organization structure. He splits the Client Leader role into two: Key Account Manager and Project Manager.

The Key Account Manager will focus on understanding the client's business. This person will have the strategic mindset of a McKinsey consultant and the commercial savvy of a CFO.

The Project Manager will focus on project delivery. This person will manage a project team of twenty and have the execution power of a COO.

Next, Jack creates a shared center of excellence and fills it with the meanest badass performance marketers that he can afford. Some of them are barely fresh out of school. They will hone their specialized skills using the best new techniques in data-driven online advertising systems.

Jack essentially broke down the top-down, hierarchical, command-and-control structure and created an agile, acentric network of highly empowered teams that can work on specific business projects and clients. His organization design looks more like Hollywood movie production teams and less like the traditional corporation. People come together to tackle projects, then disband and move on to other assignments once the project is delivered.

3. Open Heart: What difficult emotions are you ignoring?

Before, Jack's employees were doing the jobs of two or three people. Too much was going on. Working in this overwhelmed state is fine for a short time, but doing it over a prolonged period is not sustainable. People start dropping balls. People start burning out. People leave before they lose ALL their hair. Hiring and firing won't solve the real problem. The hiring process is a huge cost in terms of money and time. Jack hires them, trains them, then fires them. Or they resign. And the cycle continues. Jack ends up running very hard, but going nowhere. And *everyone* is traumatized from the experience.

When Jack redesigns the organization structure, instantly, the talent sourcing pool expands. As he moves the blocks around the board to find the optimal organization design, the names of certain individuals keep popping up. They are the ones everyone seems to turn to for expertise: "You need to get person X on the call to explain why it's done this way and how to fix it."

These individuals are diamonds in the rough. They are already performing. They are already motivated. But because of the hierarchical nature of the organization structure before, they were hidden in the matrix. Now, they have emerged into the light. The new structure gives them the space to grow, and they will rise to fill it. They can hit the ground running.

Jack assigns them to the newly created roles. He sends them for expensive specialized training, which wouldn't have been possible in the past because of their job grade. Deciding which training to go to is no longer an employee perk based on your job grade. It is now a business imperative based on business needs.

4. Open Will: What hard decision are you avoiding?

Before, Jack was on a mission to search for unicorns. The problem is: unicorns do not exist. Wishing for unicorns who will fly in and solve all your problems paints it as a people problem instead of an organizational design problem.

Maybe this organization structure was enormously successful in the past. That is how it has always been done. But it no longer works now. Advertising has become mind-bogglingly complex, and it can no longer be managed entirely by imperial decree.

Initially, the new team model looks like the "before" version of Mighty Ducks — twelve people showing up in different gear, not knowing where to go or what to do. There is no precedence to this — no process or SOP (standard operating procedure) to follow. It is complete disorganization. Jack is just relieved to have people who are willing to put the longevity of their careers on the line to bet on his hare-brained idea.

Jack watches in total amazement as they self-organize. The team sets their own goals and makes their own decisions within the context of the project, reversing the traditional top-down structure where the leader sets the goals, creates the standards and tells people exactly what to do. This allows for dynamism and agility. The team can respond much faster to the client's changing needs and demands without going through rounds of approvals. They can make better decisions because they have eyes on the ground. Jack's role is to identify and smash through the obstacles that prevent the team from doing their jobs.

In the past, Jack would get sucked into the drama when things turn pear-shaped and are escalated to his attention. With this new highly empowered team structure, Jack is liberated from the day-to-day operations to focus on the big picture; things like strategy, vision and culture. There is a bigger game afoot. Jack now has the freedom to do the job stated on his business card, rather than being dragged down to do other people's jobs.

5. New Mindset: People are your ONLY competitive advantage

These individuals will go on to form part of Jack's executive leadership team. They are battle-tested and ready for anything Jack throws at them. They are bulletproof. Jack's business unit gains credibility and trust across the organization that is visible in the market. Jack becomes well-known within the industry for creating the future of the digital business unit.

His way of working is cutting-edge and completely different from the rest of the industry which have been doing things the same way for 20 years. Jack no longer needs to worry about the talent shortage. Top talents want a seat on this rocket ship.

You simply can't hire and fire your way out of complex problems. Looking externally for a unicorn paints it as a people problem. You hire and fire. That's only chipping away at the tip of the iceberg. The changes are superficial. Deep transformation does not happen.

When you're dealing with complexity, you want to retain the people who understand the legacy problems that are unique to your organization. If they leave the organization, they bring all their institutional knowledge with them. Someone new coming into the organization will need time to understand the intricacies of your business. It's more effective to figure out how you can utilize the potential of the people you already have in your business. Previously, these individuals were hidden in the matrix. They are diamonds in the rough. When Jack opened up the matrix, he found them, polished them, put them in the light and, boy, did they sparkle. When you do this, you unlock the human potential within your people and your organization. Maybe unicorns do exist after all! They were under Jack's nose the whole time, but he couldn't see them because he was fixated on looking for a white stallion with a long spiraling horn on its forehead!

Identify people who are already motivated, and support their growth. This will become the source of your greatest pride and joy: taking B-players and turning them into rockstar A-players. If you hold the space for people to grow, they will rise and fill that space. You put them to the challenge, trusting that they will break through. The idea may be simple, but it's not easy to implement. It may mean doing away with how the industry has organized work for a long time.

6. Practical tips

Optimal structure. When throwing more people at the growth problem no longer works, it may help to relook the team structure. The skeleton of a cub can't hold up the muscular flesh of a full-grown lion.

Bad hire. There can be so much pressure to hire that job candidates can talk themselves into roles; effectively lowering the bar on talent just to fill up seats. Hiring the right person for the job is never easy, but dealing with the fallout from a bad hire can be even more challenging. Better to keep them out in the first place.

Accelerate leadership. Instead of adding competition to the talent shortage situation in the market, focus on increasing the talent supply. Invest in developing your employees. Identify employees that are already motivated, and support their growth.

Acknowledge. Acknowledge your employees' gifts and talents. Actively notice when your employee is doing something right. Notice how they light up as you affirm their positive view of themselves. They are more likely to repeat it.

Unicorns. If you're experiencing high employee turnover, check if you're searching for unicorns — some magical creature who swoops in and solves all your problems. Instead, be specific about the core skills you need. Hire the best people you can find with those specialized skills.

7. Related chapters

Chapter 10   Job Hopping

Chapter 19   Scaling Your Business

25

Transforming Your Culture

*"It does a company no good when its leader never
shares his leadership functions with his
lieutenants. The more centres of leadership you
find in a company the stronger it will become."*
— David Ogilvy

A nne is the head of one of Asia's fastest-growing advertising groups when it is acquired by a global advertising network. Externally, the message is very positive, with lots of song and dance. But internally, Anne faces a complex challenge around the integration process. The organization is more like a hodgepodge of advertising agencies, from eclectic boutiques to entirely honorable corporations — the consequence of an enormously successful growth strategy through acquisition. But Anne is now faced with a dilemma. How is she going to align 20 brands and 1,700 people behind the new global advertising network without anyone leaving?

As part of the integration process, the Human Resources (HR) from the global advertising network sends Anne the organization's global vision, mission and values. They assume it will be cascaded down to the 20 brands. A 500-slide Powerpoint document, with fancy images. Anne already anticipates strong resistance internally from the brands. The organization functions more like a diverse assortment of fiefdoms rather than a united force. The lack of cohesion is a consequence of acquiring agencies and then allowing them to operate relatively autonomously. Many of the brands are still run by the founders themselves and their founding teams. They have a strong brand identity and are fiercely protective of it. There is a strong "me versus them" mentality. Already, Anne and her team are seen as the "big brother," enforcing rules and regulations, slowing them down. Best kept at arm's length. The brands prickle with indignation when they see any directive coming from the mothership. *Just leave us alone.*

Anne speaks to the Chairman, the owner of the organization. He sees it differently. He does not see an issue. Just cascade the parent organization's 500-slide Powerpoint presentation. He assumes all the brands will comply. The Chairman has a gregarious controlling personality with a traditional, autocratic leadership style. He does not see a need for discussion. When Anne persists, he says, "If anyone has a problem, tell them to talk to me."

1. Old Mindset: Command and control

It seems there is not a word in management literature that is as divisive and controversial as the word "empowerment." It is thrown around loosely, well-meaning but misguided, and ends up confusing people.

Traditional management literature carries a hidden assumption that people are not fit to do their job, and that they need to be "empowered" to fulfill their responsibilities, feel more committed and be more engaged. The organization tells people exactly who they are, what to believe and how they should behave. To motivate them, the organization dangles the carrot and gives the inspirational pep talk, "You can do it!" — in a Club Med environment serving all-you-can-eat buffets and twenty types of water.

That is not empowerment. That is command-and-control, dressed up as empowerment. People are told they are empowered, but when they make mistakes or speak the uncomfortable truths, it's met with stern judgment, punitive consequences and public shame. What the organization is really saying: *Don't think. Don't feel. You can't trust your intuition. It's unreliable.* The organization thinks it knows their people better than they know themselves, as informed by organization theory, which is rooted in concepts developed during the beginnings of the Industrial Revolution more than a 100 years ago. Now that's disempowering.

2. Open Mind: What uncomfortable truth are you denying?

Anne is in a complex situation with the Chairman. On one hand, his edict makes her job easy. Take the 500-slide document and cascade it downwards to the 20 brands. Set some KPIs (key performance indicators) to make sure that they execute on it.

He's the boss. He must be right. But inside, her wisdom kicks in. It'll just be another paper exercise. It'll make them feel busy, but it won't make a real impact, other than the new fancy signboard hung at the reception. Fundamentally, nothing changes. It's still "me versus them."

Anne does not want to be a military dictator and impose the parent organization's will on the 20 brands as decreed by the Chairman. But she also understands the motivation behind the Chairman's decree. He needs to show quick wins to the acquiring company. He needs to be seen to be integrating the businesses. His next payout only happens when the integration is completed.

Taking a top-down approach to the integration process is surgical and efficient. Taking a more grassroots approach will be difficult. It'll take more time, you can get lost in the corporate maze, and the results are not immediately apparent.

Everything must go through me. If a CEO thinks this way, the business is not going to go very far. People won't be inspired. They stop thinking. They don't take responsibility for their actions. *I'm just following orders.* Your best talents leave. The smarter the talent, the less interested they are in following orders. The organization becomes constrained by the CEO's personal capabilities. Ego is a big thing.

Anne may lose her job going against the wishes of the Chairman. But she can't *not* do it. She can't help but feel that they are failing to seize an unbelievably golden opportunity to unite the hodgepodge of fiefdoms to become an irresistible force to be reckoned with.

3. Open Heart: What difficult emotions are you ignoring?

Anne wants to empower the 20 brands. But neither does she want to introduce anarchy. The common misunderstanding is that you empower people to please them. *Go ahead, do whatever you want.* In the hope that they remain engaged enough so that they won't quit. That will be going to the other extreme end. Without any constraints, the advertising agency could very well turn into a coffee shop.

You don't empower people to please them. Instead, you empower people so that they can make better decisions for the organization. The best solutions are not created in the ivory tower. The best solutions emerge organically as a result of countless good decisions made by purposeful individuals across the organization based on their direct engagement with the real world and whatever information that is available to them at that point in time. The solution that emerges is inherently realistic and sustainable, and thus more likely to succeed.

Empowering people means providing them with a clear mandate. The priorities are so clear that people *feel* empowered to make the right decision. It also means providing people access to the relevant information at a local level so that they can deal with problems quickly without the need for anyone's permission. When people are empowered to make better decisions, this makes the organization more resilient to change and more agile to cope with challenges. It's as much about empowering people as it is about empowering the organization.

4. Open Will: What hard decision are you avoiding?

At the operations level, Anne works closely with her HR partner. Both of them agree that for the integration to be successful, they have to empower all the brands to focus on the overall corporate mission. This requires real change in people's behaviors; they've been operating in their silos for so long. Anne and the HR partner identified critical leadership and collaboration skills that everyone needs to adopt to facilitate this transformation.

The HR partner helps Anne understand that she plays an important part to be the authentic voice that helps people understand all the changes that are happening around them. Anne also plays the part of a role model, setting an example of what being empowered and mission-driven looks like. This makes it safe for everyone else to adopt the new behaviors.

It's a partnership. Anne at the front-end inspiring people to come onboard this transformation journey. The HR partner at the back-end facilitating that transformation. *Wonder Twin powers, activate!* The HR partner develops a flexible framework that can be tailored to meet the different needs of the brands. He conceptualizes a six-month roadshow to roll out the framework to all the 20 brands.

For brands that are strongly protective of their brand identity, the HR partner centers the conversation around continuous engagement and reassurance. *This is not about changing you. It's about aligning us.*

For brands that have never done this work, the HR partner centers the conversation on education to build their understanding of leading the business with a common purpose. He helps them define their mission in their own words and align it with the global mission.

In the end, Anne and the HR partner successfully align the 20 brands behind the global mission. They got 1,700 employees to take one small step in a common direction, enabling the organization to accelerate growth and performance. This was made possible by helping them embrace the change, rather than have change forced upon them.

5. New Mindset: Empowerment

Transforming culture takes time, and it gets pushed to the last. After spending significant time and money on strategy, processes and technology, whatever is left is funneled to retrain people. At this point, organizations are scraping the bottom of the barrel. They have run out of time and money. And they assume people will adjust. *Get on with it.*

People always come last. Why? Because senior leadership needs to show quick wins. They need to be *seen* to be doing something, and it needs to be very visible. It's so legit to talk about empowering people. But many fall into the trap of believing that *saying* the right thing is the same as *doing* the right thing.

You don't empower people to please them. In fact, empowerment can feel disorienting. People have gotten so used to being told what to do. Instead, you empower people so that they can make better and more timely decisions for the organization.

Nobody comes to work to suck at their jobs. Everyone wants to make lives better, create an impact and deliver results. Those are the things most employees find truly motivating. Those who don't will bounce. An empowered workforce is a competitive advantage. When you create a culture that empowers people to make quicker and better decisions, you will create an agile organization that can spin on a dime. People can take an idea — *any* idea — and make it great. The best talents want to join your organization. Your organization will be known as that place with an amazing culture. There's nothing more thrilling than being part of a high-performing team moving in the same direction.

6. Practical tips

Vision. Most leaders fail to clearly articulate the vision and priorities for their organization. How clear do you need to be? Well, clear enough such that people *feel* empowered to make the right decision for the company. It's more common to hear people complain about top-down management and being disempowered. Instead, when you provide a clear vision and priorities, you're giving them a goalpost. Everyone wants to win. You're helping them to help themselves.

Employee engagement. Too often, engagement implies free flow of food, slides and meditation rooms. It totally misses the real driver of employee engagement: love for the work itself.

Context. Understand the context before adopting "best practices" of other organizations. Google implemented the 20% rule not as an employee engagement strategy but because managers were not allowing their engineers to work on pet projects. The irony of benchmarking is that you're telling people to try to be someone else. Instead, try to be more like yourself in your best moments.

Guard rails. Create an environment that allows people to take risks and make mistakes, but not irresponsibly. Provide guard rails. *You can do what you want in pursuit of the mission except for these hard limits.*

7. Related chapters

Chapter 7   Dealing with a Difficult Boss

Chapter 14   Dealing with a Difficult Employee

Chapter 36   Culture of Innovation

26

Learning at the Speed of Business

"The illiterate of the 21st century will not be those who cannot read and write, but those who cannot learn, unlearn, and relearn."

— Alvin Toffler

Jacqueline is a client lead for a large advertising company. One of her most important clients is not happy with the work that is being produced by the project team.

This problem is not new to Jacqueline. This is a new and fast-growing area; there is a very limited pool of talents with the relevant skills. Most of them are barely fresh out of university. The head of learning and development (L&D) has been suggesting to her for the last six months to send the project team for training. But Jacqueline couldn't afford for the project team to take time off work.

Jacqueline knows she's only kicking the can down the road. She finally bites the bullet and asks the L&D head to organize the two-day workshop for the project team.

The feedback Jacqueline receives during the workshop:

"Gosh! Two days. It is too long."
"The training is disengaging."
"The venue and food are horrible."
"The facilitator is boring!"

Even though some of the project team members had a powerful learning experience during the training, it did not translate to changed behavior back on the frontline. Back at work, it seems like nothing has changed: deadlines are still not kept, work is still shoddy and problems are still unresolved. Jacqueline asks if the project team has been practicing what they learnt, and they reply: "Oh, I'm too busy."

It looks like the workshop was a waste of everyone's time. This dilemma is not new to Jacqueline or her organization. Companies have invested billions of dollars on learning and development, and employees are not using them. Even if they are using them, very little gets retained or translated into new behaviors at work. It's no wonder that we've started noticing a silent and sinister revolt on L&D. Training is met with dry cynicism and skepticism. It's a love-hate relationship with L&D. Is there a better way?

1. Old Mindset: Learning in the classroom

For decades, learning and development has been big business, thanks mostly to the lavish support of modern organizations and partnership with universities. In the 1980s, companies started building universities or academies, hired faculty and college professors, and sent their employees for training with them. Companies curated their own MBA programs.

The university or academy was the epicenter of knowledge and excellence. The "high potentials" of the organization would spend time here learning all about the organization, its customers, products, organization structure and processes — everything they need to know for the next job 2–5 years down the line. Employees would fly in from all over the world to sit in front of deep experts to learn about computer engineering, software, design, customer service and business management.

Being the epicenter of knowledge and excellence, most of the programs were designed to be comprehensive and complete. As the modern business world became more complex, the programs became more convoluted. What you have today is a quicksand of possibility, and volumes of near-pontifical complexity explaining everything, full of contradictions.

These programs are exorbitantly expensive, so they can only be made available to the top 1% of the organization. The theory goes, train the most senior leaders, and the effects will trickle down, from the C-suite to middle managers, and, ultimately, front-line employees. But this top-down model doesn't work. Not only that, it's the antithesis of inclusion, since most employees aren't included.

2. Open Mind: What uncomfortable truth are you denying?

Just having intellectual knowledge does not change behaviors. When people try to change things, they're usually tinkering with behaviors that have become automatic. The workshop may have been mentally stimulating, but old habits die hard. In the safety of the classroom, we may be able to perform the desired behavior. But when we are back in the stressful and demanding work environment, we automatically revert to old habitual behaviors. So long as old habitual behaviors are not inhibited, the changes will remain superficial. Deep transformation does not happen.

Jacqueline no longer wants to chip away at the tip of the iceberg. She wants real solutions that will permanently address her problems. That means diving below the surface of the ocean and going to the bottom of the iceberg.

In consultation with the L&D head, Jacqueline realizes that what the project team lacks is not technical skills — which can be picked up on "Youtube University", if you're motivated enough to search for it. What's really lacking is a broad spectrum of social and behavioral skills, which are more complex, emotional and experiential. It's not that Jacqueline's people are incompetent. The organization is growing faster than its people. For example, Jacqueline hired a designer fresh out of university, and within two years, this person is managing a team of 50.

With Jacqueline's inputs, the L&D head customizes a client leadership program specifically for their business context. The program is designed to build six specific leadership capabilities, like design thinking and holding creative conversations. The core of the program focuses on gaining real-world experience — learning through doing.

Many leadership development programs assume a one-size-fits-all leadership model, regardless of the situation. Also, leadership models are developed based on reflecting on past experiences and studying the successes of previous leaders and organizations. Sometimes the experience of the past is not very useful. Sometimes it becomes the very obstacle that stops you from coming up with a new way to respond to a situation.

3. Open Heart: What difficult emotions are you ignoring?

Jacqueline believes that the project team have the leadership "muscles." They just need to train and exercise those muscles. Whenever Jacqueline sees the right behavior, she acknowledges it. She's basically catching people in the act of doing the right thing. When we're trying to adopt a new behavior that is different from a habit that is already ingrained, we first need to learn to "feel" it. Then when we have a taste of it, we can do more of it and become better. If we practice without first learning to "feel" for the right muscles, we will end up reinforcing the wrong muscles.

This is very different from off-the-shelf programs in the market, where we're spoon-fed one-size-fits-all model answers. We're judged and evaluated against the leadership model, told where our gaps are and given the training to bridge the gaps. It becomes an exercise of piling on the "security blanket" in the form of a certificate for attending the training — layer upon layer. Leadership development is not about training people to conform to a model answer. It's about training people to become better versions of themselves. No one else knows what you should do. The experts don't know, because none of them are living your life — with your talents, challenges, experiences and connections. Every leadership journey is an exception to the rule. It's not one-size-fits-all. It's deeply personal.

If this approach is more effective, then why don't we see more of it? Developing programs that are personal is not efficient. It means that the programs must be as unique and agile as the individuals. The cookie-cutter approach is a lot more scalable. Leadership development is certainly big business, but in institutionalizing leadership development, we may have unintentionally nurtured the delusion that leadership qualities are something that can only be acquired in MBA school, rather than coming from our own reality and experiences. Like we need someone in a white coat to tell us whether we've got "it." That we need to be told what is right and wrong, good and bad, what we should and shouldn't do. Somewhere along the way, we learn to stop thinking for ourselves. We become disconnected. No matter how many certificates we acquire, "leadership qualities" will continue to be elusive. We go into a catatonic shock when confronted with a dubious situation that does not come to its own model answer sheet.

4. Open Will: What hard decision are you avoiding?

The L&D lead subsequently scaled the programme into a 6-week virtual course for the entire department. Every week, everyone is trained on a specific leadership skill and given tools to help them discover answers for themselves "in the wild." Thus, the real "classroom" is the workplace, and the "teachers" are the ecosystem of clients, colleagues, bosses, mentors, peers and subject matter experts from whom they can learn from. In other words, you're not giving them the fish; you're teaching them to fish.

Learning in chunks over time allows people to learn one thing, apply it at work, and then come back and learn the next thing. This can't happen with a two-day in-person workshop. Instead, you'd leave with pages of 'to dos', which end up not getting done.

When designed well, virtual learning trumps in-person training. At an organizational level, you're talking about real change in weeks, not years. Simply put, you're shifting from a model of teaching a few people a lot of content slowly, to teaching a lot of people just enough content quickly.

5. New Mindset: Learning in the flow of work

This is not *another* training program that provides model answers and one-size-fits-all solutions. This is a whole new approach to learning and development. In the good old days, the universities were the center of knowledge and excellence, and we went back to school to learn. Today, the center of knowledge and excellence is the ecosystem itself. Your employees learn from the ecosystem, the intersection of complex social, political, economic and institutional forces, and they evolve through the ecosystem — thereby changing the ecosystem itself. They grow as the ecosystem grows.

This approach is not a substitute to the traditional approach. Instead, this new approach is about learning to develop our wisdom and expertise as the ecosystem continues to evolve. In other words, we learn how to learn, unlearn, and relearn. This approach brings us closer *towards* the natural workflow of the organization, instead of pulling people *away* from their work for long periods of time to learn. Learning and development becomes a lifelong process of tripping over the truth as the future emerges. Every advance reveals a new shortcoming. You're never done.

Learning in the flow of work is a lot more effective in accelerating leadership through the organization. This approach is highly aligned with business objectives, with sponsorship from the business leaders and the CEO, who deem this a strategic and high-value priority. This approach is also cost-effective, making it accessible to more people. This goes beyond relying on the top 1% to implement new behaviors and cascade it down the organization. Now, that's empowering!

6. Practical tips

Strategic-specific. Build out what you need. Tailor the training program to address the business context and build specific leadership and business capabilities. It's about supporting people to perform in their jobs now — not the job five years down the road.

70-20-10. We learn 70% of our knowledge through doing (taking on challenging experiences and assignments), 20% through others (developmental relationships), and 10% through formal training (in-person or online). At the moment, learning and development focuses on formal training. Instead, shift more focus to facilitating real-world learning experiences in the moment of need. Create structures to facilitate more learning through doing.

Learn, unlearn, relearn. In a rapidly changing world, the ability to unlearn and relearn matters more than ever. We need to *actively* stop thinking one way — the dominant thought — before another train of thought can arrive. It's not about adding to your suitcase of skills; it's about learning to let go.

7. Related chapters

Chapter 27   Leadership Development

Chapter 36   Culture of Innovation

Part 6

Transformation Tools: What Is Your Leadership Brand?

27

Leadership Development

*"Our deepest fear is not that we are inadequate.
Our deepest fear is that we are powerful beyond
measure. It is our light, not our darkness that
most frightens us."*

— Marianne Williamson

Think positive. Set goals and OKRs. Avoid loser talk. Look at the bright side. Suppress your negative emotions. We've heard these types of advice for performing under stress. They make a big part of leadership development. When things get harder, our automatic response is to work harder and longer. *Go big, or don't go home.*

The problem? These toxic positivity strategies simply don't work. While there are substantial research that positivity is beneficial under many circumstances, but during periods of high stress and high demand, tactics like positivity and suppression are not merely ineffective, they can be actively damaging.[1]

Positivity and suppression are failed strategies. That's because positively reframing an experience when undergoing stressful or demanding situations takes up a lot of cognitive power — mental energy that you've already burnt out. And it's cyclical and exponential. As your focus fades, you get triggered more easily. You react by trying even harder to be positive and stop the loser talk. This sucks up even more cognitive power. And through all this, you're making unintended mistakes. Stress ratchets up, and your mood worsens. You react by leaning harder into these failed strategies. You're spiraling downwards, and you simply can't help it. In other words, you're working very hard to stop yourself from getting out of the funk!

The solution is simple. When working harder is not getting the results that you want, maybe it's time to change that strategy. This is not about squeezing and pushing your way to the top. That's too exhausting and you burn out sooner or later. Instead, find your sweet spot for performance.

Set ambitious goals, think better and faster, be more positive — it all matters. But that's only half the story. Operating in your sweet spot for performance means being fully present in the face of *everything* you have to deal with as a mighty corporate warrior. Through good and bad. Through pleasure and misery. Through hope and despair. Through greatness and adversity. You don't deny the uncomfortable truths. You don't ignore the difficult emotions. You don't avoid making the hard decision. You manage it. You're dancing on the edge of greatness. It can feel like the edge of despair, but this is exactly where the magic happens. The energy you waste on toxic positivity and ruthless suppression can be channeled more effectively to lead with grace and power.

1. Why it works

People work at their best when they are appropriately challenged and stretched. That's the sweet spot for performance. They experience just the right amount of positive stress. *Not too hot, not too cold, but just right.* This is where we experience our greatest trajectory for performance. But there's a limit beyond which the stretch becomes unproductive, even destructive. Our threat response kicks in — the more automatic, primitive part of our brain — and we get pulled into playing the small game.

Learning to operate in the sweet spot for performance means gaining deeper self-awareness of the old dysfunctional behavioral habits that keeps us playing the small game, and establishing new ones that keep us playing the big game in a consistent and sustainable way. It's about becoming better versions of ourselves. This is a continuous evolving process — it's a practice.

The sweet spot for performance is not something you can buy off the shelf or get from reading a book. No one else can do it for you. It requires an individualized approach. Individuals vary in terms of the stretch they need to feel engaged and alert — or tip them over the edge. This is not about getting you to conform to a one-size-fits-all leadership model. There is no certain type of person that you must emulate. It's not about changing yourself to fit a job description. Instead, this is about owning your influence in the world. Greatness requires a personal commitment. Your leadership brand is a representation of your personal commitment to scale your impact in the world. Discovering your leadership brand requires slowing down and having a strategic conversation about the most exciting topic in the world: YOU. Bring out your X-factor — that *je ne sais quoi.* The answers come from within. It's deeply personal.

READY
Frame your learning edge.

SET
Define your leadership brand.

GO
Activate new leadership habits.

Figure 27.1: Making leadership personal.

2. What blocks us from doing it?

People can work hard for many years but never *free up* enough to get into the sweet spot for performance. They can never *let go* enough to get there. Growth requires a balance of stress and rest. *Stress + Rest = Growth.* But this experience feels alien to us. We are trained, hardened corporate warriors. We're more familiar with feeling busy, stressed and burned out. We think this is normal — a mark of achievement, even. We don't have a problem turning it on — the *Stress* part of the equation. We have trouble turning it off — the *Rest* part of the equation. We don't give ourselves the space to rest or reflect. We're always ON! ON! ON!

The next time you're stuck no matter how hard you push, try this instead: stop trying. Take a break. Surrender to your sweet spot for performance. Remind yourself: Rest *IS* work. Give yourself the space to reflect and generate breakthroughs.

3. How it works

Making Leadership Personal has three steps (see Figure 27.1):

1. READY: Frame Your Learning Edge (see Chapter 28).
2. SET: Define Your Leadership Brand (see Chapter 29).
3. GO: Activate New Leadership Habits (see Chapter 30 to 35).

28

Frame Your Learning Edge

"This is the true joy in life, being used for a
purpose recognized by yourself as a mighty one.
Being a force of nature instead of a feverish,
selfish little clod of ailments and grievances,
complaining that the world will not devote itself
to making you happy."

— George Bernard Shaw

Every day, you encounter challenges at work. You throw yourself into overcoming them. It gets you pretty far. But every so often, you get stuck. No matter how hard you try, you can't figure it out. You think you've fixed the problem, but a new problem arises. You seem to be fighting the same fires but on different days. *Same, same, but different.*

When we hit a roadblock like this, our habitual reaction is to work harder. But we could be reinforcing a dysfunctional behavior pattern that has become automatic but is no longer relevant, which keeps us stuck.

When you reach this point, though it seems counterintuitive, the best thing you can do is stop trying. Instead, hold the space to reflect and learn from the experience. Take that deep transformation journey. Frame your learning edge.

This book covers the most common difficult situations that leaders face. Each chapter guides you through a deep transformation journey. Pick the chapter relevant to your situation. Sit back, relax, read the chapter and tune in to your gut. Feel all the feels. Be guided by your intuition to frame your learning edge. These are NOT model answers. They simply serve as a mirror to reflect your own experience. Become more aware of the dysfunctional mindset that keeps you stuck playing the small game. This mindset may have worked for you before; it got you here. But now it's no longer relevant, and holds you back. Frame a new positive mindset that keeps you playing the big game. Roll out your rocket booster. Step towards your learning edge. Connect with your inner authority and operate from the sweet spot for performance.

1. Why it works

We're obsessed with fixing problems and getting things done. Unfortunately, the modern corporate world is filled with problems, and we can end up getting lost in the details. We lose our sense of perspective and develop tunnel vision. In this disconnected state, we don't even realize that we've fallen into autopilot mode focusing on the wrong answers, which have become the dominant, habitual thought. Changes are superficial, real transformation doesn't occur.

For real transformation to happen, you need to LET GO of the wrong answers so that the right ones can emerge. This explains why we often gain breakthrough insights while we're doing something else, like showering or strolling. You see how the old mindset has kept you playing small.

Instead, you come up with simple and creative ideas to *permanently* solve your insidious chronic problems.

2. What blocks us from doing it?

Change is not easy. When undergoing change, we're tinkering with finely-tuned behaviors that have become automatic; we do it without thinking. The brain hardwires everything it can — any behavior or thought that is repeated — so you literally don't have to pay it any more attention. Change involves getting out of this autopilot mode into more conscious thinking. This requires some cognitive effort. It *feels* uncomfortable, and may even be perceived by our brain as a threat.

Change may *feel* scary, but it's not dangerous. It may be the safest thing for you to stay relevant. Pretending the problem doesn't exist doesn't make it go away. The villain here is denial. Instead, when you give yourself the space to reflect on the situation — without blame, judgment or over-reactivity — you may be surprised that the solution has been in front of you all along. A good night's sleep can have that magic effect, too.

3. How it works

i. Read the relevant chapter

Identify a difficult situation that you faced recently or deal with regularly. Read the relevant chapter. For example, go to Chapter 14 if you had to deal with a difficult employee recently. These stories do not provide model answers. Instead, I hope that they trigger some epic moments in your own

Figure 28.1: Frame your learning edge.

extraordinary career. As you read, notice what resonates with you, negative or positive. If you don't feel anything, also take note of that.

ii. Unpack your situation

Now unpack your situation using the change frame in Figure 28.1. Follow the steps below to frame your learning edge.

(1) **Situation:** Describe the situation. What is happening? Who is involved?

(2) **Open Mind:** Think big, act big, and you'll grow smaller. What uncomfortable truth are you denying? Where are the disconnects and blind spots? Are you trying to solve a gravity problem?

(3) **Open Heart:** If you are not actively empowering people, then you're disempowering them unintentionally. What difficult emotions are you ignoring? How are you disempowering people, albeit unintentionally?

(4) **Open Will:** What looks like a people problem is usually a situation problem. What hard decision are you avoiding? What old habitual behaviors are keeping you stuck in the past? What new behaviors do

you need to adopt? How are you complicit in creating the situation that you don't want?

(5) **Old Mindset:** What is the dysfunctional belief that is keeping you stuck in the past and playing the small game?

(6) **New Mindset:** What is the reframe? What is the fresh and compelling belief that aligns with the bigger game and the emerging future?

(7) **Practical Tips:** What are small easy steps you can take *right now* that will help you sneak up to the future? What is going well today that you want to **continue** doing? What are you not doing today that you need to **start** doing? What is no longer relevant that you need to **stop** doing?

iii. Reflect often

Take action on the small easy steps. Learn it, process it, practice it. Let go of the old mindset. Let the new mindset emerge. It may feel strange initially. Reflect and fine-tune the change frame again and again until it becomes more natural. Put the change frame where you can see it all the time. Rewire your brain. This becomes your set play.

This is how you show up powerfully in the world. Connect and act from your inner authority. Hit that sweet spot for performance. You do less and accomplish more. This is not delusional thinking. It's in the realm of possibility, but it requires you to do things differently. Hold the space to reflect and learn from your experience. Recognize the disconnection that keeps you playing the small game. Perfect the reconnection to your inner authority that helps you elevate your game.

There is a learning curve to this. Initially, there will be some degree of gawkiness. Don't worry. Keep at it. With practice, you develop "muscle" memory which is connected to different parts of your brain. When this wide-scale mental connection is well-established, your brain can easily find the sweet spot and reconnect. Your brain will thank you for it. It thrives on learning and growth. It hates being stuck.

When you've tasted how pleasurable it is hitting the sweet spot for performance, and you can see how productive it is, you can't imagine doing it any other way. Operating any other way will feel unbearable.

29

Define Your
Leadership Brand

*"We don't get burned out because of what we do.
We get burned out because we forget why we do it.
Purpose keeps you fresh."*

— Jon Gordon

Greatness requires a personal commitment. Your leadership brand is a representation of your personal commitment to scale your impact in the world.

Your leadership brand reflects your unique point of view. It represents your values; what you believe is important. Your leadership brand is personal. It's not the same for everyone. It's not one-size-fits-all. Because you have something very special and unique. You have something worth saying. It can't be taken from you because it's essential to who you are. And you can lead people with that. You can scale and build on that, whether it's a career, a team, or a company. It's the thing you believe you are uniquely positioned to do. The thing you fundamentally believe you are the best person in the world to do. Where you have a unique proposition, given your story, to solve that challenge.

You will not act according to your leadership brand for every single decision every single day. We are complex human beings. There are multiple versions of you, depending on the role you're playing, the people you're with, even the time of the day (when you haven't had your lunch, and you're hangry: hungry and angry). But you know what your values are, and it's something you can always return home to.

1. Why it works

Your leadership brand provides direction. Your leadership brand is like the North Star that points you towards your ambitious future. Use it to take consistent bold steps every day, come rain or shine. You rely on your leadership brand to make complex decisions. The decisions we make every day are rarely clear-cut — we deal with complexity every day, and people change their minds. Use your leadership brand as a lens to turn disadvantages into advantages. With your leadership brand, you become an intentional, unimpeded trajectory through the quagmire of corporate life. Without your leadership brand, you will react to every situation in an ad-hoc manner. For example, accepting a job offer for a little more money and then regretting it two years later. *The money looked good, so I signed on.* Or not accepting a job offer from a small startup and then regretting it two years later when it goes IPO.

Your leadership brand can scale. Your leadership brand can be applied by others to drive the results that you want, even without you being physically present. It is impossible for you to be in every meeting room, micro-managing every decision being taken. But your leadership brand can. Over time, a commonly shared set of values will emerge. People's actions will be value-driven. These values and behavior patterns become your organization's culture.

Your leadership brand attracts talent, customers and investors/ sponsors. Your leadership brand reflects your values. You stand for something. When you can clearly articulate your values, people who stand for the same values will gravitate towards you. Your energy and enthusiasm inspire the same in them. You will stand out from the crowd. In their eyes, you snap out of the blurriness into sharp relief. Like when the camera comes into focus. *Snap!* Talents will want to work for you. Customers will want to buy more from you. Investors and sponsors will want to invest time and money into your projects. Because of your shared values.

Your leadership brand helps you prioritize. Your leadership brand guides you to identify the tasks that really matter. This way, you get more *out* of your work, rather than cramming more "stuff" *into* it. More importantly, it helps you to say no to the tasks that make you feel busy but don't get you results (and drains your energy). We all have our vices. Mine is "internet research" (endlessly scrolling on social media). Just by being more aware of it, you can stop. And you end up with more than enough time for what matters and a sense of peace and spaciousness that the constant activity has kept outside your reach ... until now.

The leadership brand is captured through four leadership principles. Applying these leadership principles gives you an intrinsic reward — a positive boost of energy you get directly from your work. It keeps you engaged in your work and energizes you to keep performing at your best. There are four sources of intrinsic reward:

PASSION is the feeling of excitement and enthusiasm you experience when your work aligns with your values. When you're doing what you love, naturally you'll find your work energizing.

PURPOSE is the feeling you get when you believe you're on an important mission. You're committed to something that you believe matters to others — whether at an individual, organization or society level — and to yourself. Your work is meaningful.

POWER is the accomplishment you experience when you skillfully perform your work. You feel agency to influence the world around you.

PRIZE is the DOPE feeling of exhilaration you experience when you're operating in your sweet spot for performance. You act from an inner authority. You source validation, approval and control from within. Consequently, you're able to perform at your peak in a consistent and sustainable manner.

The four leadership principles are inter-related. They work together like a system to help you *stay* in your natural state of being: the sweet spot for performance. It's a self-management process to direct your activities towards achieving your desired outcome (see Figure 29.1). It's like the lane markers at the bottom of the competitive swimming pool. *Swim in your own lane.* Ambling from day to day, trying to do everything and please everyone, is the alternative.

2. What blocks us from doing it?

We're barely scratching the surface of our potential. Achieving greatness does require a personal commitment. That X-factor comes from within. At the moment, we're so disconnected from the work because we're so singularly focused on external rewards. We get our fix of validation, approval and control from external sources. Here are some common examples.

Boss-centered. Your bosses can be the greatest source of inspiration, but working to please them above everything else can turn your life into a nightmare. And when things go wrong, you say, "It was not my idea. I was just following orders." Seniority does not preclude you from making this faux pas.

Process-centered. You follow the standard operating procedure even when it's no longer producing the results that you want. You justify the lack of results by saying, "But I followed the process!"

Results-centered. You are so obsessed with winning at all costs that you take shortcuts, backstab and do things that are not in the best interest of the customer or organization.

Surrender the obsessive compulsion to do everything and please everyone. Relinquish the robotic impulse to control everything and everyone. Stop going through the motions, and start leading from your leadership values.

A little warning. You're not going to live up to your leadership brand all the time. It's a lifelong practice, and it only gets better. Remember, it's not an intellectual exercise. It's all about the *feels*. When you directly experience how being powerful is our natural state of being, you can't imagine working any other way.

3. How it works

You use your leadership brand as a lens to shift mindsets, thought patterns and behaviors; not for self-promotion. Your leadership brand guides you

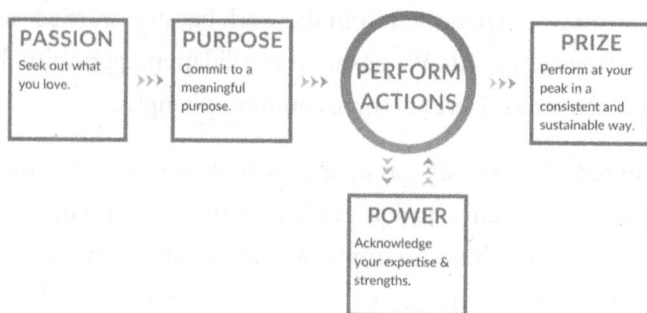

Figure 29.1: Self-Management process.

to perform at your peak in a consistent and sustainable way. How do you know when you've got it? It's part science, part art. Framing your leadership brand is an ongoing process. It is never *done*. Use the self-management process in Figure 29.1 to refine and validate your hypothesis. That's the science part. There is also an intuitive approach to it. As with all matters of the heart, you'll know when you find it. Just reading it gives you goose pimples. *That's me!*

Passion. What do you love?

Do not try to be someone else. Embrace yourself, with your miseries and your strengths. Accept it, you cannot be but just you, and that makes you extraordinary. Unleash your PASSION.

Passion is a strong feeling of excitement and enthusiasm — it makes your heart sing. It reflects our sense of fairness and "doing the right thing." It fires unrelenting drive. When you speak on a topic you love, you radiate enthusiasm and stand a much greater chance of persuading and inspiring others.

Example:

I love solving problems quickly and efficiently.

Your passion can also reflect a new way of thinking or doing things. Use the structure below to create the reframe. The reframe highlights the old mindset that is holding people in the past and the new mindset that allows the future to emerge. The best reframes make people uncomfortable. They are considered "wrong" by most people precisely because they go against the conventional wisdom.

Typically, when people think of (*domain*),

They think (*the old mindset*).

I think differently.

I think (*the new mindset*).

When you do this (*a small change in behavior*),

You will achieve (*a better result*).

When you don't do this (*a small change in behavior*),

You will get (*a worse result*).

Ultimately, (*the new mindset*) empowers you to (*elevate the performance to a whole new level, a game-changer*).

Example:

Typically, when people think of (_Interior Design_),

They think (_it is just aesthetics. It's a look_.)

I think differently.

I think (_Interior Design affects how we feel and behave_).

When you (_approach Interior Design as a thought process_),

(_It transforms the lives of the people who live in and enjoy that space_.)

When you (_focus just on aesthetics_),

(_The space becomes a superficial expression of good taste_.)

Ultimately, (_design is a tool to enhance our humanity_.)

Purpose. How do you create meaningful impact?

Your work matters. It does, and that is why you are part of a team doing something greater than yourself. This will give you PURPOSE.

You serve a purpose larger than yourself. It is why you are here. It is what gives your life meaning. It's about being part of something bigger than yourself and impacting many lives. It acts as a guiding star to direct our effort towards a meaningful goal. Purpose helps us thrive when things are going well, and it helps us stay focused when things go wrong. Purpose sustains us through the long and hard journey, no matter what happens at the end. It's the lamp illuminating the dark tunnel.

Example:

I'm here to help my organization solve outstanding challenges.

Maybe you've been thinking about your purpose and you have a ton of ideas. Use the template below to distill your ideas to its essence.

We are here to help (*customers*) who face (*a specific challenge*).

We help them achieve (*results*) by providing (*solution*).

Get (*solution*) in three steps:

1.
2.
3.

Example:

We are here to protect (*humankind*) from (*anthropogenic extinction such as climate change, global nuclear annihilation and biological warfare*).

We help (*save the human race from extinction*) through the (*colonization of Mars*).

(*Colonize Mars*) in four steps:

1. *Run scouting missions.*
2. *Drop off a full-scale fuel factory.*
3. *Send the pioneering human mission to Mars.*
4. *Colonize Mars.*

Power. What are you great at?

For each obstacle you come across, take action to fix it. In doing something, you gain experience, which gives you POWER to influence the world.

This is your domain expertise and how you make an impact. It is what you perform skillfully and what people are willing to pay for. It's about translating vision into reality and making things happen. Knowing that you're great at something instils confidence. It gives you a sense of power that you can influence the world around you.

Apart from your domain expertise, you also have significant achievements under your belt. You may have been involved in the design and sale of something completely new. You may have structured innovative deals, secured access to valuable resources or completed a project. Share your stories (see Chapter 32 Storytelling).

Example:

I am great at holding the space for people to learn and grow. For 20 years, I have led highly empowered teams to create innovative customer-centric technology services across Asia and Europe.

Prize. What are you like, at your best?

Take charge of your own success. Be responsible for yourself. The results you are getting today are because you wanted them. Own your PRIZE.

This is who you are at your best and most fulfilled. You source validation, approval and control from within. You care deeply about the work and want to do it well — even when no one is watching. It's where you feel in the flow, what gives you your edge and what helps you to create breakthrough solutions. You act with courage and find your strongest and most inspiring voice. You hit your sweet spot for performance. This is how you perform at your peak in a consistent and sustainable manner.

Example:

I'm at my best when people count on me to be optimistic and to see their potential.

4. Exercise

i. **PASSION:** What do you love?

Fill in the blank: "I am/love _____"

ii. **PURPOSE:** How do you create meaningful impact?

Fill in the blank: "I'm here to _____"

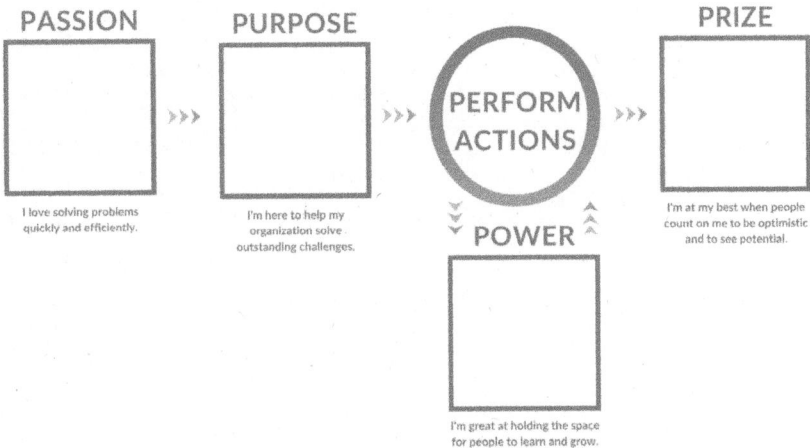

PASSION   PURPOSE   PERFORM ACTIONS   PRIZE

POWER

I love solving problems quickly and efficiently.

I'm here to help my organization solve outstanding challenges.

I'm great at holding the space for people to learn and grow.

I'm at my best when people count on me to be optimistic and to see potential.

Figure 29.2: Your leadership brand.

   iii. **POWER:** What are you great at?
       Fill in the blank: "I'm great at _____"

   iv. **PRIZE:** Where are you at your best?
       Fill in the blank: "At my best, I _____"

    v. Fill in the self-management process diagram with your leadership brand (use Figure 29.2).

Personality profiling tools like MBTI and DISC can be a great source of inspiration. Use them as a starting point to set you off on your self-discovery journey. Remember, they are not model answers. No profiling tool can tell you exactly who you are. Every human is an exception to the rule. It's deeply personal. You are the editor-in-chief.

Take the Leadership Readiness quiz:
leadership-readiness.me

30

Clearly Articulate
Your Vision

The biggest challenge organizations face today in promoting or hiring leadership is the alignment of the leader's personal vision and the organization's vision.[1] From my experience, the confusion is around what "alignment" means. Alignment is not about squeezing into a certain leadership mold, or bending to fit a job description, or chanting the corporate slogan. The sycophantic glorification of the corporate mantra hints of cultism, no matter how persuasive the performance. It's not about becoming Steve Jobs or Elon Musk. That's not alignment; that's conforming.

Alignment is a process of discovery through the maze of possibilities with different stakeholders to find a place where you belong within the organization — a home. It isn't just a job that pays the bills. You have a vision of how your personal influence can contribute to the organization's mission. The organization mission is not just a handful of snazzy acronyms with no connection to what you do every day. You feel personally connected to it. You can clearly articulate your vision — of yourself, your team, your department — to others.

Clearly articulating your vision requires high-level thinking. It doesn't happen automatically. It requires us to distill our ideas to its simplest essence: what is it really about, and why does it matter? You capture people's attention by highlighting the essentials, and ruthlessly remove everything that distracts from the essentials. We don't give ourselves the time to do this high-level thinking. Instead, when we share our vision with others, the essentials are drowned in a sea of details, or worse, completing missing in the dense cloud of smoke.

1. Why it works

Your vision bridges the abstractness of the corporate vision and the harsh realities of the day-to-day. Your vision takes into account the local context, which makes it more meaningful to the people on the ground, and therefore more actionable.

As a leader, you want everyone on your team to feel empowered to make decisions that are right for the organization. You do that by making sure that the vision and priorities are so clear that people feel empowered to make the right decisions in their day-to-day work.

2. What blocks us from doing it?

One of the biggest leadership mistakes we make today is not clearly articulating our vision. It requires us to distill our ideas to its simplest essence. We don't do it. As corporate warriors, we're trained to be comprehensive and thorough when exploring a new idea. We have to think of everything. But when it comes to sharing our ideas, everything is the last thing people want to hear.[2] We present counter-arguments, possible

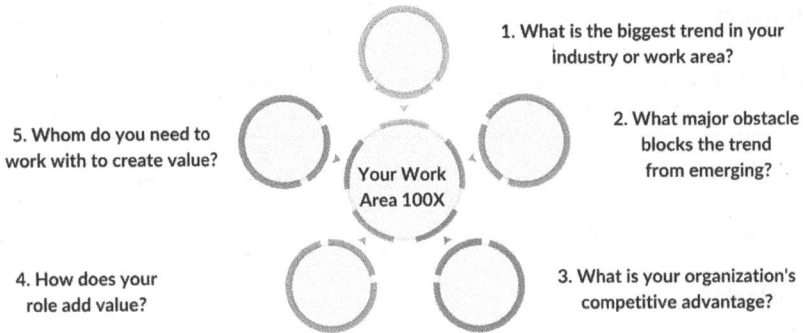

1. What is the biggest trend in your industry or work area?

5. Whom do you need to work with to create value?

2. What major obstacle blocks the trend from emerging?

Your Work Area 100X

4. How does your role add value?

3. What is your organization's competitive advantage?

Figure 30.1: Clearly articulate your vision.

points of failure, potential unintended consequences and the details of the execution plan. All these are critical aspects of any big idea, but not useful when first sharing it with others.

This is the sad fact of innovation: nobody will ever be as interested in our great idea as we are — until we get them hooked, that is. If you want to get people hooked on your idea, you have to invest the huge effort to make your idea inspiring and interesting for them. That means distilling your idea to its essence. After clearly articulating your vision, you then engage them in generative conversations to expand the idea. You hold the space for sparks of collective creativity. Through the conversations, you start to co-create the future together and unlock trust.

3. How it works

Use this mental model to distill your idea to its simplest essence (see Figure 30.1). This is a creative and generative process. We're not looking for model answers. We're looking for your unique perspective on things. To see the extraordinary out of the ordinary.

Industry:

What is the biggest trend in your industry or work area?

_____

_____

Example: Livestream shopping.

Obstacles:

What major obstacle blocks the trend from emerging?

_____

_____

Example: Setting up the back-end fulfillment infrastructure.

Organization:

What's your organization's competitive advantage?

_____

_____

Example: Huge user base and rich content.

Role:

How do you (or your team) add value to the organization?

_____

_____

Example: Leverage partnerships instead of building the back-end infrastructure from scratch.

Stakeholders:

Who do you (or your team) need to work with? What existing resources can you leverage? Whom can you partner who have the resources that you don't?

_____

_____

Example: Identify strategic partners.

4. Exercise

The next time you are presenting an idea, use this mental model to distill your idea to its essence. Capture ONLY the essentials. Very few things matter. Remove EVERYTHING else that distracts from the essentials.

Note:

- If you want to bring out your X-factor during a job interview, clearly articulate your vision.

31

Create A 100-Day Impact Plan

Congratulations on your new leadership role. You have been given an ambitious mandate. It is a moonshot, and to achieve it, you need to build a firm foundation. You know that if you can't get all the ducks in a row in the first 60 days, you will not hit the 12-month gate. There is no honeymoon period. You're hitting the ground running. The stopwatch has started.

Onboarding is challenging. Whether you are doing precisely the same job but in a different organization, or another job in the same organization, there will be a steep learning curve. If you go in with a "business as usual" mindset, the highly complex existing processes will overwhelm you.

A 100-day impact plan is not a vision or mission statement. It's a high-level and practical set of milestones that gives the journey some shape. It acts like a map that helps you navigate towards your destination and brings the moonshot into the range of possibility. For example, a goal of "raising $5 million" may seem impossible until you have broken it down into practical steps. It helps you to manage risk and not avoid it altogether.

A 100-day impact plan is not a fancy PR document to make you look good. Having a 100-day impact plan helps you focus on what needs to be achieved and be intentional. It gives you the courage to say no to anything that does not contribute to it — and explain why. It stops you from being pulled an inch in a million directions. You get to stay on top of the business — working *on* the business — instead of drowning *in* it.

A 100-day impact plan is not a to-do checklist. The 100-day impact plan provides a higher-level order to what actions need to be taken first: first things first. If you use a to-do checklist, you may become overwhelmed and end up taking unnecessary action. For example, you might spend weeks developing a business proposal and submitting it to your client, who then tells you that what you have proposed is way beyond his budget. If you had an earlier action plan to gather information, you might have saved weeks.

1. Why it works

Most of us already have some form of a 100-day impact plan in our heads, but it probably looks more like a to-do checklist. It lists the *details* of our daily work, and thus it seems endless, like the deep dark forest where the panic monster lurks. It gives us ulcers and keeps us awake at night. We can get so caught up in our checklist that we can't see the forest for the trees. We get lost in the details.

Details have some sort of superpower over us that demand all our attention, especially when we're under stress. The fight-or-flight response kicks in. We get "tunnel vision," focusing on problems and details. Having a 100-day impact plan keeps the panic monster at bay. It helps us to regain perspective and not drown in the details.

2. What blocks us from doing it?

The act of writing down the 100-day impact plan is something new for us. We are more familiar with acting from what we think. We hold a long to-do checklist in our heads. We're constantly thinking and updating our checklist. We think it's faster this way. In our youth, we might have gotten more done this way. But things are more complex now; the to-do checklist is too long and detailed, thus the deep dark forest.

Writing down the 100-day impact plan takes time and requires super-brainpower. Planning and prioritizing require high-level thinking. It might seem like writing it down is too tedious and slows you down. It helps to remember that you're slowing down in order to go fast.

3. How it works

Strategic priority. Decide on three strategic priorities that you will work on for the first 100 days. Having three different strategic priorities focuses the attention on the three areas where you can make the greatest impact in the first 100 days. Your biggest challenge will be to shortlist it down to three. You will be tempted to have seven strategic priorities. Be ruthless, prioritize it down to the three most important priorities.

Milestone. Break down each strategic priority into a step-by-step process to achieve it. This is also an opportunity to brainstorm new ways of thinking and doing things. Without planning, you are likely to tackle the work in the way you always do.

Action. Each milestone breaks down into action items. This is your to-do list. When you have the right strategic priority and a plan that works, the actions you need to take become obvious.

Figure 31.1: 100-day impact plan.

There is a cadence between the strategic priorities, plans and actions that helps you stay on top of the game. There is a clear and logical framework that allows you to know where you are at any part of the journey. See Figure 31.1.

32

Storytelling

We have our own experience of witnessing the most skilled orators. They project that fabled "reality distortion field." They draw us out of our neuroses, and we fall hopelessly under their mesmerizing spell. I've had my fair share of falling in love with these magicians spinning their web of fantasies and luring me into doing things that I wouldn't normally do, like happily spending Christmas Eve chasing a Purchase Order from a client instead of sipping champagne at a party.

I've been observing these devious but magnanimous magicians for a long time. I've fallen under their spell too many times. And I've noticed a commonality: storytelling. Instead of dreary PowerPoint slides, they spin tales that win over the hearts and minds of people.

If you're someone who needs people to buy your products, invest in your organization or follow your lead, then storytelling can help. Good storytelling helps you land your message. Your message becomes more persuasive and memorable. People fall under your deep and beguiling spell.

1. Why it works

Our brains love good storytelling.[1] We love stories. We grew up with them. Stories connect with us in ways that facts can never do, and in reading them, they shift the way we look at the world. We're never the same again. We're more likely to agree with the storyteller's point of view than we normally would — thus that fabled "reality distortion field."

A captivating story captures and holds our attention — a scarce resource in the brain. It brings us to the peaks and valleys of the protagonist's experience. We come to share the protagonist's emotions, and after the story ends, we are likely to mimic the feelings and behaviors of the protagonist. This explains the feelings of not-so-humble world domination after watching James Bond movies.

2. What blocks us from doing it?

People think that, within a professional context, they shouldn't display emotion. They remove all the feelings and personal experiences from their presentations and amp up the business jargon and data. That's how they fall into the "professional boring mode."

Emotion is what makes your message memorable and incites people to act. We think we need to be serious to be taken seriously. We think that showing emotions will make us look weak and vulnerable. It might seem counter-intuitive, but speaking naturally and informally, with genuine emotion, makes us sound more confident and engages the audience's attention better.

Omit emotions and personal experiences, and your story will fall flat like a dry recitation of facts, or worse, a flagrant display of self-promotion. Obviously, this is not your intention, but disobey the rules of good storytelling, and you'll be doing it unintentionally. You've been warned.

Those skilled orators make storytelling look so natural and effortless that you may be tempted to "wing" it. DON'T BE FOOLED. What seems to you like off-the-cuff anecdotes would have been rehearsed at least a dozen times. Even the most skilled orators experience gawkiness when they first rehearse their lines. It's paradoxical, but it takes hard work to make it *look* so effortless and off the cuff.

3. How it works

Compelling stories follow a specific structure: a plot. It's a sequence of events in which the protagonist is put into a challenging situation that forces the protagonist to make increasingly difficult choices, driving the story toward a climactic event and resolution.

The plot contains specific elements that are ESSENTIAL if you want to engage your audience. These key elements bring movement, conflict and fluidity to your story. It brings your story to life. Figure 32.1 shows how a plot breaks down into seven elements.

i. **Opening scene:** At the beginning of the story, you describe the existing situation. This shows your audience what "normal" is. That way, they will know what's wrong when we hit the next step.

ii. **Conflict:** Conflict is an event that throws the protagonist into a challenging situation, upsetting the status quo. The event can be something that happens externally or internally. This is the beginning of the story's movement.

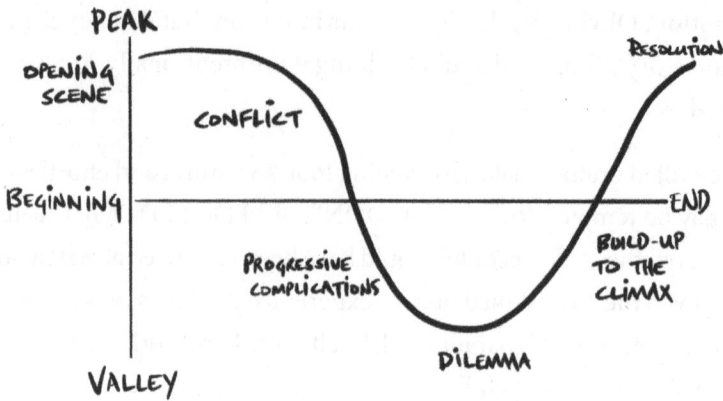

Figure 32.1: Elements of a plot.

iii. **Progressive complications:** This is the largest part of the story, and where most of the challenges take place. Here's where you raise the stakes. It's crucial that the conflict resonates with the audience and they know what's at stake here. Weak progressive complications, weak story.

iv. **Dilemma:** This is the real heart of the story — the most important element. The story has been building toward this point. This is the moment when the protagonist is put into a situation where they must make a hard decision. If you set the dilemma up skillfully, it creates a frisson of excitement in the whole story, setting your readers on edge.

v. **Build-up to the climax:** Having made the hard decision, the protagonist commits to a path and drives the outcome of the conflict. You can have new characters coming into the picture like a motley crew of eccentric personalities or an apparent magical mentor. Most action, drama and changes happen here.

vi. **Resolution:** This is where the story ends, and the main problem is resolved; the open-ended questions are answered; the loose ends are tied. Now, at the end of the story, you establish the new "normal." Stick the landing. Don't let the story trail off and leave the audience confused or unsatisfied.

vii. **Moral of the story:** Emotionally wrap everything up so your audience can happily tuck the story in their mind palace for easy retrieval in the future. It's a scene-closure with enough finality to deserve those two words: The End.

4. Exercise: Outline the plot

1. **Opening scene:** What is "normal" at the beginning?

_____

_____

Example: Richard has been climbing the corporate ladder and enjoying the high life of a corporate executive.

2. **Conflict:** What has upset the status quo? What is the conflict?

_____

_____

Example: Richard feels like something is missing, but he's ashamed to admit it.

3. **Resolution:** What is "normal" at the end of the story? After the storm passes and the water calms, what has changed? (Note: Establish the

beginning and ending first. This bookends the story. When you know where you're heading, you can plan better.)

_____

_____

Example: Richard takes on a risky role within the organization to build a new business from scratch. From managing 110 people, he becomes an independent contributor.

4. **Progressive complications:** What's at stake? What's the cost if your main character blows it?

_____

_____

Example: Richard is always exhausted. He is distracted at work. He is distracted at home.

5. **Dilemma:** What are the alternatives, especially if they are equally undesirable?

_____

_____

Example: Richard can continue pretending everything is fine until he gets disrupted, or he can make a change.

6. **Build-up to the climax:** Who does the protagonist team up with? How do they face the conflict together? How does it all come to a head in the climax?

_____

_____

Example: Richard has always harbored dreams to be an entrepreneur. He used to think that it was too risky. He starts having conversations with business leaders within the organization.

7. **Moral of the story:** Why did this happen? How was it meaningful? What positive aspect can you gain from the experience?

_____

_____

Example: Life is not just about looking successful. Life is an adventure to be engaged.

33

Listening

Have you ever had a deep conversation with someone where you feel transformed by the end of it? Something shifts during the conversation; the griping at the beginning of the conversation turns into a sense of awe and wonder. Both of you are no longer the same person from the beginning of the conversation. You are transformed: happier, stronger, more confident.

I've had my fair share of such experiences. How did it happen? I might like to think it's because I'm such a wonderful conversationist, my oratorical flourishes so amazing, or my wisdom so utterly profound. My ego will like that, but that won't be the truth. The truth is: I was transformed because my conversation partner was such a great listener. I felt seen, heard, and valued. It's the greatest feeling.

What makes a great listener? Well, it's not so much what you say or do, but what you make the other person *feel*. You make them feel like they are the most important thing in your life at that moment. Not only do you attend patiently to their gripes and tirades about their coma-inducing work, their cantankerous boss and their non-existent social life, but you notice something else as well: the arrival of their highest future possibility. It's so subtle that most people miss it in the dark cloud of pessimism. And by shining a light on it, you help them break free from their obsessive narcissism, and they sparkle like a star again. Great listeners draw out our best selves. It's like they are willing our best nature to manifest. In their presence, we feel like a million bucks.

1. Why it works

When we're brainstorming for ideas, what's the first thing that usually happens? Nothing. Nothing happens. Their first reaction: *I don't know*. Or you get the same old, same old responses. People's default thinking is to reconfirm what they already know. The conversation goes in circles, repeating the same message, but in different words. But sometimes, in the midst of the gripes and tirades, there's a pause. The silence is deafening. But from that awkward pause, something new emerges. It's like magic. The creative breakthrough arrives at its own schedule. It needs space to emerge. Great listeners hold the space for creative breakthrough to emerge.

Breakthrough insights are more likely to occur when people are reflecting on deeper thoughts and not paying much attention to the external world.[1] A great listener is quiet and listens attentively. The silence creates a state for reflection, without which the conversation never deepens. It just skims the surface and never reaches a turning point.

2. What blocks us from doing it?

One of the biggest leadership mistakes we make is not listening. We might think that we're listening. But really, our attention is on judging what the other person is saying, identifying problems, figuring out what to say next or trying to sound smart. It may look like two persons are talking to each other. I think it's more accurate to say that they are talking *at* each other — two massive and rather insufferable egos, each locked up in their own bubble, so self-conscious to the point that they are only listening to themselves.

This might sound simplistic, but it rings true: If you want to listen, you must stop talking. And I don't mean talking out loud. I'm referring to the compulsive demonic chatter in your head, so violently possessed, like hungry ghosts breaking out from the gates of hell every seventh month of the Chinese lunar year. Most people are not even aware of their inner banshee droning. We speak at a rate of about 100 words a minute, and our too-noisy mind throttles at 300–500 words a minute. Active listening is a very *active* task. It takes strict discipline and lots of practice to quieten the too-noisy mind.

3. How it works

There are four levels of listening[2]:

i. **Level 1: Downloading.** This type of listening is limited to reconfirming what you already know — the inner banshee droning. Nothing new penetrates the droning. Your attention is not actually focused on what the other person is saying but on your own inner commentary. For example, while the other person is still speaking, you are already planning what you will say next.

ii. **Level 2: Listening for new data.** You are curious about what the other person thinks, and you actively look out for disconfirming information that conflicts with your pre-existing ideas. Argue like you're right; but listen like you're wrong. Suspend your habit of judging or identifying problems. Instead, you adopt the viewpoint of an innocent and open your mind. Hold the space that allows everything — *everything* is data. Don't judge it as good or bad. Just experience it as it is. Your attention moves from listening to your inner voice to actually listening to the person in front of you.

iii. **Level 3: Listening for emotions.** As the conversation deepens, you use your feelings and your heart as a sensing organ to tune in to the other person's perspective. You step into their shoes. You feel their emotions as keenly as if it is your own. You start to see the situation through their eyes.

iv. **Level 4: Listening for potential.** This is the learning edge. You listen for the creative breakthrough — the highest future possibility. You hold the space for what is unknown and emerging. The silence can be so uncomfortable that you just want to fill that space — don't jump the gun! This is the edge of a breakthrough. Once the person finishes, you clarify back the *essence* of what you heard. It's like you've sifted for the gold in what the person said, polished it, and then held it up for their consideration.

Most of our conversations happen at Level 1 listening: downloading. At the same time, Level 4 listening isn't always the right answer. Each situation is unique. The magic trick here is to be aware of the quality of your listening and to adapt the quality of your listening to what is needed in each situation. For example, Level 1 listening may be appropriate for a meeting to discuss debugging issues. You want to deepen the listening to Level 4 when you're brainstorming for visionary ideas. Be watchful when these meetings are back to back; you don't bring that rat-tat-tat Level 1 listening to the next.

4. Exercise

Practice listening to someone for two minutes without interrupting them. Give them your full attention, as if every word they say conveys a special meaning. Be aware of the quality of your listening: which level are you listening? Notice when your own thoughts creep in or when you find yourself drifting off into other thoughts. Notice the difference when you're listening at each of the four levels.

34

Acknowledgment

"The happy phrasing of a compliment is one of the rarest of human gifts, and the happy delivery of it another."

— Mark Twain

One of the most heartbreaking things about the modern corporate world is that people don't feel as valued for their work as they would like to be. From my experience, this is because people feel awkward about praises — whether giving or receiving them.

We are much more familiar with being hard on ourselves and others. We hold black belts at beating ourselves up. We have a childish, merciless tyrant in our heads that constantly analyzes and criticizes our work: *it's too big; it's too small; it's too strong; it's too weak.* We also have bosses, employees and colleagues who constantly offer their terribly intelligent opinions on what we're doing wrong and what we should do to improve. Without invitation. We are so familiar with fault-finding that we imagine criticisms coming from others even when there is none.

When we receive a compliment, or somebody affirms and praises our work, we dismiss it: *Oh, it's nothing.* It slides off like melted butter on a Teflon skillet. Or we see it as a cue that criticism might be coming next and brace ourselves for the punch in the stomach. Or we think the person is being sarcastic and is actually mocking our work.

1. Why it works

Acknowledgment is about catching people in the act of doing things right. It's about noticing and pointing out what's going right and what's right about them. The effect on the person can be truly transforming. They experience being seen and valued. Their self-confidence builds up. They feel good about themselves. That feeling of power, excitement and energy — it's addictive. They will want to repeat that behavior. Not only do they feel good, they are also more likely to think clearly and be solution-focused. It's a precious leadership moment that unlocks trust between the leader and other people.

Acknowledgment can be as simple as saying:

"Hey, I saw what you did there. That's special."
"I'm really proud of you for taking on the challenge."
"What you did really raised the bar for everyone. Well done!"

From a neuroscience perspective, positive feedback is a signal to the brain to do more of something. The brain sees the positive feedback as a reward, which helps to reinforce any new habit the other person is trying to develop.

2. What blocks us from doing it?

The mistake leaders make all too often is skipping over these precious leadership moments. When a generous thought comes to mind, we don't say it aloud. We think their achievements are expected; they are not worth mentioning. It's that "spare the rod, spoil the child" mentality. Spoiling people does not make them go soft. They become more motivated and energized.

We also worry about how others may perceive us when we sing them praises. We are terrified of coming across as clumsy, fawning or patronizing. As it turns out, the other person doesn't care about that. They just care how nice and kind the compliment is. We significantly underestimate how happy the other person would be to hear the praise, and significantly overestimate how cringe-worthy they would find the encounter.[1]

Acknowledging people is a very active task. It also takes guts, particularly if you work in an environment where "constructive feedback" is valued over acknowledgment. *Criticism is good for you; it makes you better.* It's not true. Negative feedback rarely leads to improvement.[2] And guess what? Verbal praise is more effective at increasing productivity than cash bonuses.[3] It's incredible how something so small can have such a big impact!

Constructive feedback is necessary, and is received well when it comes from a place of genuinely wanting the other person to improve. There is no blame or finger-pointing. There's consequence, but no punishment involved here. There is no stern, moralizing judgment. You can sing praises AND give constructive feedback. *Good, good. Try again.*

3. How it works

There are three levels of acknowledgment.

i. **Level 1: Acknowledge the tangible achievement.**
   Example: *Well done for completing the task!*

ii. **Level 2: Acknowledge the difficulty.**
   Example: *Well done for completing the task! I know you had to deal with conflicting priorities.*

iii. **Level 3: Acknowledge the learning and growth.**
   Example: *Well done for completing the task! I know you had to deal with conflicting priorities. This is a real breakthrough and game-changer for the organization.*

4. Exercise

Set a goal to give one acknowledgment a day. Go with the flow. Observe and see what the experience feels like for yourself and the other person.

i. **Acknowledge your employees.** Actively notice when your employee is doing something right. Notice how they light up as you affirm their positive view of themselves. If you want your employees to adopt a new habit, acknowledge their efforts, and they are more likely to repeat it.

ii. **Acknowledge yourself.** Be gentle and kind to yourself. This also opens you to receive acknowledgment from others. When someone acknowledges your work, consciously let it in. Accept it graciously and say a simple "Thank you."

iii. **Acknowledge your boss.** This surprises most people. But bosses need positive feedback too. It validates their own intuition that they are heading in the right direction. Think of three things your boss is really good at and share them with your boss. It opens up a conversation for both of you to become creative collaborators.

35

Uncomfortable
Conversations

"Either you run the day, or the day runs you."
— Jim Rohn

I magine a conversation where people discuss, debate, and, above all, decide on a lot of stuff in a fraction of the time. They leave the meeting feeling energized and enthusiastic like they've accomplished something, and they can't wait to share it with others.

Sounds rather far-fetched, airy-fairy, delusional. Surely, you're not describing a corporate meeting. Sounds more like a bonding session at an ayahuasca therapeutic retreat.

We are more familiar with this:

Leaders dominating the conversation and discouraging contradictions.
People denying inconvenient truths.
Sycophants chanting the corporate mantra.

Feudal lords politicking and jostling for power.

Corporate assassins arrowing one another, playing the blame game.

Aah, we're playing in the drama triangle...

The key to an effective meeting is to run them with a human touch, and not like some bureaucratic management meeting issuing military orders. The differentiating factor is the quality of the conversation. The conversation flows and connects. It's playful and energetic.

This does not happen on its own. To bring the magic to life, you must be prepared to be comfortable being uncomfortable. You create the space for a creative conversation to happen. You hold the space for deep and diverse views, without the usual blame, anger and moralizing judgment. And from this space, a collective tangible result emerges: a decision, a plan, a list of great ideas to pursue, a shared understanding of the work ahead.

1. Why it works

It boils down to trust. Do people trust each other enough to speak truthfully? And not be worried about being judged or punished? A team simply can't get to the performing stage without trust.

When there's trust in the team, people are more willing to raise tough issues. Problems are seen as an exciting challenge to be overcome. There is stress, but it's a healthy stress; *eustress*. They think more creatively, stay focused, collaborate better and make better decisions. They experience the DOPE effect.

When people feel threatened that they may be judged or punished, they will cover up their mistakes and not be honest about them. It's a natural self-defense mechanism. When something is wrong, nobody dares to speak up. It becomes this big open secret that is discussed and debated at the office water cooler and in private. But that voice remains silent in the boardroom.

Neuroscience research tells us that if trust is not established, or if it is damaged, our limbic system is more likely to be aroused, which sets off the threat response in our brain. *Don't speak up, it's not safe.* The threat response pulls energy away from the prefrontal cortex, the executive brain. We experience *distress*. We find it harder to think and work toward solutions. Instead, we focus more on problems and drama. We fall back to old childish behavioral patterns that keep us stuck playing the small game.

2. What blocks us from doing it

We are not familiar with having empowering, creative conversations. We are much more familiar with meetings that are tense, disempowering and put everyone in an away state.

One of the biggest leadership mistakes we make today is avoiding the uncomfortable conversations. We shy away from talking about the uncomfortable truths. It feels safer to perpetuate the comfortable lies. When the conversation comes too close for comfort to the truth, we say, "Let's take this offline." Or we change the subject, "Anyway..." Just when we're a hair's breadth away from a breakthrough, we completely lose the plot. The conversation never deepens. It goes back to being polite and superficial. Kicking the can down the road once more. The organization debt mounts up.

If you want powerful, truthful conversations, then you have to be prepared to be uncomfortable. Hold the intention to focus on what matters. Make sure that people feel safe to have an open and truthful conversation. You don't need to have the loudest voice in the room. It's those quiet moments when you confidently open yourself to the discomfort — without the moralizing judgment and blame — that can make all the difference.

3. Shift from Hero to Coach

Instead of trying to be the hero to everyone, you become a coach who makes everyone a hero. You hold the space for people to figure out their problems for themselves.

When people are triggered or disconnected, our tendency is to jump in with the solution or fix the problem for them. Instead, empower them to solve their own problem. Support them to make their own decisions and learn from their mistakes. This is the essence of leading people.

i.   **Pause.** Start by bringing attention to the person and simply listening without interrupting until the person calms down.

ii. **Ask questions.** After the person has calmed down, ask quality questions to understand the situation from the person's perspective. Hold the belief that they are capable of solving their own problems, but they are triggered at this moment.

iii. **Provide options.** After you get where the person is coming from, provide meaningful, easy-to-accept options to support the person. This gives the person a sense of autonomy and control.

For a startup founder, this subtle shift makes all the difference whether you have a founder-led or product-led organization. Stop problem-solving everything yourself; focus on providing guiding principles for the organization.

4. Shift from Villain to Challenger

Instead of playing the villain, you become a challenger.

Instead of blaming or criticizing, you articulate your vision and priorities in such a clear and compelling way that people feel empowered to do the right thing for the organization. This is the essence of innovation and being a visionary.

i.   **Acknowledge the challenges.** Address the elephant in the room upfront. You're not sweeping the inconvenient truth or harsh realities under the carpet. People will feel heard and validated; they know they are not alone.

ii. **Bring it back to the vision.** Once you've acknowledged the difficulties, clearly articulate your vision and priorities to all your stakeholders.

iii. **Build camaraderie.** Encourage people to expand your idea. Create a safe space for people to add their own insights.

This is exactly what entrepreneurship is about — turning disadvantages into advantages. Precisely because these are challenging times that the organization can do something extraordinary!

5. Shift from Victim to Creative

Instead of playing the victim, you become a creative. You exercise your curiosity and creativity to find better solutions with partners, instead of feeling powerless about what is happening — or not happening — to you.

This is the essence of empowerment. You source validation, approval and control from within.

i. **Disconnect.** Give yourself the space for rest and high-quality thinking. Self-hero a little; watch your favorite Netflix show, enjoy a good meal, exercise, go shopping.

ii. **To reconnect.** When you catch yourself saying "I can't", that's a win because you are now aware of that automatic habitual thought. Saying "I can't" is actually covering up fear. The fact is not that you "can't", but merely that you're afraid. Reframe it to say "I can't, yet." This opens up a possibility.

iii. **Positive stretch.** Take a small concrete action towards your goal in the next week. Something so small that you can't fail, but moves you one step closer towards your long-term direction.

This shift from victim to creative is foundational. The learning never ends; it only gets more important. For founders, as their company grows, from startup to scaling, they also need to change. They have to stop doing the thing that got them here, that they're so good at, and start doing the other thing that they're incompetent in. They go from being able to do everything, talk to everyone and have a hand in everything, to the person who is a guiding principle for the company, holding everybody to a higher standard. It's like a state change, from water to gas. Everything that they are competent in, that makes them feel worthy, evaporates. It's a crisis of identity. That's why it requires a leap of faith.

6. Managing emotional drama

Here are some tips for holding the space when people are triggered in the meeting:

i   Validate their concerns. Don't minimize or dismiss their concerns by saying things like, "It's going to be okay" or "It's not that bad". And don't even try to turn it into a joke.

ii Try to understand where they're coming from before you try to reason with them. If you're being accused of something, don't immediately jump to defend yourself. Listen to their side of the story first.

iii Take ownership for the influence you have in the situation. If you can see how you are complicit in creating this situation, then you have the power to change it. You don't have to provide immediate answers. Promise to think about the issue and agree to meet again at a specific time.

7. Setting a powerful intention for the meeting

The output of the meeting is as powerful as the intention you set for it. You are creating the space for a creative conversation to happen. It enables you to unlock the magic. The magic really comes from everyone in the room — not just individually, but collectively as a whole. One creative breakthrough opens another one. It's like following the intuitive breadcrumbs to get to your big ideas. By setting a powerful intention, you are clear about the desired outcome from the meeting. You begin with the end in mind. You bring together a carefully selected group of people. Every person is an essential contributor. There are no "observers." It only takes one person banging on their laptop to suck the energy out of the room and destroy the magic.

People: Who <u>needs</u> to be in this meeting?

_____

_____

Example: Your client is not happy with the work that has been delivered and you have called a meeting with your project team to address the situation.

Think: What do you want people to think, know or understand by the end of the meeting?

_____

_____

Example: You want to acknowledge the difficulty with managing this client. It does not reflect on the team's competence. In fact, this delicate situation requires their unique talents to adapt and do better. You want the project team to know that this piece of work is critical to the client _and_ the organization, and you want to brainstorm creative ideas to do things differently.

Feel: How do you want people to feel at the end of the meeting?

_____

_____

Example: You want to have an empowering conversation. They have a breakthrough aha moment. People leave the meeting feeling re-energized.

Do: What specific action do you want people to take after this meeting?

_____

_____

Example: You want the project team to follow up on their ideas. You hold the space for the project team to take the lead. You schedule the next meeting in a week's time to address obstacles that emerge.

8. Exercise

i. **Before the meeting:** Take 15 minutes to set the intention before your next meeting. Set the timer. Don't take more than that.

a. Create the first draft of the intention for the meeting.

b. Look at your response. See what role you are playing in the drama triangle. For example, if your intention is for the project team to think the situation is no big deal, then you're playing the hero, not wanting the team to feel bad.

c. Rewrite your intention to come from the empowerment triangle. If you're playing the hero, shift to be the coach.

ii. **During the meeting:** When you find that the conversation is becoming disempowering or getting stuck, most likely the conversation has veered off-track. The moment you notice it is a win; you're aware. This is a huge mindset shift, but an important one: what you think is a failure is actually a win. Remind yourself of the intention and guide the conversation back on track.

iii. **After the meeting:** Use the intention to evaluate whether the meeting went well. If you hit all your objectives, even if it's a small win, give yourself a pat on the back. *Job well done!* We have a tendency to ruminate on that one minor detail that marred our perfect plan. We go over the events of the meeting again and again, wishing they had gone differently. Again, the moment you notice this loop of doom, remember, it's a win; you're aware. No extraordinary journey is linear. It requires strategic patience. Drop the story, and roll with the times. Keep going, keep moving, stay curious about what the next moment will bring.

36

Culture of Innovation

It's an incredible time to be working in Asia Pacific. This is a fast-growing market that truly resonates with mobile first, with a large and growing population that is incredibly young. When I talk to organizations that are on a hyper-growth trajectory, this is what I often hear: "Our organization is growing faster than its people." To capture the market growth, these organizations are adaptively redefining the way they work. And in the process, they are surreptitiously creating long-overdue change in the talent landscape.

i. Organization structure

The organization structure is evolving from a vertically integrated organization structure to an agile system of networks and ecosystems. Asia Pacific comes with its unique set of challenges. For example, if you want to build an e-commerce infrastructure across Southeast Asia, you can't just think about the typical supply and demand of the marketplace. You also need to think of the payments infrastructure, the logistics underlying the business, and the barriers across language, culture and geographical lines. Hierarchically structured organizations designed around traditional top-down management thinking — where global headquarters imposes their way of working and dictates what the region can do — does not work. It creates busy work for everyone and little results. What's working? A structure that empowers "think global, act local".

ii. Leaders

As these organizations move away from a structured top-down hierarchy to a more agile one, they require a different type of leader. In the system of networks and ecosystems, groups of leaders are forced to work together in new ways, creating a culture of collaboration across generations, geographies, functions, job grades, personalities, and internal and external teams. They lead, not by fiat, but by inspiring trust through a shared sense of passion and purpose. The fast-changing market landscape also requires a new breed of leaders who have an entrepreneurial mindset; comfortable dealing with ambiguities and willing to challenge the status quo.

iii. Leadership development

The traditional pyramid-shaped leadership development model is simply not producing leaders fast enough to keep up with the demands of business and the pace of change. The theory goes, train the top leaders, who would then train the next level down, and so forth. The effects should trickle down, from the C-suite to middle managers, and, ultimately, front-line. But this top-down model doesn't work. Not only that, it's non-inclusive, since most employees aren't included. Post-pandemic, leadership development is shifting from a model of teaching a few people a lot of content in person sequentially, to teaching a lot of people a little content virtually at the same time. At an organizational level, you're talking about real behavioral change in weeks, not years.

iv. Learning & development (L&D)

L&D is moving away from formal courses that takes you away from work to learn how to address an issue that may not be relevant until months or years later. Instead, it's moving towards offering in-the-moment support for a situation at hand in the flow of work. Deciding which training to go to is no longer just based on the job grade. It is a business imperative based on business needs. You work towards instilling a culture of ongoing reflection and individual learners taking responsibility for recognizing

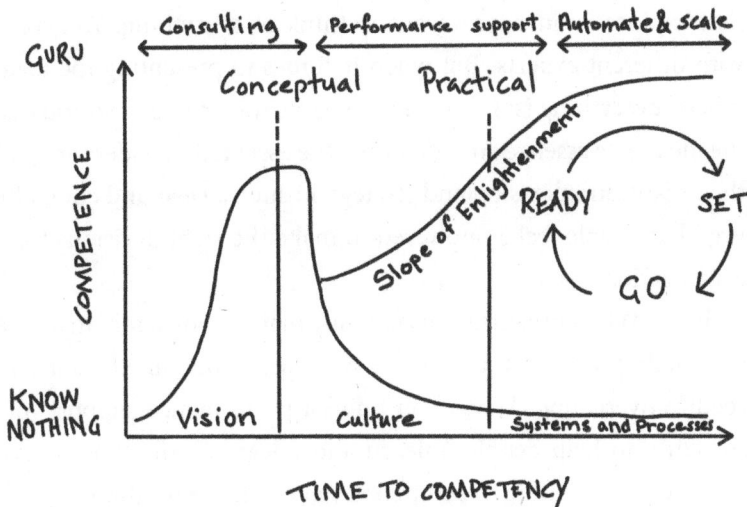

Figure 36.1:   The drama triangle.

their own development areas. This puts learners in the driver's seat. It harnesses the power of technology and the diverse wealth of instantly available external content (like "Youtube University"), to offer a great user experience for learners.

1. Why it works

With a culture of innovation and continuous improvement, your organization has the agility to spin on a dime. Your people can take an idea — any idea — and make it great. But instilling a culture of innovation and continuous improvement is not an overnight job. It is a process, and it takes time to scale (See Figure 36.1).

i. **Vision & Strategy.** There is clarity on where the organization wants to be in the future and what needs to be done to get there. When you first explore an idea, you want to think of everything. You consult with different experts. But when it comes to presenting the idea to others, everything is the last thing people want to hear. So you distill the idea to its essence and offer only the essentials. Leaders articulate the organization's vision and strategy in such a clear and compelling way that people feel empowered to make the right decisions for the organization.

ii. **Culture.** When organizations face any major change initiative, there is a high probability that there are deeply ingrained habits that require overriding. When you build a performance support infrastructure to help people unlearn and relearn in the flow of work, they shorten the time to competency and achieve on-the-job performance faster. When the change happens in the flow of work, the solutions that emerge from *within* the complexity are inherently realistic and sustainable. Employee engagement goes up because people feel they are making a difference.

iii. **Systems & Processes.** Wherever you see bright spots in the change initiative, you capture it and scale it. You embed or automate the new skills and behaviors into systems and processes to drive the desired results at scale. This is where you realize the true value of organization transformation.

2. What blocks us from doing it?

Moving from a top-down hierarchical organization structure to an agile system of networks and ecosystems is difficult. The neat lines of the organization structure create silos; it imposes a collaboration tax. It makes it more difficult for people across generations, geographies, functions, job grades, personalities, and internal and external teams to collaborate.

We also tend to confuse Culture with Vision & Strategy — like it's the one and same thing. When an organization needs to undergo change, they first pay half a million dollars to management consultants to tell them how to strategize their business. Next, they spend another million dollars on a new software to implement a new process or system. Whatever dollars they have left — we're scraping the bottom of the barrel here — they spend it on people.

We don't pay enough attention to people — it's left to chance. We all have attended the kumbaya offsite strategy sessions where we experience the most profound insights and commit to change. But once we're back in the office, we automatically go back to habitual modes of working. We fall into the valley of despair (See Figure 1.1 on the Dunning Kruger Effect). Without performance support, that initial euphoria from the vision-setting exercise fizzles out over time (See Figure 36.1). Changes are superficial, deep transformation does not happen, and we say the strategy session was a waste of time.

We ignore the human side of transformation. We assume that if we have a clear strategy and a new system or process in place, people's behaviors will magically change — and we're surprised when it doesn't. We know that people are different — we respond to changes and challenges in different ways — and yet organizations often make and implement change plans as though everyone was the same. For example, most organizational cultures value and encourage the detached, logical and unemotional approach: *It's just business, it's not personal.* The problem? It creates an organizational blind spot. Real and difficult issues get swept under the carpet. When we implement new systems or processes with this organizational blind spot, we run the risk of automating old ways of working. The consequence? The organization would have spent a significant amount of money and time taking a giant leap... into the past. And we blame people for resisting the change.

3. How it works

There is a misconception that people resist change. It's not true; people change all the time. What people resist is having change imposed on them. Instead, if you intentionally hold the space for people to shift their mindsets — unlearn their old habitual ways of working and relearn new ones — the change can happen much faster than you expect. When you win over the hearts and minds of your people, change becomes inevitable. Then the challenge will be on senior management to keep up!

Here are some practical tips that you can tweak to instill a culture of innovation and continuous improvement.

i. **Vision & Strategy.** Tailor the vision & strategy for your stakeholders. Many times, leaders leave the vision & strategy at a high level. They share the same message to all their stakeholders — spraying and praying, hoping something sticks. An empowering message would be one that takes into account the audience's context, explains how the change will impact them personally, and provides guidance to help them make the right decisions for the organization.

ii. **Culture.** Don't keep the vision at a high level. Reach down to the team and individual levels to foster highly engaged teams of employees doing work they love. This goes beyond relying on the top1% to implement new behaviors and cascade it down the organization. Instead, identify the critical behaviors that *everyone* needs to adopt in order to drive transformational growth for the organization. It's that FOMO — people change when they think *everyone else* changing. Support people to align their personal vision with the organization vision. This requires self-awareness and good communication skills; support people to pick up skills on how to communicate the good, bad and the ugly in an authentic way, and not shy away from difficult or uncomfortable conversations. Don't assume people will do it automatically just because they know it's important. Also, this alignment of personal vision and organization vision is a continuous process — things change.

iii. **Systems & Processes.** In order to scale, you have to first do the things that won't scale. Handcraft until it hurts, then only automate. For non-product-related tasks, use the tech, don't build the tech.

Implement tools to measure and manage desired behaviors or mindsets that align with the business strategy. For example, if a growth mindset is an important trait, then embed it into your hiring process — screen for it during job interviews. It's easier to hire someone who already has the growth mindset and encourage them to improve than to hire someone with a fixed mindset and then train them to shift it.

37

Conclusion

"Be not afraid of greatness. Some are born great, some achieve greatness, and some have greatness thrust upon 'em."

— William Shakespeare

C ongratulations, you have reached the end of the book! But in some ways, it is also a beginning. Because this is where you must make a conscious choice. This is where you decide to start. To dance on the edge of greatness.

It's time. To dream boldly and imagine possibilities. To travel between two worlds. Between the world that is possible and the world that it is. Between pleasure and misery. Between hope and despair. Between success and failure. Between greatness and adversity.

Why? Just for that rarest of moments when you touch perfection. To hit that fabled "sweet spot" for performance. You're dancing on the edge. *Not too hot, not too cold, but just right.* You're in control, but you're so close to losing it. That's where you feel most alive. This is your natural state of being. You remember the natural born leader you once were when you were a kid, and you had to be yelled at to slow down. You have forgotten what it is like. But it is all still there. You just have to reconnect with it, and often.

No extraordinary path is linear. Things change, disruption happens, as they do. With change comes the need for adaptation, for fresh thinking and sometimes a total reboot. So many things can change — bosses, employees, products, customers, market conditions. So does our families, friends, thoughts, opinions, moods, feelings. It's overwhelming. It can feel like the edge of despair.

When you're overwhelmed, it can be hard to tell the difference between a failure and something that is shifting your life in a different direction. "Failure" can be the gateway to adaptation, to having a fresh perspective, and sometimes a total reboot. This is also the edge of greatness. They are two sides of the same coin. So follow the footsteps of your mind. Be open to your heart's meanderings. They will quietly lead you to make your most important decisions, and the rest will fall into place. It will dawn on you: *Oh, I'm only just beginning.* It is exhilarating to be at the top of your game and feel like you've only now just learned how to lead.

The villain here is disconnection. Being disconnected has become our default mode. There is nothing glamorous about being an always-on, burnt-out corporate warrior. We are forlorn and ignorant strangers to love and delight. But we don't need to stay there. Something better is available to us.

When we're in our natural state of being, we don't rush through firing someone because we feel uncomfortable. We don't throw a tantrum because the presentation deck is in the wrong font. We don't ignore inconvenient business facts so that we can recklessly present a bright and sunny PR picture. We can calmly accept the changing realities of our vile and immensely exciting modern corporate life without the usual fear, blame and resentment. If we do this, maybe fewer of us will lose our way in burnout, depression, alcohol or abusive relationships. Instead, we'll come to recognize an inner authority acting upon us, guiding and leading us. In that space, we recognize ourselves as powerful beyond measure. This is the performance of your life. *Sparkle like you mean it.*

Change is in the air. The opportunities are there, but it requires your existential participation. It requires your commitment to claim your authority as a leader. It has the potential to transform us if we give ourselves the space and time to reflect and dance with it.

There has never been a greater need for leadership.

To keep an open mind.

To keep an open heart.

To keep an open will.

So turn off your email and stop checking your traffic light scorecards. Stop worrying, and start leading. It's time to begin. The whole process of creating the next big thing and becoming a great CEO, of being revered for your bold vision and electrifying charisma — this is not up to you. It's not your call to make. Your job is simply to show up powerfully. Today.

And make it look effortless.

About the Author

You can say that **Sophia Chin** is a leadership expert, based on her experience designing and delivering human-centric leadership development programmes to scale high-quality impact. However, she prefers to see herself as a student or scientist observing outstanding leadership. She is deeply curious about what makes a great leader and the tough decisions they make for the things they love. She has 21 years of coaching and consulting experience, tiptoeing the corridors of power, from government agencies to global MNCs and startups, including Apple, crypto.com, Google, Grab, HP and Media.Monks. Today, she is the lead consultant and co-founder of leadership development company PERSONNA. Sophia spent the formative years of her career in growth strategy consulting firm Frost & Sullivan and Singapore industrial space developer JTC Corporation.

Find out more about leadership branding:
personna.me

Acknowledgments

I f you haven't already noticed, I'm infatuated — ardently, feverishly, fervently in love. This book essentially is an homage to the object of my affection: leaders. This book was inspired by your tales of courage and mayhem. It brings the leadership theories to life. Thank you for inspiring me with your greatness. Abhi, Aman, Shonna, Andre, Andrew N., Ben T., Byron, Anne, Sham, Bianca, Gloria, Siew Lee, Dan, Bruce, Caitlin, Carl, 'Ain, Carrie, Christine T., David S., Sharan, Dwayn, Dylan, Gen, Jin, Gerald, Shao Wen, Emeline, William, Hwee Hoon, Cheng Lang, Sarifah, Kumari, Janice, Jacqueline, Stephen, Charles, Alex, Chika, Jasmine, Su Lee, Rina, Kay, Hernie, Rachel, Linah, Adeline, Hilda, Azura, Oonagh, Ben, Suhairi, Herriot, Karen L., Howard, Lorinna, Ishan, Jim, Prisca, Jo, Rayne, Manuel, Andrea, Levent, João, Melissa, John Lee, Karl, Geraldine, Angela K., Olivia, Ming, Danielle, Vikas, Nitin B., Prashant, Matt S., Ed, Eigerim, Mike, Pamela, William, Molly, Tim, Monica, Nicholas, Nicole, Tommy, Rachel & the team in Red Schoolhouse, Rinor, Russell, Simon, Cat, Yvonne, Ben, Marilyn, Jo, Phil, Jacob, Stephen J., Joji, Natassja, Valerie, Walter, Lein, Yves.

I grew up standing on the shoulders of giants. Thank you, mum and dad, for providing the stability *and* the stretch for me to reach the stars. Thank you for being an inspiring beacon of boldness, ingenuity and kindness. Thank you to my bosses for guiding me, mentoring me, and pandering to my grandiose vision of success: Thurai, Patrick, Andrew, David, Geok Tin, Soon Eng, Lit, Foong Leng, Cecilia, Manoj, James, Steven.

Thank you Chris Newson for being such a gentleman and an advocate for my naïve dream of publishing a book. I hope you spot your penetrating editorial prose peppered through the book.

Thank you Hong Koon for casting a divine glow over the book and keeping the faith. The Bible is the perfect moonshot. Just lifting off the ground with this book will be an incredible achievement.

Triena, you brought that touch of ballroom class and glamour to the book. I can't thank you enough.

Nicole, Jimmy, and the team at World Scientific, thank you for bringing this book to life. What we do in the dark puts us in the light. And how the book sparkles!

Ben, Alex, Sam, love, love, love you. You're my best teachers. Thank you, Evelyn, for keeping a wonderful home for us, and your wickedly good lasagna. Thank you, Ching, Chris, Sam, Kit Fai, for the Tomahawks and the ridiculous Christmas gluttony.

Thank you, Roger, for being my hero, and keeping me happy. The black hole is a ravenous beast. The vow said for better, for worse, for richer, for poorer, I didn't realize how profound it would become. As we plunge into the vast, unplumbed abyss together, the more deeply I fall in love.

Endnotes

Chapter 1

1. Jamie Lee, "OCBC offers safehouse for 'rebels' to hatch breakthrough ideas", *The Business Times*, 22 May 2017.

2. Goh Yan Han, "MRT train leaves Ang Mo Kio station with door open; station manager suspended", *The Straits Times*, 12 March 2019.

3. Boris Ewenstein *et al.*, "Changing change management", McKinsey & Company, 1 July 2015, https://www.mckinsey.com/featured-insights/leadership/changing-change-management.

4. Anirban Chowdhury, "Unique talent: Air hostesses to turn pilots at Airasia", *The Economic Times*, 23 July 2014, https://economictimes.indiatimes.com/industry/transportation/airlines-/-aviation/unique-talent-air-hostesses-to-turn-pilots-at-airasia/articleshow/38883513.cms?from=mdr.

5. Mary Slaughter, "How the psychological effects of power explain harrassment", Neuroleadership Institute, 12 February 2018, https://neuroleadership.com/your-brain-at-work/how-the-psychological-effects-of-power-help-explain-harassment/.

6. Tony Fernandes, *Flying High: My Story From AirAsia to QPR*, Portfolio Penguin, 2017.

7. Zhaki Abdullah, "No 'deep-seated cultural issues' at SMRT, says its new CEO Neo Kian Hong", *The Straits Times*, 16 November 2018, https://www.straitstimes.com/singapore/transport/no-deep-seated-cultural-issues-at-smrt-says-its-new-ceo-neo-kian-hong.

8. "What are emotions?", Paul Ekman Group, https://www.paulekman.com/universal-emotions/

9. Ng Jun Sen, "Ong Ye Kung apologises for a 'rough and stressful' night of MRT train breakdowns", *Today Online*, 15 October 2020, https://www.todayonline.com/singapore/ong-ye-kung-apologises-rough-and-stressful-night-MRT-train-breakdowns.

10. Rosaline Chow Koo, "Winning the Asian Human Capital Leadership Award: CXA's Journey and Learnings", Linkedin, 23 September 2017, https://www.linkedin.com/pulse/winning-asian-human-capital-award-cxas-journey-learnings-koo/.

11. John Sviokla and Mitch Cohen, *The Self-Made Billionaire Effect: How Extreme Producers Create Massive Value,* Portfolio Penguin, 2015.

12. Justin Kruger and David Dunning, "Unskilled and unaware of it: How difficulties in recognizing one's own incompetence lead to inflated self-assessments", *Journal of Personality and Social Psychology*, December 1999.

13. Axel Cleeremans, "Conscious and Unconscious Processes in Cognition", *International Encyclopedia of Social and Behavioral Sciences*, 2001.

14. For a description of the iceberg model, see Peter M. Senge, *The Fifth Discipline,* Doubleday, 2006.

Chapter 2

1. Amy Arnsten and Li Bao Ming, "Neurobiology of executive functions: Catecholamine influences on prefrontal cortical functions", *Biological Psychiatry*, June 2005.

2. "Neuroplasticity: How to rewire your brain", *BBC Reel*, 5 March 2021, https://www.bbc.com/reel/playlist/mind-matters?vpid=p098v92k.

3. Originally coined by venture capital investor Ben Horowitz in his book *The Hard Thing About Hard Things,* Harper Collins, 2014.

4. David Rock, "SCARF: A Brain-Based Model for Collaborating With & Influencing Others", *NeuroLeadership Journal*, (1): 44–52, 2008.

5. Ben Wigert, "Employee Burnout: The Biggest Myth", Gallup, 13 March 2020, https://www.gallup.com/workplace/288539/employee-burnout-biggest-myth.aspx.

6. James Danckert and John D. Eastwood, *Out of My Skull: The Psychology of Boredom,* Harvard University Press, 2020.

7. "Attitudes and perceptions of leaders towards engagement and purpose at work", Personna, 4 October 2016.

8. Vivien Shiao, "Are you comfortably miserable at work?", *The Straits Times*, 2 July 2016.

9. Kelly McGonigal, *The Upside of Stress: Why Stress Is Good for You, and How to Get Good at It,* Avery, New York, 2015.

10. Jeremy P. Jamieson *et al.,* "Mind over matter: Reappraising arousal improves cardiovascular and cognitive responses to stress", *Journal of Experimental Psychology: General* 141(3): 417–422, 2012.

11. Elizabeth D. Kirby, Sandra E. Muroy, Wayne G. Sun, David Covarrubias, Megan J. Leong, Laurel A Barchas, Daniela Kaufer, "Acute stress enhances adult rat hippocampal neurogenesis and activation of newborn neurons via secreted astrocytic FGF2", *eLife*, 2013.

12. Amy Arnsten, "The biology of being frazzled", *Science*, 1998.

13. Mihaly Csikszentmihalyi, *Creativity: The Psychology of Discovery and Invention,* HarperCollins, 1 June 1996.

14. John Kounios and Mark Beeman, *The Eureka Factor: Aha Moments, Creative Insight, and the Brain,* Random House, 2015.

15. Steven M. Smith, "Getting into and out of mental ruts: A theory of fixation, incubation, and insight", *The Nature of Insight*: 229–251, 1995, The MIT Press.

16. Matthew Walker, *Why We Sleep,* Penguin Books, 2018.

Chapter 3

1. Tom Wright and Bradley Hope, *Billion Dollar Whale: The Man Who Fooled Wall Street, Hollywood and the World,* Hachette Books, 2018.

Chapter 4

1. Pauline R. Clance and Suzanne A. Imes, "The imposter phenomenon in high achieving women: Dynamics and therapeutic intervention", *Psychotherapy: Theory, Research and Practice* 15(3): 241–247, 1978.
2. Lora Kelley, "How LinkedIn Became a Place to Overshare", *The New York Times*, 16 September 2022, https://www.nytimes.com/2022/09/16/business/linkedin-overshare.html

Chapter 5

1. "Attitudes and perceptions of leaders towards engagement and purpose at work", Personna, 4 October 2016.
2. Rufus Griscom, "HAPPINESS: Arthur C. Brooks Shares His Roadmap for Finding Purpose, Meaning, and Success", *The Next Big Idea*, 9 September 2022.

Chapter 8

1. Matthew Walker, *Why We Sleep*, Penguin Books, 2018.
2. John Pencavel, "The productivity of working hours", Discussion Paper No. 8129, Institute for the Study of Labor, April 2014.

Chapter 9

1. "Attitudes and perceptions of leaders towards engagement and purpose at work", Personna, 4 October 2016.

Chapter 11

1. Dan Marcec, "CEO tenure drops to just five years", Equilar, 19 January 2018, https://www.equilar.com/blogs/351-ceo-tenure-drops-to-five-years.html#:~:text=According%20to%20a%20recent%20Equilar,fallen%20from%206.0%20since%202013.

Chapter 16

1. Good examples of CEO message: *Airbnb News* (5 May 2020), "A Message from AirBnB's Cofounder and CEO Brian Chesky"; *Air New Zealand Monthly Update* (28 April 2020), "Air New Zealand CEO's email to staff and customers".

Chapter 17

1. Originally coined by venture capital Ben Horowitz in his book *The Hard Thing About Hard Things* (HarperCollins, 2014).

Chapter 22

1. Keith Hammonds, "Why we hate HR", *Fast Company*, August 2005.

Chapter 23

1. Good examples are *Airbnb News* (5 May 2020), "A Message from AirBnB's Cofounder and CEO Brian Chesky"; *Air New Zealand Monthly Update* (28 April 2020), "Air New Zealand CEO's email to staff and customers".

Chapter 27

1. Amishi P. Jha, *Peak Mind: Find Your Focus, Own Your Attention, Invest 12 Minutes a Day*, HarperOne, 2021)

Chapter 30

1. "Attitudes and perceptions of leaders towards engagement and purpose at work", Personna, 4 October 2016.
2. Dan Roam, *Blah Blah Blah: What To Do When Words Don't Work*, Portfolio, 2011.

Chapter 32

1. Paul J. Zak, "Why your brain loves good storytelling", *Harvard Business Review*, 28 October 2014, https://hbr.org/2014/10/why-your-brain-loves-good-storytelling.

Chapter 33

1. John Kounios and Mark Beeman, *The Eureka Factor: Aha Moments, Creative Insight, and the Brain,* Random House Publishing, 2015.
2. Otto Scharmer, *Theory U: Leading from the Future as It Emerges,* Berrett-Koehler Publishers, 15 August 2016.

Chapter 34

1. David Robson, "Why we don't dole out many compliments — but should", *BBC Worklife*, 27 July 2021, https://www.bbc.com/worklife/article/20210722-why-we-dont-dole-out-many-compliments-but-should.
2. Scott Berinato, "Negative feedback rarely leads to improvement", *Harvard Business Review*, January–February 2018.
3. Liad Bareket-Bojmel, Guy Hochman, and Dan Ariely, "It's (not) all about the Jacksons: Testing different types of short-term bonuses in the field", *Journal of Management*, 43(2),: 534–554, 2017.

Ingram Content Group UK Ltd.
Milton Keynes UK
UKHW040848090323
418276UK00004B/93

9 789811 251931